From New York to Ibadan

American University Studies

Series VII
Theology and Religion

Vol. 82

PETER LANG
New York • Bern • Frankfurt am Main • Paris

Efiong Utuk

From New York to Ibadan

The Impact of African Questions on the Making of Ecumenical Mission Mandates, 1900-1958

PETER LANG
New York • Bern • Frankfurt am Main • Paris

Library of Congress Cataloging-in-Publication Data

Utuk, Efiong
    From New York to Ibadan : the impact of African
questions on the making of ecumenical mission mandates,
1900-1958 / Efiong Utuk.
        p. cm. — (American university studies. Series VII,
Theology and religion ; vol. 82)
        Includes bibliographical references (p.   ) and
index.
        1. Ecumenical movement—African influences.
2. Missions—African influences.   3. International
Missionary Council.   4. Africa, Sub-Saharan—Church
history.   I. Title.   II. Series.
BX9.5.A37U78   1991   266—dc20   90-6213
ISBN 0-8204-1401-8   CIP
ISSN 0740-0446

© Peter Lang Publishing, Inc., New York 1991

To the All-Africa Council of Churches and its constituency, especially the Presbyterian Church of Nigeria

Keep on being faithful.

ACKNOWLEDGEMENTS

The material in this work formed the substance of my dissertation at Princeton Theological Seminary and various lectures within and outside the academy community. The notes and the bibliography indicate the range of my indebtedness to a large number of archivists and librarians in Africa, North America, and Europe.

I owe a special debt of gratitude to the Princeton Faculty, especially Professors Charles C. West, Samuel H. Moffett, Peter J. Paris, Jane Dempsey Douglass, and Charles A. Ryerson III, all of whom read earlier drafts and offered valuable suggestions. The same gratitude goes to Professor John Mbiti, University of Bern, Switzerland, Dr. Howard S. Olson, Wartburg Theological Seminary, Dubuque, Iowa, and Dr. George R. Hunsberger, Western Theological Seminary, Holland, Michigan. Dr. Hans-Ruedi Weber, World Council of Churches, Geneva, helped to focus my attention on the period surveyed in this study.

To the staff of the World Council of Churches Library, Union Seminary Library, New York, and Speer Library, Princeton, words are hardly enough to express my appreciation for their assistance in gaining access to IMC/CBMS Archives. Many African graduate students at Princeton helped to identify ecumenical figures and clarify some points relating to their particular countries. Here, let me thank in particular Kasonga W. Kasonga (Zaire), David Mosoma (South Africa), Nyambura J. Njoroge (Kenya), and Setriakor Nyomi (Ghana).

I want to thank the Dept. of Publications of the World Council of Churches for allowing me to reproduce the material in the appendixes. I am also grateful to the Inter Documentation Company (now in Leiden, Netherlands) for permitting me to quote from their microfiche collection of the IMC Archives. Unfortunately, their letter arrived too late for me to make extensive use of their collection as I would have liked.

Finally, I must thank my family: Affiong for her invaluable support and proofreading earlier drafts; Idiongo for helping to baby-sit the younger ones, freeing me to concentrate on this work; and the younger ones for reminding me of the perennial problem of generation gap, thus helping me to constantly critique my pedagogical and missiological assumptions. Knowing that I frequently think as a Nigerian but write as an Ivy Leaguer, I crave the indulgence of the reader for faults and shortcomings in the book. It will be sufficient for me if the book conveys something of the help and stimulus I have received during its production.

E.U.

CONTENTS

PART IV AFRICA AND ECUMENICAL ADVANCE AMID STORM, 1928–38

LIST OF ABBREVIATIONS

AACC	All Africa Conference of Churches
ACNETA	Advisory Council on Native Education In Tropical Africa
BMS	Baptist Missionary Society
CBMS	Conference Of British Missionary Societies
CMS	Church Missionary Society
CMSGBI	Conference Of Missionary Societies In Great Britain And Ireland
FMCNA	Foreign Missionary Conference Of North America
ICCLA	International Committee On Christian Literature For Africa
IIALC	International Institute Of African Languages and Cultures
IMC	International Missionary Council
IRM	*International Review of Missions*
PMS	Protestant Missionary Society
PMMS	Primitive Methodist Missionary Society
QIM	Qua Iboe Mission
RBMU	Regions Beyond Missionary Union
SCM	Student Christian Movement
SPG	Society For The Propagation Of The Gospel
SUM	Sudan United Mission
WCC	World Council of Churches
WMMS	Wesleyan Methodist Missionary Society
WSCF	World's Student Christian Federation
YMCA	Young Men Christian Association
YWCA	Young Women Christian Association

INTRODUCTION

This book originated in an effort to explore the relation of Africa to the making of ecumenical mission mandates during the formative years, 1900–1958. Its central theme is that Africa, like other continents, has had a determinative effect on the development of ecumenical mission mandates; and that this effect is particularly related to the formation and growth of the International Missionary Council (IMC).

Previous studies of the roots of this Council and mandates have quite naturally thought of them as a Western affair, with some proportion of Eastern imprint, and little or no building block from Africa.[1] This judgement rests upon an incorrect understanding of ecumenical development which assumes that its development was prepackaged by the missionary, and that the paucity of Africa's ecumenical credential (higher educational, technological, and cultural attainment, political and economic freedom) during this period was tantamount to Africa's lack of ecumenical contribution. This was, for example, the basis on which Roger Bassham made the unfortunate remark that Africa had little or nothing to do with ecumenical development during these colonial years.[2]

There can be no question that, throughout this period, there existed a relationship between a continent's cultural attainment and its level of ecumenical participation. And there can be no question that, during this period, Africa's inadequate modernization efforts[3] combined with colonial restriction to severely limit its ecumenical participation. However, extensive study of this period has led me to conclude that those who give excessive attention to nonAfrican factors (especially the role of missionary personalities) in the making of these mandates have ignored an important factor.

This important factor is the fact that, during this critical phase of ecumenism making, the decisive and more determinative factors which brought about the necessity for ecumenical mission thinking and acting were not missionary personalities or their agents but missionary questions or problems. This perspective does not preclude the role played by personalities at the outset of this movement and rethinking of missions. It does, however, question the disproportionate attention personalities have received in the literature, given the obvious fact that these were ephemeral, whereas the issues or problems were and are enduring, cutting across time frames, generations, and denominational barriers, and demanding several meetings and conferences to grapple with them.

Seen from this perspective, and judged by the complexity and challenge of its questions, a new picture of Africa has emerged as an ecumenical partner whose contribution, directly and indirectly, to the making of ecumenical mission mandates and the growth of the IMC was far more formative and significant than the literature has portrayed. Indeed, evidence suggests that Africa deserves more credit and appreciation than it has received for withstanding countless internal and external hurdles, and providing ecumenical building blocks to the construction of these mandates, in spite of these hurdles.

The sad part is that this African ecumenical past is not widely known, not because the evidence is lacking, but because works such as the *History of the Ecumenical Movement*,[4] in spite of their semi-official status and wealth of material, only alluded to it. Here for the first time is set forth an aspect of this African past, indicating its long journey and transition from an object of, to a participant in, missions.

STRUCTURE AND THEMES

I. Approach and method of interpretation

The approach adopted in this study reflects this belief that Africa deserves more appreciation than it has been given for helping to spread ecumenical ideas even during this colonial period. I reject the idea that colonial Africa was a creation but not a creator of the ecumenical movement, for, as recent changes in world history, including the cataclysm that is going on in Southern Africa and Eastern Europe, have shown, humans make their own history, but they do so within confines inherited from the past and within structures or boundaries not totally of their own creation. Similarly, movements, including ecclesiastical movements, do not develop and grow without important issues and challenges serving as catalyst.

This perspective assumes the sociological fact that Christianity was not planted *in vacuo* in Africa and that, in addition to countless native agents who constituted a significant link of transmission, there was incarnation and adaptation, organic growth and cross-religio-cultural fertilization. Besides, there were numerous, unexpected issues which also served as a crucial link of transmission between one generation of missionaries and the next, and between colonial evangelism and post-colonial evangelism. Africa helped to change and reconstruct some missiological views just as missionaries, doubtless, helped to change and remake some aspects of African life and culture.

Actually, this is the process and crucible Christianity has passed through as it has made its long journey from one part of the world to another, leaving behind new forms of expression yet weaved to one body of Christ. For this reason, the ecumenical movement owes its origin and growth in part to colonial Africa; and can be said, with a high degree of certainty, that the movement is more a product of the missionary encounter with African and other problems, and less a product of *a priori* unitive commitment on the part of the missionary.

There is a sense in which this approach is, in part, my own *sitz im leben*, a statement of my own faith situation and affirmation, an embodiment of my African and Western roots. Until recently, I have, due to socialization, tended to deny one of these cultures and to affirm the other. The reasons for this dubious and apparently dishonest position are not hard to come by. One, for instance, was presented to me as "authentic" and, the other, "inauthentic." Yet I know from personal experience that such bifurcation is hypocritical, inappropriate, and unrealistic. And the danger was that, until recently, I tended to lead a multiple life, as any "Westernized African" can testify. Instead of the Gospel being a liberating experience for me, it tended to be an *unsolicited burden*. I happen to believe now that there is something patently wrong with any conception that seeks to alienate the Gospel from culture, the African from the Western, equate the two undialectically, and presume that being a Christian means imbibing only the accretion of the missionary's culture and disparaging that of the missionized.

More important, this approach is also suggested by the data itself, the most important suggestion being that we need a shift in our categories of data compilation and interpretation, in order to take adequate account of the rich ecumenical fellowship and learning process which Africans and nonAfricans underwent together, throughout these colonial years. Not to mention appreciating the remarkable silent revolution that Africans have had to undergo at a pace few other people have been forced to adapt.

This approach acknowledges the fact that world conditions had made interdependence between African and Western peoples an economic and social reality, even before both peoples became highly conscious of that fact. The fact that this vital revolution was invisible and took place for centuries before the colonial era in Africa has been richly documented. Mere mention of the slave trade, which relied for its success on some African and nonAfrican cooperation, should remind us of that tragic period; and how it continues, in part, to color post-colonial relations between African and nonAfrican peoples and nations.

Several changes have taken place, ever since the end of the colonial era, that our thinking has not kept up with. It is hoped that this study would provide a means for better understanding and awareness of many ecumenical issues Africans and nonAfricans had faced together in the period under discussion, and an appreciation of their achievements, in spite of their colonial captivity.

Our method of interpretation, then, does not try to emphasize one culture at the expense of the other. It rejects attempts made by some to separate the so-called "software" (African factor) from "hardware"[5] (missionary factor) or overemphasize one at the expense of the other, claiming that there can be Christianity "without fetishes"[6] or contradictions. Recognition is made of similarities and dissimilarities in cultural beliefs and technological achievements. The end has been to try to give a fair and balanced treatment and importance to both the African and the Western, the old and the new, internal and external factors, criticizing both and evaluating their contributions, as much as possible, in terms of the colonial worldview and ethos which dominated the period under survey.

I realize that it is not always easy to be consistently fair to all sides of the issue; and that at some points the writer has had to take a position which the reader may find controversial. The point to remember is that missiology is not a "hard" science, therefore, there is bound to be divergences in hermeneutics. It is however, my hope that the book will contribute to the understanding of Christ's last command that Christians should witness so that our world will be rescued and restored to the authentic life God expects from us.

II. Unit of analysis

Because the growth of ecumenical movement and its mission mandates cannot be conceived without the conferences which provided a forum for their conception, our organizing framework or unit of analysis is the proceedings of some of the movement's early conferences and meetings. Within that framework, the analysis is done chronologically and with particular attention to shifting, external historical and sociological forces—within and without Africa—which helped to shape international mission thinking during this period.

To ensure a unified account of our findings, each chapter reflects six principal questions which guided our investigation. These questions, each of which assumes knowledge of Western and African mission histories, are:

1. What was the impact of the African social conditions on mission thinking and doing?

2. How did the persistence of indigenous cultural and primal religious values affect Christian evaluation of nonChristian religions?

3. How did the rise of indigenous African churches affect church-mission relations?

4. How did the race problem and calls for equality and justice affect ecumenical consciousness?

5. What in Africa necessitated unity in church and civil life on the one hand, between mission and church, and on the other hand, mission and government?

6. Who were some of the principal figures, "adopted" as well as "African Africans," and how did they reflect on, and respond to, these questions?[7]

The number representing each of these questions is mnemonic. This is an important methodological concept which makes it possible for the reader to make comparisons from conference to conference. Also, it should be noted that not all Conferences gave equal attention to all the questions. The text reflects, as accurately as possible, this variation.

Clearly, the interrelationship between these questions cannot be overemphasized and to some extent they are inseparable. However, the benefits of delineating and appropriating them as analytical and delimiting tools far outweigh the danger of their imposing artificial unity on the analysis. In addition, I have employed extra-conference resources to shed light on conference discussions and resolutions. These are, among others, unpublished reports and memorandums written by both the officials and nonofficials of the IMC.

III. Scope and limitations

With these questions, I am only probing one dimension of Africa's relation to the development of contemporary missiology and ecumenical experience, and in so doing, my hope is that it would contribute to a larger and better understanding of post-colonial (after 1958) ecumenical mandates and the birth and growth of regional, ecumenical bodies such as the All-Africa Conference of Churches (AACC). This, then, is a background study, a point of departure rather than a point of destination. A still larger task remains—namely, the description of the various activities of the IMC brought about by African conditions and the religious experience of countless men and women who encouraged unity, directly or indirectly, with their personal devotion to Christ.

It must be emphasized that this work deals with Black Africa's connection with the development of the Protestant ecumenical enterprise. More specifically, it deals with Black Africa's contribution to, and impact on, the making of the "missionary wing" (IMC) of that unitive quest[8] which became integrated with the World Council of Churches (WCC) in 1961.

Although, geographically, this region is vast, ecumenically, and, for most of the years with which this study is concerned, the region's activities were severely restricted by lack of political independence. At the same time, the focus of the study cannot be limited to what we call today West Africa, East Africa, or any one contemporary African nation-state. For the missionary world did not think of Africa in such terms. Not infrequently, and even after Edinburgh 1910, the birth place of modern ecumenism, Africa was looked at as one "country," not a "continent" with diverse cultures and peoples. In fact, the missionary convention of the time was to compare the whole of Africa with India, China, or Japan as if, geographically and politically, they were similar. It would also be noticed that substantial reference is made to black American relation to this movement. By doing this, I am also following the missiological convention of the period as well as the historical fact that colonial Africa cannot be understood without reference to Africa's Diaspora.

In view of the complexity and interconnection of the political and ecclesiastical histories of modern Africa, emphasis is placed on the "religious." This does not mean that sociopolitical events are altogether sidetracked or overlooked. It means that, while references are made to them where, by contrast to the internal ecclesiastical events, they illuminate the discussion, they are, however, not a primary reference group.

Similarly, given the fact that modern ecumenism was largely spearheaded by Protestantism until 1961, when the nonProtestant world[9] signalled its interest, directly or indirectly, in this unitive crusade, this study is limited to that early Protestant initiative. In this sense, this study is not a history of the whole subject of missionary cooperation or of the IMC in Africa. Its chief interest has been to see how African questions related to, and helped to shape, the development of the conciliar-ecumenical mission theology during these colonial years. Yet, because during these years the development of ecumenical mission theory and praxis were intertwined, I have made use of one to explain the other and vice versa.

IV. Definition of terms

One point needs to be mentioned, and it concerns the definition of some of the terms employed in this work. The word "missionary" is consistently used in this study in its Old-School connotation, that is, a person sent out to a foreign country to preach, teach and evangelize. Where change is warranted by the context, I have used the term "ecumenical worker" or "workers" to indicate the change. The word "conciliar" or "conciliar-ecumenical" refers to the WCC and its affiliated bodies.

Without denying that there are evangelicals within the conciliar circles or vice versa, the word "evangelicals" refers to that wing of the Protestant party affiliated with the Interdenominational Foreign Mission Association or the Evangelical Foreign Missions Association. Unless suggested otherwise, the terms "theology of mission," "missiology," "theory of mission," and "ecumenical mission mandates" are used interchangeably to refer to those ecumenical statements and principles which provide specific guidelines to Christian workers or evangelists, associated with the IMC and later the WCC, regarding how they were and are to conduct missions in the world.

Throughout the text, we employ the "ecumenical shorthand" for each of these meetings: New York 1900, Edinburgh 1910, Le Zoute 1926, etc. Although a list of abbreviations is provided, an attempt is made to avoid contracting the names of mission societies and organizations, and to help the reader place geographical names in their chronological and geographical setting.

To appreciate Africa's role from one conference to another, this work is organized in terms of a journey, with a determination to arrive safely at our destination without missing necessary roadside attractions and inescapable detours.

Divided into five parts, Part I provides a profile of the beginning of the search for twentieth-century warrants for missionary work, taking the reader from New York City (1900) across the Atlantic Ocean to Edinburgh, Scotland (1910). With much of Western Europe in mental ruins after the first world war, Part II discusses why another ecumenical trip to the United States was necessary as well as the first post-war meeting in England in 1923, held appropriately at an ecumenical way-station, Oxford. Part III brings to light four area Conferences; two of these were held in England (High Leigh 1924 and London 1925), while the others were held in New England (Hartford, Connecticut, 1925) and the Continent (Le Zoute, Belgium, 1926). Together they document the momentous efforts on the part of the IMC to redefine the missionary aim in Africa, given the powerful Reports of the Education Commissions to Africa. Part IV takes our journey to the Holy Land (Jerusalem 1928) and the East (Madras, India, 1938); and, in light of the underlying theory, examines ecumenical advance amid the storms of world events. Part V chronicles the effect of the second world war and the resulting stops which this ecumenical train made at Westerville (Ohio), Whitby (Canada), Willingen (Germany), before it arrived on the African soil—Accra (Ghana) and Ibadan (Nigeria). The study concludes with an interpretative essay in which an attempt is made to give a theoretical hook for hanging the text together.

Appendixes which give insight into some conference and extra-conference information are provided. These include impressions of the Le Zoute Conference (appendix 2) from the perspectives of two observers: African and nonAfrican.

This study spans over five decades, visits numerous world cities—some well-known and some not well-known, makes interesting detours, notes enduring attractions on the way, and ends, both symbolically and literally, at the Ibadan All-Africa Church Conference of 1958.

NOTES

[1]See, for example, William R. Hogg, *Ecumenical Foundations: A History of the International Missionary Council And Its Nineteenth Century Background* (New York: Harper, 1952); R. Pierce Beaver, *Ecumenical Beginnings in Protestant World Mission: A History of Comity* (New York: Thomas Nelson, 1962); Amba Oduyoye, "The Development Of The Ecumenical Movement In Africa With Special Reference To The All Africa Conference Of Churches 1958-1974," *Africa Theological Journal* 9, 3 (1980): 30-40. Oduyoye concedes pre-1958 ecumenical developments as "a Euro-American endeavour" (p. 31); cf. Charles Amjad-Ali, "A Theory of Justice for An Ecumenical Praxis: A Critique of Eurocentric Pseudo-Universals" (Ph.D. dissertation, Princeton Theological Seminary, 1985), pp. 1, 82–83 *passim*. For a study of the relation of the East to ecumenical movement, see Hans Ruedi Weber, *Asia and the Ecumenical Movement 1895–1961* (London: SCM, 1966).

[2]Rodger C. Bassham, *Mission Theology: 1948–1975 Years of Worldwide Creative Tension Ecumenical, Evangelical, and Roman Catholic* (Pasedena, CA: William Carey, 1979), p. 136.

[3]Notice that modernization in some parts of Africa, for instance, Southern Nigeria, was not coterminus with Western missions in Africa as often thought. See, for example, Kenneth O. Dike, *Trade and Politics in the Niger Delta 1830–1885* (Oxford: Clarendon, 1956); D. Forde, ed., *Efik Traders of Old Calabar* (New York: Oxford, 1956); A. J. Latham, *Old Calabar 1600–1891: The Impact Of The International Economy Upon A Traditional Society* (Oxford: Clarendon, 1973); K. K. Nair, *Politics and Society in Southeastern Nigeria 1841–1906: A Study of Power, Diplomacy, and Commerce in Old Calabar* (London: Frank Cass, 1972).

[4]Ruth Rouse and Stephen Neill, eds., *History of the Ecumenical Movement 1517–1948* (Philadelphia: Westminster, 1954); see also its sequel, Harold Fey, ed., *Ecumenical Advance: A history of the Ecumenical Movement 1948–1968* (Philadelphia, Westminster, 1970).

[5]See, for example, Lamin Sanneh, *West African Christianity* (Maryknoll, New York: Orbis, 1983), pp. 243–4.

[6]See, for example, F. Eboussi Boulaga, *Christianity without Fetishes* (Maryknoll, New York: Orbis, 1981).

[7]These are variants of the questions I have used in other works. See, for example, Efiong S. Utuk, "An Analysis of John Mbiti's Missiology," *Africa Theological Journal*, 15, 1 (1986): 3–15. In phrasing these questions, I have also benefited from Lukas Vischer, ed., *Church History in an Ecumenical Perspective* (Bern: Evan-

gelische Arbeitsstelle Oekumene Schweiz, 1982); and Robert Berkhofer, *A Behavioral Approach to Historical Analysis* (New York: Free Press, 1969), pp. 32–44.

[8]In any event, the other early ecumenical bodies—the World's Student Christian Federation (WSCF), The Faith and Order Movement, The Life and Work Movement, The Young Men and Women Christian Associations—did not have substantial early African connection.

[9]By the nonProtestant world, I include the Roman Catholic and the Eastern Orthodox Churches. The Ethiopian Orthodox Church was one of the founding member-churches of the WCC in 1948.

PART I

AFRICA AND ECUMENICAL BEGINNINGS, 1900–1910

1

BIRTH PANGS: NEW YORK 1900

When on Saturday, April 21, 1900, the Ecumenical Conference on Foreign Missions opened at Carnegie Hall, New York City, certain African conditions and questions were among the currents that led to its organization. Ecclesiastically, the rise in West and South Africa of Ethiopianism, a new mobilizing-doctrine, dressed in the garb of African *dramatis personae* and couched in the language of prophecy and fulfilment, helped to shape its planning and agenda. Politically, it organizers were not unaware that Pan-Africanism (a movement which sought to bring into closer touch with each other the peoples of African descent in the United States, West Indies, Africa, and Europe), was in the making.

Within and without Africa, the redrawing of the world's political map was an ongoing project either through belligerency, as in the case of Britain in South Africa and the Yoruba Kingdoms, or outright colonial occupation, as in the case of America in the Philippines.

Accordingly, New York was called to confront these and other changing world conditions,[1] and to tackle the unfinished business of Protestantism's fragmentary approach to missions which had dominated the nineteenth century. Conscious that Protestant missions could no longer be insulated from the reorientation of Western social thought, its sponsors, the Foreign Mission Conference of North America[2] (FMCNA), reasoned that, regrettable as were these sociopolitical disturbances in themselves,

> the time had come for the Church, as a whole, to grapple with the problems incident to the world's evangelization, and to realize that the responsibility of meeting these problems could no longer be cast wholly upon administrative boards at home and missionaries on the field, far in advance of the great body of the Church as they might be. The solution of these problems required the united thought of Christendom.

Attended by 2500 delegates (including several black American missionaries in Africa as well as a native (South African) National Baptist pastor, E. B. P. Kote), New York was not a legislative body. However, its format was determined in a way that enabled many thoughtful Christian men and women who were concerned with working out "the many-sided problems of human progress" to unite and "make the results of their study and experience contribute"[3] to the expansion of the Christian missionary enterprise.

Therefore, like the Comity Conferences,[4] New York was a place in which missionary workers all over the world could share the fruits of common experience in a larger induction. However, unlike the Comity Conferences, New York delegates were more determined to restate the traditional missionary appeal in "conventional thought-forms."[5]

Comity Conferences had forgotten that mission societies were not Church *per se* and had negotiated comity agreements with or without the assent of their respective denominations. New York sought to have nothing to do with such anathemas. Its burden was to put a stop to any surreptitious attempt to split the Church from its *raison d'etre*: world-wide missions. Its name "Ecumenical Conference," according to its organizers, was coined, not because all portions of the Christian Church were to be represented in it by delegates, but because "its proposed plan of campaign" was international and covered the whole area of the inhabited globe.

1. Social conditions at New York

At New York, Africa was visible as a significant player in this first attempt to propose ecumenical plan for missionary advance. This was first reflected in the plethora of social questions on New York's docket: Can Christianity be planted in Africa without education and literacy? Is it missiological to be concerned about modern industry and agricultural establishments? What do we do with slave labor in East Africa and land rights in South Africa?

Whereas, in the nineteenth century, thought was not given, on a continuing and sustaining basis, to how the expressed ideal of transforming the old African social order[6] could be reduced to actual implementation, New York said that this must no longer be the case. It felt that Christianity's future in Africa could not be secured without a sustained attack on illiteracy. Thus, in view of pressing economic and religious reasons, New York endorsed Western education as a "civilizing tool."

On the economic side, it declared that literacy was necessary so that African Christians, like nonAfrican Christians, can be able to read the "advertisements of soap and shoes" and come to appreciate "newspapers and magazines." On the religious side, they were to learn to read so that the "Christian Bible" would not remain a closed book.

While this understanding may strike one as overly Western-oriented, it was consistent with the largely triumphalist, missiological mentality of the time in which, in spite of evidences to the contrary, many missionaries believed that being a Christian largely meant being a Westerner in thought and action. It was also consistent with the idea that the Bible was largely, if not wholly, the infallible word of God, behavior largely moral or amoral, and the world largely inhabited by Christians and non-Christians, the former being "civilized" and largely Westerners and the latter being "barbarians" and largely non-Westerners.

Despite this instrumentalism, New York placed emphasis on the fact that, however many schools missionaries were able to conduct, and to whatever heights of grade they were able to reach, these schools should be of high quality.[7] Here we see the beginning of a new educational value which, though still utilitarian, modified the attitude that prevailed in the Comity Conferences (e.g. London 1888), particularly the view that any parochial school system was good enough for Africa. Interestingly, the planting of schools, like the building of hospitals was seen as an integral part of the biblical warrant for mission.

Although critics were already at work, claiming that too much mission strength was being given to education, the majority opinion was that Africa calls for more, not less, of what conciliarists call today "social action" programs. This majority commitment to educational mission would become a vexing and perennial issue as its consequences became manifest in the ensuing years, necessitating more united missionary effort than some delegates had foreseen or hoped for in this Conference.

A related African social matter discussed at New York, largely because its demand was outstripping its supply, was medical missions. Like educational missions, New York saw medical missions as a means through which the heart of the "uncivilized" Africans could be won for the "Word and the Gospel of Light," even though that did not mean a total abandonment of traditional medicine by African converts.

Various descriptions of the native response to this Western science or "witchcraft," as some natives called it, were made. Although the language was still idealistic, with the finger of God seen as present in every healing process, medical science was put forth as something that could unite all missionaries and could be used as a weapon to break down superstition, to open the way for ministering the word of God, to enable these African people come nearer to the great hope of the world—the Love of Christ. Here can be seen the unmeasured language and rising confidence in medical science as a missiological factor, a reflection of the optimism and bouyant confidence which characterized missionary work at the turn of this century.

Thus, New York tried to appropriate latest scientific and cultural studies for understanding African social conditions and enhancing missionary unity. This was evident in its approach to the challenge posed by Africa's nonindustrial status in which, contrary to conventional thought, a fairly balanced analysis of its present and future status was made.

Although the extent of the application of such studies was limited, it was different from the nineteenth-century in which critical examination of missiological suppositions was largely seen as antithetical to evangelistic spirit and adventure. This was a good indication that African missionary romance was beginning to face African missionary fact.

In discussing this African nonindustrial status, New York prompted missionaries to see that it makes no sense to have intelligent Christians when their means of livelihood are uncertain. Past missionary nonchalant attitude towards industrial missions was in part critiqued. Absent, however, was any recognition of the fact that Africans themselves were, in some city-states such as Old Calabar, Nigeria, initiating social improvement schemes which were partially unrelated to missionary work.[8] Still, New York saw that how the advance in industrial science was appropriated, and natural and life processes were interpreted, could have an enduring impact on evangelism in Africa.

Appropriately, an unusual statement was made. This statement declared that it was the appropriate time to raise the question as to whether an advance may be made in the scope of industrial and technical training. This statement was necessitated by New York's acknowledgement that the so-called Christian nations have no monopoly and copyright of the world's knowledge. This was a critical acknowledgement because it shows that, already at the turn of this century, there were missionaries who were willing to admit the fact that the so-called "Christian nations" did not have the blueprint to every and any problem in life, despite claims to the contrary.

Yet the primary question for New York vis-a-vis industrial missions was who will take the lead in interpreting this industrial, scientific orientation in Africa, Christians or nonChristians? Not surprisingly, many delegates believed that, if Christians fail to take initiative and spread their understanding and interpretation of nature and of nature's God, nonChristians will take up that initiative.

Looked at from our own age, the reason given for this view was at once missiologically and industrially insightful in that New York delegates knew that the non-Christian world will seek to catch up with Western scientific and industrial advance. Thus it was said that the nonChristian world stands on tiptoe to catch the "glints of the morning of science," and that, with this science, a new social order will soon emerge for millions in Asia and Africa. When that happens, delegates added, "Christian nations" would not have to complain that they were not given adequate opportunity to extend their influence.

To avoid such a missed opportunity, New York counselled missionaries to develop a positive attitude toward industrialism and to capitalize on the apparent industrial gap between the "Christian" and "nonChristian" nations for evangelical purposes. A statement urged missionaries to recognize that the one institution that would give the missionary prestige and power in Africa, Japan, China, Korea, India, Turkey, and Persia would be powerful institutes of technology and the best and latest in science. Therefore, it was mandated that all mission societies should take technology seriously, for it will help to fill their school halls, make their classes enthusiastic, and provide profound and far-reaching influence in all mission stations.[9]

Here was a straightforward admission of the relation of economic and industrial power to missions, an apparent expression of fear that, without Christian people maintaining their industrial advantage, the prestige of Christian missions would be impaired. It was a recognition that, in Africa, industrialism could not be avoided or prevented. Instead, its side-effects were to be held in check, "redeemed and enlightened" by what the Conference called "the pervading spirit of Christ." Thus, ecumenical workers were to ensure that this industrial spirit was properly directed to become the champion of liberty, the handmaid of education, the auxiliary of the gospel.

However, doubts were also expressed as to whether such hopes could be realized. In other words, New York was theoretically willing and open to seeing African social conditions in some realistic fashion. That Africa will become industrial was as certain as that it will survive the colonial era. The larger question asked then, which is both interesting and may be a surprise for some today, was this: shall Black Africa become materialistic, hard, defiant, hopeless, and godless, with nothing to soften and mitigate the severity of its life, with hundreds of New York East Sides and London East Ends (pockets of affluent neighborhoods amidst widespread poverty and illiteracy) in its cities?

New York did not directly answer this question. Rather it postulated that, normally and ultimately, the "West Sides" and "West Ends" become what the "East Sides" make them. Also, it recognized that poverty and affluence are related and that missionaries must work to overcome what the Conference called "wrong and neglect." Implicit here was, clearly, New York's aversion to Africa developing its own "East and West Ends." Also implicit was the idea of political and economic emancipation for the downtrodden, or, in recent parlance, "liberation." While this idea was not pushed to its logical conclusion, the interdependence of the "East and West Siders" was recognized. Hence, it is reasonable to assume that some delegates were aware of the interlocking system of the world economic order and interdependence of all peoples, though they said very little about it.

However, New York fell short of a comprehensive anti-oppression, ecumenical policy. Instead, reflecting the feelings of its Protestant constituency, it directed most of its anti-colonial polemics against the Arabs, the French, and the Belgians, while implying that British colonialism in Africa was qualitatively different from the ones it attacked. First, it regretted the oppressive condition brought on the African natives by the Arab slave trade. Second, it warned against the danger posed in Madagascar for Protestantism by the hoisting of the French flag and, therefore, the changing of missionary configuration and balance of power between Protestants and nonProtestants in that island country.[10] Third, it deplored the Belgian slave labor machinations in the Congo. The time, however, had not yet come to press charges against colonial governments or to see their presence in Africa as, ultimately, counter-productive to Christian world mission.

To be sure, at this point in time no serious qualms were expressed toward colonialism in Africa, not to mention questioning its legitimacy. Instead, it was seen as benevolent and providential primarily because the Colonial Powers (e.g. Britain, France, Belgium) were in part helping missions to accomplish that which was impossible in some mission stations: the penetration of Africa's hinterland.

However, there were voices indicating that the dark blot that rested on Leopold's Congo was also resting on the whole mission enterprise. "We," it was said, not "they," "owe Congo much. We have robbed her, killed her, destroyed thousands of her sons and daughters."[11] In such a state of unspeakable rape and social violation, New York saw mission as reparation of European debt to Africa and believed that it was unconscionable to have a divided Protestant approach to defraying that debt. Yet nothing was proposed as to how to overcome the apparent fact that multitudes had responded, in various parts of Africa, to the invitation to better their condition up to the full limit of the missions' ability and willingness to provide facilities. This inability to meet the full need and rising African expectation would remain a perennial problem and an unfinished agenda throughout the period under survey.

2. Primal religions at New York

The presence and persistence of African primal religions was also an issue which helped New York in its attempt to chart a new course for Christian understanding of nonChristian religions and peoples. Controlled more by apologetics rather than anthropology or sociology, the discussion of this question reveals that New York, while conscious of African primal religions, was more preoccupied with the challenge posed by the so-called other great and book religions of the world—Islam, Buddhism, and Hinduism.

This reflected, of course, the continuing relative respect that Western missionaries at the time were paying to Oriental and Islamic civilizations. Still, New York was scornful of those "book" religions and social systems. However, it spoke even more disdainfully of African primal religions which, according to the hierarchical classification scheme of the time, occupied the bottom end of the religious scale and was marked for outright replacement. If the so-called nonChristian book religions were "misguided" and "partial lights," bookless African religions were largely "pagan" with little or no religious utility.

However, there were those who signalled their discomfort with the idea that, in classifying religions and determining their "superiority" or "inferiority," as the case may be, it is sufficient to appeal to the moral and social fruits of Christianity. Some voiced that Western infidelity must not be brushed aside. Others warned that to be wise-hearted missionaries should not proclaim that Christendom was perfect and picture their denominations as the stainless bride of Christ, but should strive to give the missionized African a full vision of Christ and Christ alone. How such a disembodied picture of Christ was to be presented was not worked out.

The discussion which ensued brought out a laundry list of social and personal vices which were common in the so-called Christian nations. These included careers of vice and villainy, liquor and human traffic. Because these vices counteracted the evangelical message and undermined the holier-than-thou attitude with which some missionaries presented the gospel to Africans, the mood at New York on this question was somber and lamentative. Some hoped that this public acknowledgement of Western cultural imperfection would lead to "candor, frankness, and modesty" in missionary circles.

Unfortunately, the days for candor, frankness, and modesty, as far as Christian/nonChristian encounter was concerned, were still far away. The dominant attitude was still that of Christianity over against other religions. Tied more to the nineteenth than the twentieth century, New York delegates believed that missionaries should see Christendom as "the argument for Christianity" and, consequently, the condemnation of heathenism, paganism, and primal religions. Consequently, while, on the one hand, New York sought to make adjustment to the world in which religions meet, on the other hand, the position it felt most comfortable with remained that of Christianity uprooting the old African social order with the "stream of Christian civilization."

As the center was still holding and things had not yet fallen apart (Chinua Achebe), New York mirrored Ernst Troeltsch's *The Absoluteness of Christianity and History of Religion*, a highly acclaimed work at the turn of the century and known far beyond the narrow borders of academic theology. The days for compromise and tolerance were at least a decade away (see Edinburgh 1910); syncretism was, of course, still a highly dreaded idea.

3. Indigenous churches at New York

New York found that the rise of indigenous African churches affected how evangelism was to be conducted in Africa. It brought to the fore, though in a lackluster manner, the importance of native African participation in church planting. Discussed together with the missionary aim in Africa, this theme brought the understanding that Protestant forces must abandon the feeling that the Western missionary is the end-all and cure-all. It was clear to some participants that no one, however "civilized" and "mentally fit," could single-handedly bring the sub-Sahara into the Christian orbit.

Also self-evident was the fact that not even all the missionaries combined, with all their paraphernalia and supposed sophistication, could accomplish such a task in a short time. Here we see an attempt to grant foreign missionaries only that which they deserved—and no more—rather than inflating their role out of proportion to what they, as individuals, can actually accomplish in the field.

Thus the position occupied by the natives in the evangelical chain was found to be important and worthy of further encouragement and expansion. The discovery of a vast unoccupied region along and between the Congo River and Old Calabar, with its millions of inhabitants, was seen as beckoning for more, not less, native involvement in the transmission of the gospel so that such vast unoccupied areas could be reached with the gospel in the shortest possible time.

New York heard that many Africans were already, not unlike the age of Tertullian, finding that the blood of the martyrs is, indeed, the seed of the Church, given the fact that some native Christians were being persecuted and killed because of their faith and support of Christian expansion in Africa.

An American Baptist missionary, Henry Richards, working among the Bantus brought to the notice of this Conference the incalculable gift of faceless natives to the evangelical process. The Christians at Mbanza Manteke, Congo, he said, being naturally averse to stinginess and, in spite of their poverty, gave in 1899 one hundred and sixty British pounds (a substantial sum by that time) for the expansion of the work.

Lest it be said that native churches could not stand on their own, Dr. A. Schreiber of the Rhenish Missionary Society, brought to New York's attention that at Cape Colony, ten churches "numbering 15,000 souls" were self-supporting. Schreiber let it be known that his Society was not giving even a farthing to support those churches. The only thing the people required, he added, was the availability of those who could teach and pass on the evangelical knowledge to native Christians.

Unfortunately, New York did little to tap more of this outburst of native evangelical zeal. Instead, discussants appear to have been surprised at the rate some of these indigenous churches were clamoring for more participation in making missionary policies through the Ethiopian Movement, a religio-political umbrella through which some African Christians sought religious and political franchise.

This is why the mood of the Conference was changed when the Reverend Charles Morris of the National Baptist Convention in South Africa, sought to move the discussion away from negative to positive results of this Ethiopian Movement. As a black American and one who was sympathetic to its rise and growth, Morris saw the Movement as a warning sign that African native workers must be given more, not less, ecclesiastical recognition and opportunity. The Movement, he added, was not simply a blind attempt or rebellion on the part of the natives to get out from under European control.[12] The problem was that the spirit, which actuated the first generation of African missionaries (e.g. Livingstone, Moffat, Mary Slessor), had given way to naked discrimination against Africans.

It was a movement which believed, rightly or wrongly, that metropolitan Protestantism was indictable for sacrificing racial equality at the altar of political and economic expediency. For its leaders, the fact that race had become the apparent controlling category in determining ecclesiastical power questions was sufficient sign of Protestant apostasy and loss of ethical direction. The time, they reasoned, could not have been more appropriate for black folks to, in the words of the Psalmist, stretch forth their hands to God in both the Old and the New Worlds.[13]

Morris urged the Conference to see that the quest for separation advocated by the Movement stemmed from the injudicious manner in which white missionaries were treating some of the natives. Believing that God in His providence has been intending and preparing black people, especially black Americans, to assume a large place in the evangelization of Africa, Morris saw this Movement as God's action in history. Morris hoped that the whole Conference would see the movement in a positive light and be prepared to open the door for more native and black American participation in evangelization.[14]

This subject of native and black American participation in the evangelization of Africa was underlined by other delegates. C. F. Harford-Battersby, a member of a

Sudan missionary party who had been on three tours on the Niger, spoke of his encounter with a native who had translated and written out the Gospel of John from Arabic into Hausa in ten days, without ever seeing an Englishman before. Harford-Battersby said that this in an attempt to correct the misconception that native Christians could not do anything without supervision from foreigners. This translation of the Scripture was seen by Harford-Battersby as an example of the intelligence of some of the native people, and one of the most "striking instances [of] indigenous civilization" he had ever known. Africa, he said, is an opportunity for black Americans who had been exposed to the gospel in a way that is "unexampled in the world's history" to go and evangelize.[15]

4. Race relations at New York

Tied to this discussion on native churches and African participation in the making and execution of missionary policies was the undercurrent of race discrimination which had shown its ugly head in several mission stations, mainly east and south of the Sahara. New York was, therefore, challenged by the race problem and African calls for fair-play in social relations. While it made no special attempt to make an in-depth and explicit study of this issue, and largely took for granted the racist prejudices of its age,[16] it is possible to glean from its proceedings the beginning of the understanding that there is nothing that Africans cannot do if they are given a chance.

Some missionaries (see individual contributions below) testified to their new understanding of Africans as a result of their firsthand contact with them as opposed to the myths they were taught about them prior to this firsthand encounter. Many decried the fact that the Church which should be the agent of change was itself caught up by the pseudo-science that some Social Darwinists were advancing at the turn of the century as explanations for the differences which characterize peoples and cultures.

Still, because this Conference took place in 1900, not 1990, we must not downplay the fact that it was difficult for some delegates to move beyond the conservative beliefs of their denominations and national sensibilities. Furthermore, while on the individual level, there were those who were opposed to Social Darwinism and racial antipathy, on the collective level, it was not yet possible to fashion out a unanimous resolution condemning all forms of racial discrimination.

On the whole, while stereotypes died hard, New York made a try to search for an alternative image of Africa. This new image was to be positive at least in part, respecting the fact that not all Africans were benighted and sunk in savagery as was previously thought.

5. Cooperation and unity at New York

At New York, it was the enumeration of unsavory examples of comity breaches and discourtesies in African and other mission fields, which helped to arouse several pleas for mission unity. One keynote futurist noted that twentieth-century Africa demands that missionaries be Protestants not "contra-testants" and that, while controversy among Christians may be needful, they are most unprofitable in the mission field.

Unfortunately, all the talk of comity kindling a missionary *corps d'esprit*, and accustoming Protestant folks to a *solidarity of missionary interests* was far from becoming a reality. Here there was no magic formula for curing entrenched parochialism and denominational interest. What had accumulated over the centuries was not going to be undone by a year's ecumenical orientation, let alone a ten-day convention. Denominational rubrics and "practice and procedure" die hard; and, as later Conferences came to discover, national sensibility was, regrettably, thicker than the common element of the Gospel. Little wonder, then, while some attempts were made (e.g. advising missionaries to form cooperative medical and industrial projects) to move beyond comity, no fundamental cooperative accords were reached.[17]

6. Some individual contributions at New York

At New York, missionaries with firsthand knowledge of the sub-continent, together with the native representative, were Africa's mouthpiece and advocates. Although we have noted some of them in passing, consider the following. The native representative, E. B. P. Kote, spoke on Christian Missions from the native African standpoint and was largely thankful for the work of the National Baptist Missions in Africa.

Kote was happy because native Christians were enthusiastic in shouldering the responsibility of their local congregations. He urged the Conference to see Christianity in Africa the way the natives saw it as a religion with remarkable social responsibility. The fact that the natives were embracing Christianity with enthusiasm, he said, was not without its difficulties. Ethiopianism, he said, had brought to light some of the social difficulties that Africans were having with the new generation of missionaries who were more interested in social positions than in service. However, Kote preferred to call the difficulties in race relations a spiritual disaster, urging the Conference to regard Ethiopianism largely in that sense. The implication of this conception of Ethiopianism was clear: the missionary community was to put its house in order by becoming more concerned with the spiritual needs of the native Christians, rather than the social mobility of a few self-conscious missionaries.

With this brief but historic presence and presentation at New York, Kote helped to usher in a new century and ecumenical pilgrimage for Africa and Christian missions. It is very likely that Kote himself was not fully aware of the precedent he had created with his appearance at this grand missionary occasion in a brand new century full of possibilities and problems no one could fully foresee. However, from our vantage point and the benefit of hindsight, Kote left behind an indelible mark or trail on the sands of ecumenical time, a trail many native Africans would later follow, crescendoing until the missionary movement reached a new era at Ibadan 1958.

Another divine, A. O. Whitman, spoke on "The Debt of Christendom to Africa." Seeking to capitalize on the guilt many missionaries felt about the enslavement of Africans, Whitman did not allow the Conference to forget the fact that Western debt to Africa was a high priority, still largely undefrayed, and probably irrepayable. Whitman appeared unconventionally frank and straightfoward. By importing new diseases and liquor into Africa and turning it into a killing field, Whitman thought that Westerners had abused the privilege that God gave them to exploit resources in Black Africa. Whitman wanted more sacrifice on the part of missionaries so that "Christendom" will quickly pay its debt.

None of these contributions, however, was as influential as T. Wakefield's. As a missionary associated with the United Methodist Free Churches, the modifying effect Wakefield's speech had on the delegates, and helped in framing a largely positive attitude toward Africans, can only be fully grasped in retrospect.

From the start of his missionary pilgrimage in Africa in 1861, Wakefield recalled, the prevailing opinion of the African as *tabula rasa* had no basis in reality. Missions had, without hermeneutical suspicion and prophetic imagination, subscribed to ethnocentric theories that prejudged and shortchanged the African capacity. The myth of their inequality with other peoples, the doubts concerning their humanity, and the reservation expressed concerning their power to acquire knowledge were but serious misperception and misdoing on the part of the Church.

Wakefield remembered how a good number of his friends were very skeptical when he decided to become a missionary in Africa, arguing that it was no use at all for him to go and preach in Africa, because Africans could not be converted or regenerated. Some of his friends, Wakefield disclosed, told him that the African was not a man but something between manhood and brutehood, and that to carry the gospel to Africa would be like pouring a cup of oil in an ocean. Others, he continued, argued that Africans have no mind enough to understand the gospel; and that, even if they have mind enough to understand the gospel, they have no moral consciousness. Why, they asked, should one waste one's time, resources and energy on a people who would not respond to the gospel no matter how it was presented to them?

Wakefield knew from personal experience that his critics were not only skeptical but also absolutely pessimistic. After several years in Black Africa and personal encounter with its people, Wakefield was ready to confront his critics with bare empirical facts and experience, not unnecessary arguments. Wakefield assured them that the African has intelligence enough to understand the gospel; that there was no lack of intellectual power or acumen in the African; and, that, concerning mental capacity, the African was quite equal to the skeptics.

While Wakefield thought that the African should not be unfairly compared with others, he also argued that, given time, the African, once he is on his feet, will stand as "high" as any nonAfrican. Nothing convinced Wakefield of Africa's bright future as its children. He had found that African children were "remarkably sharp, very clever, superior to some . . . English children here in the power of acquiring knowledge." In addition, Wakefield found that in whatever he attempted to teach these African children they were quite ready and eager to learn. "It didn't," he affirmed, "matter what it was."[18]

With all this experience, some would think that Wakefield should have scolded his audience; he did not. Instead, Wakefield appreciated the pervasive role socialization and other nontheological factors play in how we see ourselves vis-a-vis others and how, not infrequently, cultural variables are mistaken for genetic constants and vice versa. No textbook, he remarked, can change that misperception *in toto*. Experience is its only antidote.

By far, his was a powerful *testimonium* to cross-cultural experience and a crack on the powerful fortress of microcosmic vision that passed for so long as empirical truth.

Similarly, in a perspicacious manner, the Reverend H. B. Parks, Secretary of the African Methodist Episcopal (AME) Church, told the Conference that Africa, through Ethiopianism, had signalled how it wanted contemporary Protestant mission thought and practice to proceed. The problem, according to Parks' diagnosis, was that missionaries were overly negative in their reaction to this development, like parents reacting to their assertive children who, anxious for recognition, would stop at nothing to get their way.

That its development was a crisis, Parks admitted; that it meant a paralysis for mission advance, he rejected. Crisis, he averred, always comes with judgement and opportunity, a damaging as well as a cleansing effect. The question was not only whether mission societies could see the handwriting on the wall, but also whether they could peruse and decipher its message and promise for missions, and utilize it to the optimum advantage of ecumenism making.

Parks did not think that the evangelization of Africa was ever more hopeful. He saw contemporary conditions as favoring more expansion not retreat. This is why he regarded the Ethiopian Movement in Africa, which the established churches were deploring so much from one standpoint, as being one of the hopeful signs of the speedy evangelization of the African people. Indeed, Ethiopianism to him, spelt "the opening of the door" for more enthusiastic Christian expansion in Africa by the natives.

Recalling the numerous remarks which were made concerning the missionary status of the native and black Americans, Parks employed his acquaintance with the AME's surprising rapid growth (largely because of its indigenization scheme), to affirm the significance of native participation in mainline denominations as a cogent missiological factor for the twentieth century.

Confident and verging on the exaggerative, like the nineteenth-century African patron saint, Bishop Samuel Adjai Crowther of the Niger Delta,[19] Parks did not fail to tell New York how it was God's election to reserve the black son of that continent to disseminate the gospel and convert his unchurched "brethren on the dark continent."[20] Parks made no mention of the daughters of Africa. Unfortunately, at this point in time, he did not see God's election including black women as missionaries.

Summary

Overall, New York found that Africa has helped Protestantism to recover and reaffirm the fundamental convictions of the gospel. With its questions, the Protestant mission enterprise, which was, to say the least, largely individualistic and chimerical enterprise began to search for unitive bases for evangelization. There were indications that Africans were not the only victims of racism, and that rivalry among European peoples themselves affected the discordant notes which were heard loud and clear at the Conference.

The Germans, for example, registered their complaint against some Anglo-American Societies which equated the Continent with the nonChristian lands, thus necessitating missions in that part of Europe. The problem was serious enough to justify the Conference being reminded that Germany is the land from where Luther came. Apparently, it was still too early for the idea of Christian witness in six continents.

Because it recognized its limitations and sought to present the differing opinions on the various points under discussion, New York moved with its age. Its ecumenical suggestions were not to be taken as ironclad rules. Rather, as premonitions, they called for abiding thought and search. Still, with all its innovative propensity and attempt to update Christian mission thinking, New York was only a beginning.

For the first time missiology realized, in a serious manner, that it was impossible to continue to shut the door against the Enlightenment thought and sought, like other theological disciplines, to appropriate such intellectual values for mission work. Yet, although it was willing to open up its missiological suppositions to scrutiny, New York did not throw the whole door wide open.

Every effort was made to tap, for apologetic exercises and in a selective manner, the rich promises of historical criticism. For example, when an aspect of the teaching of Professor Max Muller, a pioneer of comparative study of religions, supported Christian assumptions, the Conference did not hesitate to capitalize on it. Thus Muller's belief in the supremacy of Christianity over other world religions was cited in support of the credo of Christianity's "immeasurable pre-eminence."

Indeed, this rationalist motivation which operated prior to, and at, New York helps to explain why the Conference avoided making resolutions. For it was impossible to predict how delegates would react to this first attempt to restate mission mandates. In this sense, Robert Speer's post-mortem evaluation was on target when he wrote that the Conference was able to reassure those who feared what would become of Christian missions in a time when conceptions have changed greatly since the days when the Protestant missionary enterprise made its earlier appeals in different parts of the world. "The very impression," Speer added, "which this Conference produced as it restated the missionary appeal in terms of the thought of the present day, showed how much more powerful that appeal has become."[21]

Still, by recognizing ecumenicity as the reaching after some method of concerted action in such an attempt to Christianize the nonChristian portion of the inhabited earth as shall be commensurate with the vastness of the undertaking, New York symbolized the birth pangs of ecumenical mission thinking. It knew that the dawning of the twentieth century brought possibilities for far-reaching mission gains; yet it had no quick-fixes for past missiological blunders occasioned by hasty conclusions and excessive emotionalism.

Its findings were incorporated into its "Address to the Church," in which it hinted that adequate mission patterns will come as piety and learning are not seen as mutually exclusive, and in which it urged the Protestant Church to abandon the indifference which characterized its missionary beginnings. The unknown and unopened world, it said, was becoming known and open. The evangelistic burden laid squarely on the doorstep of the Churches.

In its own way, New York helped to initiate the process of *thinking* with, not *condemning* Africa.[22] At Edinburgh that legacy became manifest and irresistible.

NOTES

[1]The Conference noted that, although these disturbances in themselves were regrettable, they helped to widen the circle of thought, and resulted in an increased appreciation of the condition of the nonChristian parts of the world. See *Ecumenical Missionary Conference New York, 1900*, 2 vols. (New York: American Tract Society, 1900), vol. 1, p. 10; hereafter cited as *New York 1900*.

[2]Notice, however, that by this time the FMCNA itself was only seven years old and was still struggling to be on its feet. For more on its development, see Lesslie Moss, *Adventures in Missionary Cooperation* (New York: Foreign Missions Conference of North America, 1930), pp. 7–13.

[3]For this and the preceding citation, see *New York 1900*, vol. 1, p. 9. For more on the rationalist temper and what thoughtful men and women were saying at the turn of the century, see, for example, H. Stuart Hughes, *Consciousness and Society: The Reorientation of European Social Thought 1890–1930* (New York: Vintage, 1977).

[4]There were several of these Comity Conferences, beginning with New York 1854. To gain perspective on what these were about see, for instance, *Report of the Centenary on the Protestant Missions of the World held in Exeter Hall (June 9th–19th), London 1888*, 2 vols. (London: James Nisbet, 1888). Hereafter cited as *London 1888*.

[5]*New York 1900*, vol. 1, p. 9.

[6]For a declaration of this ideal see, for instance, E. A. Ayandele, *The Missionary Impact on Modern Nigeria, 1842–1914* (London: Longmans, 1966), pp. 4–5.

[7]*New York 1900*, vol. 2, pp. 168–9.

[8]See, for example, *Memoirs of Captain Hugh Crow of Liverpool* (London: Frank Cass, 1970); John Adams, *Sketches Taken During Ten Voyages To Africa Between The Years 1786–1800* (New York: Johnson Reprint Corporation, 1970); Robin Hallett, ed., *Records of the African Association, 1788–1831* (London: Thomas Nelson, 1964).

[9]*New York 1900*, vol. 2, p. 166.

[10]The man who reported the conditions in Madagascar, the Rev. W. E. Cousins of the London Missionary Society fame, was inexplicably balanced in his judgement. It appeared to him that Catholic and Protestant Frenchmen had chosen that island, which is much more spacious than France itself, to settle old scores. *New York 1900*, vol. 1, pp. 473–5, 467–8. See also, Stephen Neill, *Colonialism and Christian Missions* (New York: McGraw-Hill, 1966), pp. 337–58.

[11]*New York 1900*, vol. 1, p. 469.

[12]Ibid., p. 470. On this problem, New York was only told half the story. Its causality was much more complex than that or as recent interpretations have allowed. In South Africa, this Movement was cast in the worse possible light, especially after the founding (in 1896) in Pretoria of a branch of the African Methodist Episcopal Church. In West Africa, it was seen as a case of irresponsible and arrogant children who, anxious to take their parents' place, would not wait for nature to take its course. Cf. G. Shepperson, "Ethiopianism: past and present," in *Christianity in Tropical Africa,* ed. C. G. Baeta, (London: Oxford, 1968), pp. 249–64.

[13]Mojola Agbebi offers us a glimpse into the Ethiopian literature of the time:

> "When we look for no *manifesto* from Salisbury Square, when we expect no packet of resolution from Exeter Hall, when no bench of foreign Bishops, no conclave of Cardinals, 'lord over' Christian Africa, when the Captain of Salvation, Jesus Christ Himself, leads the Ethiopian host, and our Christianity ceases to be London-ward and New York-ward but Heaven-ward, then will there be an end to Privy Councils, Governors, Colonels, Annexations, Displacements, Partitions, Cessions and Coercions. Telegraph wires will be put to political vocabulary of the . . . African Native." As cited in Ayandele, p. 174. Undoubtedly, this was tough-talk.

[14]*New York 1900,* vol. 1, p. 470; G. Shepperson, pp. 249–264.

[15]Notice that Harford-Battersby referred to the indigenous culture as "civilization," indicating a change in the evaluation of African culture. In the nineteenth century African culture was largely seen as not meriting such a sociological designation. Philip D. Curtin, *The Image of Africa: British Ideas and Action, 1780–1850* (Madison: University of Wisconsin, 1964).

[16]For example, the rise of "mixed races" born in some Western cities was characterized as proof of licentiousness. *See New York 1900,* vol. 1, pp. 347–354. Cf. Felix N. Okoye, *The American Image of Africa: Myth and Reality* (Buffalo, N. Y.: Black Academy Press, 1971).

[17]*New York 1900,* vol. 1, pp. 233–238.

[18]Ibid., p. 462.

[19]Crowther was present at London 1888. For his contribution at that meeting, see *London 1888,* vol. 1, p. 272 and passim.

[20]*New York 1900,* vol. 1, p. 472. Notice that Parks, though a black American, spoke of Africa unqualifiedly as "dark continent" and that in general, despite feelings of racial identification with Africans, many black mission supporters accepted

Western stereotypes about African savagery. For an extensive commentary on black American attitudes (including Parks') toward Africa, see, Walter L. Williams, *Black Americans and the Evangelization of Africa* (Madison, Wisconsin: University Press, 1982), pp. 104–140.

[21]*New York 1900*, vol. 1. p. 63. Robert Speer (1867–1947) was one of the leading missiological thinkers for the first part of this century. Because of his missiological influence, the library at Princeton Theological Seminary, New Jersey, is named after him.

[22]See a book with that title which is a collection of essays by African and non-African leaders. Milton Stauffers, *Thinking with Africa* (New York: Mission Education Movement, 1927).

2

AFRICA AND THE BIRTH OF THE ECUMENICAL MOVEMENT: EDINBURGH 1910

I. BETWEEN NEW YORK 1900 AND EDINBURGH 1910

New York 1900 was succeeded by numerous world events which necessitated the missionary world to continue to come together, and to realize more and more that, in every department of thought and action, African problems were passing out of the stage in which mere dosing out of Christian moral injunctions was becoming completely inadequate. One of these events was the economic and colonial rivalry which continued at a feverish pitch in Africa. Another was the naval race which unleashed more conflicts in Anglo-German relations, and later helped to plunge the world into the calamity of World War I.

Missiologically, an outstanding event, during this decade, was the fact that some churches were beginning to come out of their closets, and the missionary movement which was not a traditional power-center began to recognize the importance of organizing to influence the course of political events. The meeting which embodied this rediscovered group ethic, awakened the latent political power of the churches, and served as a prelude to Edinburgh was the Second Hague Peace Conference (1907). It was at this Conference that the first "modern attempt of the churches to cooperate in international practical matters was manifested."[1] There some European and North American church and mission leaders, prodded by a band of Christian activists (notably Allen Baker, a Canadian Quaker and manufacturer), signed and placed a petition before the statesmen who had gathered to plot, among other things, how to maintain the balance of power in Africa and other parts of the world; and so perpetuate the relative peace that Europe was experiencing.

This Peace Conference was followed by another extraordinary event: the exchange of visits by German and English ecclesiastics between May 1908 and June 1909. These visits (which were premised on the belief that international problems could be solved, if there were only greater opportunities for personal contact and personal knowledge between the peoples of the world), were designed to lessen tension between the two peoples, in view and in spite of the fact that their governments were busy fighting over spheres of influence in Africa.

Together they served as another indication of ecumenical beginnings, marked the first public "reentry of the churches into the concerns of this world since the Reformation,"[2] and led to the most important event that followed New York: the World Missionary Conference held at Edinburgh in the quiet summer of 1910.

II. THE BIRTH: EDINBURGH 1910

If the nineteenth-century Comity Conferences were but bumps, New York 1900, a noticeable tremor, Edinburgh 1910, was the earthquake that necessitated and triggered the birth and nurture of ecumenism and full commitment to espousing acceptable mission mandates in a rapidly changing world. What gave Edinburgh the explosive capacity it engendered? And what made it the prototype for subsequent ecumenical conferences?

A New Way To See Missions

The answer, first, to the second question can be summarized in one word: organization. Unlike all previous missionary conferences, including New York 1900, Edinburgh's delegates, 1200 strong, were not only mission enthusiasts but also official delegates of more than one hundred and fifty-nine mission societies. Judged by attendance and personalities, Edinburgh was predominantly a Conference for the "mother churches." One need not go through the list of official delegates to discover the celebrated names of world Christianity of the time: Drs. John R. Mott and J. H. Oldham, two figures who helped to bring the meeting about and served as its Chairman and Secretary respectively; Bishop Brent of the Episcopal Church in America and later the brain behind the Faith and Order Movement; Dr. Eugene Stock of the Church Missionary Society (CMS); and Basil Mathews of the London Missionary Society (LMS).

Also, one need not be surprised to discover that representing Africa were hundreds of Western missionaries and four black Americans. These four black Americans were the Reverends W. W. Brown and J. G. Jordan of the Foreign Mission Board of the National Baptist Convention; and the Reverend J. W. Rankin and Miss H. Quinn Brown of the Foreign Missionary Society of the AME Church.

Edinburgh's quintessence, however, was not the representatives as such but the subjects and method of its study. Unlike New York, eight commissions were set up to critically examine Protestant conduct of mission. As if appointing commissions was not enough, a preliminary circulation of the fruits of that survey was made public prior to Edinburgh's opening session. Besides, as we shall see, Edinburgh made recommendations that no other non-Roman, non-Orthodox conference had ever ventured.

As for what gave Edinburgh its explosive character, the answer lies in understanding its epicenter: the fields. Yet when these fields are compared, no other field generated more shock waves than the African field. Pre-Edinburgh opinion about the Asian field was far more positive, respectful, and even predictable. Some missionaries knew that it will not surrender lying down. Prior to Edinburgh such was not necessarily the expectation from Africa.

It is against this background that we must understand the shock which gripped Edinburgh's delegates as many of them heard, for the first time, that the evangelical challenge in Africa was far more demanding than earlier imagined. This shock was made doubly painful after many delegates discovered that missionaries were, by no means, closer to fulfilling the hope of evangelizing the world in their generation, contrary to what many were led to believe by the watchword "the evangelization of the world in this generation," popularized by the Student Volunteer Movement.

1. Social conditions at Edinburgh

Whereas the Comity Conferences (and New York 1900, in particular) were largely satisfied with inviting various experts to "lecture" on African conditions and, for the most part, to project a rationalist image of Protestant missions, Edinburgh sought to move beyond projection and to call things more as it saw them. In a world where the geography of Africa was just becoming plainer, the first shocker came from Edinburgh's general survey of the continent's social conditions as well as its readiness to examine whether or not societies were arrayed to wage a prolonged "campaign of evangelization adequate in scope, in thoroughness, and in power."[3]

Edinburgh found that African social conditions, because of their preindustrial status, called for special, concrete missiological intervention. For example, the climatic conditions and diseases, capable of reducing the missionary band as quickly as it was replenished, called for alternative strategy. In short, without rehearsing the familiar litany of the evils of the so-called "dark continent" and contrasting them with the best of the so-called "civilized continents," Edinburgh was unconventionally candid and matter-of-factly. Missionary work in Africa, the Conference declared, was at the brink of collapse and in danger of drowning; and that, without a calculated, unitive attack on these conditions, its ruins will be unsalvageable, its drowning a devastated blow to Christian missionary enterprise, and its meager gain irreplaceable.

Although Edinburgh regretted how pre-Edinburgh missions approached African social conditions, it did not seek to overturn everything that had gone before. Instead, it built on it by seeing, for example, that compounding the African missionary situation, was the presence of Western commercial and governmental interests. Edinburgh also wanted missionaries to take cognizance of how immigration from Europe was changing the African landscape, and how this brought new problems for any evangelistic effort. For example, the task of having to convert not only Africans but also the increasing number of nonChristian Europeans who migrated to East and Southern Africa largely because of economic, not religious, reasons.

If, in the past, some missionaries tended to give some Africans the impression that all Westerners were Christian, this immigration of nonChristian Europeans to these African regions (where they began to compete with the natives for food, land, and other necessities), drastically changed the missionary situation in Africa. Because this was a new situation of which the Protestant missionary societies had little or no experience, either collectively or separately, Edinburgh cautioned that a divided missionary approach would do more harm than good in the long run.

Further, Edinburgh found that the development of large centers of industry in the cities further spelt a bad omen for divided Protestantism. Threatening the home life of mission stations, this industrial and urban wave called for broadening missionary perspective on economic issues with their inevitable impact on African social cohesion and stability. Here Edinburgh made missionaries to be aware that missionary work cannot be effectively conducted in an atmosphere of economic or political instability; and that to be concerned about the welfare of the missionized and to ensure social stability was a prudent missiological move calculated to preempt disruption in evangelistic efforts.

This teaching was certainly in accordance with the belief of many African peoples, including the Ibibios of Southeastern Nigeria, who believe that a hungry person cannot listen attentively to God's message. Or, as Edinburgh itself put it, missionaries were obligated to pay attention to the "economic basis for prosperous community" life and to technical and industrial training, particularly with regard to agriculture, in order to succeed in their Christianization efforts. Clearly, this statement was an affirmation of New York's social position. However, Edinburgh appeared poised for more, not less, social Christianity than New York was willing to advocate.

Edinburgh's review of past missionary attempts to deal with modern education in Africa revealed that the situation was not something to write home about. From Cape Colony came evidence that educational programs were becoming, at the time, a disintegrative rather than an integrative factor. Some young people were becoming discontent with their village life; and displeasure with, and breaking away from, traditional family control was becoming rampant. The verdict from Sierra Leone was equally discouraging. Book knowledge, the Sierra Leone report card said, was "disappointing," repetitive, and a very one sided venture touching only a part (spiritual) of a child's nature. The evidence from Uganda, concerning an industrial educational experiment, showed that it was too spasmodic to be effective, suffering severely from want of proper equipment on "an adequate scale and from lack of support."[4]

While ensuing discussion showed that the New Testament contains no regulative prescriptions concerning missionary methods, Edinburgh reaffirmed New York's conviction, that the most effective means for Christianizing the sub-Sahara was the Christian school. This reaffirmation did not preclude medical and industrial missions. To be sure, societies were encouraged to set up commercial and industrial companies and operate them on sound commercial lines. Named as prototypes for ecumenical emulation were, inter alia, the Scottish Mission Industrial Company and the Church Missionary Society Uganda Company.

As part of its commitment to formulate specific missionary mandates for ecumenical workers to follow, Edinburgh encouraged societies to extirpate past policies which made Christianity exotic in African eyes. Specifically, delegates made seventeen daring recommendations vis-a-vis African social problems. These recommendations included the importance of careful planning and concentration of effort, and the necessity of economizing resources based on certain courses of action.

Among the courses of action suggested were united effort in studying educational, industrial, and agricultural problems and the maintenance of union educational institutions. In light of these African challenges as well as challenges from other fields, Edinburgh introduced the idea of "the whole Gospel by the whole church to the whole world."[5]

Clearly, this recognition that evangelism is for all people and for all the inhabited world was a significant ecumenical development and an apparent modification of New York's nineteenth-century geography and simplistic bifurcation of the world into Christian and nonChristian. Thus, recent emphasis on *Witness in Six Continents*, with its bipolar concern for both soul-winning and social action, has its root here at Edinburgh, contrary to what Harvey Hoekstra and Ernest Lefever would have us believe when they attribute the so-called demise of evangelism to the integration of the IMC and the WCC after the second world war.[6]

Similarly, it is evident that the present concern for social justice is not the product solely created by the Third World Churches with their Liberation/Political Theologies as Amjad-Ali[7] claimed, because Edinburgh itself indirectly laid the foundation for the emergence of such theologies.

2. Primal religions at Edinburgh

At Edinburgh, the making of ecumenical attitude towards nonChristian religions received a boost from Africa. On the surface, its conclusions about African primal religion were similar to New York's. However, beneath the surface, the similarity was no more than approximate. Actually, New York's attitude was far less precise. The same cannot be said of Edinburgh's. Though members consistently employed E. B. Tylor's antiquated appellation "animism" to refer to all primal religions, Edinburgh's disposition was heavily influenced by a phenomenology that recognized the empirical credentials of this belief system as religion *sui generis*. In so doing, primal religious value was acknowledged.

Although primal religious ideas may appear to the missionary as absurd, Edinburgh mandated missionaries to first look at the bright side of this religion. In the first place, Edinburgh called attention to the fact that this religion has performed an unsolicited duty for Christian missions. Although its external manifestation has taken the form of extensive pathos of wailing at funerals, a desperate attempt to ward off spirits considered as capricious, and a persistent atmosphere of phobia and fatalism, its adherents are not irreligious or atheistic. They may lack what others consider a dense concept of the transcendent, but they are by no means thoughtless. They may be expressing a preponderant concern for the here-and-now—averting illness or misfortune, praying for good harvest and victory in skirmishes and warfare and so on, but they are not, by any stretch of imagination, expressing an inveterate opposition to Christianity.

Edinburgh saw that this religion, like all religions, is not without some effect on social morality.[8] In this, Edinburgh was making an irresistible plea for better appreciation of this folk-religion, and wanted missionaries to remember their pagan ancestry; for today one can see some of its memorials, its altars, and tombs at Salisbury Plains (Stonehenge), England.

Yet the apparent simplicity and unsophistication of primal rituals, warned Edinburgh, did not imply, as earlier thought, a quick knockout for Christianity. Because there was no evidence to suggest that all primal religionists were dissatisfied with their religion, Edinburgh found that there were several hindrances which made cooperative action urgent.

The first hindrance was moral in character. Edinburgh concluded that, as long as Christianizing Africa meant conversion from past to present, old to new life, it should not be unrealistically expected that the converted African will immediately meet moral standards fashioned in metropolitan Christian centers, after centuries of social struggle and casuistry.

In Edinburgh's understanding, moral renovation was not to be the sole barometer for religious change. The two, it said, are related, but not inseparable, and should not dictate catholic missionary policy, given the fact that moral renovation may follow rather than precede religious conversion. For this reason, Edinburgh mandated missionaries to bear in mind that the moral conduct of new Christians may remain unsatisfactory for a long time. However, missionaries were not to doubt the reality or sincerity of the religious experience of new converts solely because they exhibited slow moral progress.

The second hindrance was intellectual in origin and was rooted in the challenge of Western and African cosmologies or, more specifically, the encounter of a Copernican cosmology with pre-Copernican cosmology. Edinburgh reasoned that the question was not, as often thought, whether preindustrial thought is also "prelogical" or "illogical." The question, said Edinburgh, was that of worldview: fate versus causation. This was quite an interesting understanding of how one's worldview, can, consciously or unconsciously, affect one's view of right and wrong, especially as it appears to another person trained and brought up in a different cultural background.[9]

The third hindrance of equal gravity was social in kind. It stemmed from the gulf between a social structure in which the unit is the group and one which extols the self. Some wondered whether reliance must not be placed on other sources of influence (such as targeting the group or clan) rather than helpless individuals. Missionaries were forewarned that "it may be that actually the Christianising of these [African] people will be another instance of salvation by 'the remnant.'"[10]

The fourth and final hindrance was the increasing tendency on the part of the natives to perceive Christianity, rightly or wrongly, as an Occidental religion and a religion in which the natives must always be "subordinate to the Europeans." Edinburgh warned that, as long as this image of Christianity prevailed and missionaries continued to be regarded as agents of foreign domination, a political and religious time-bomb was inadvertently being planted. This was a timely warning in light of the events, during and after World War I, in which some radical African nationalists, in order to generate popular support for their emerging political views, branded some missionary groups as agents of foreign oppression.

Consonant with its desire to be "progressive," Edinburgh had sought to ascertain from its African and other correspondents whether contact with primal religionists had altered, in form or substance, their impression of Christianity's central dogmas. Understandably, most respondents resoundingly said no. However, they also acknowledged that, as a result of their physical presence in Africa and personal encounter with its people, they had made new discoveries and had broadened their perspectives of Africa. Most had gained a deeper appreciation of the dogma of grace and justification. One was inclined to lay increasing emphasis on eschatological themes—resurrection and *parousia* (the Second Coming of Christ). Another had acquired a deepened belief in God as Spirit, the doctrine of reward and punishment, and Jesus as the determinant of humanity's destination. One had come to understand in a new and urgent way the necessity of attending to the economic conditions in which the people live. Many more had begun to come to grips with the oneness of the Church and had become increasingly tolerant and respectful of other religions. Equally received were telling notes of disappointment caused by "an unyielding wall" of the old African order and absence of visible and immediate results.[11]

Consistent with these discoveries, Edinburgh recommended the following for ecumenical embracement:

a. That the time has come to put away prejudice and study and get to know the African religion from inside out. Missionaries were to strive at understanding the local conception of things by learning from the natives themselves. For to pursue it otherwise is to attempt to hang a ladder in the air. This process was to be informed by a painstaking ethnocentric method, more akin to contemporary data collection methods than the nineteenth-century arm-chair deductionism practiced by E. B. Tylor and his disciples, especially after the publication of his *Primitive Culture* in 1871.

b. That the missionary must recognize that to lighten a dark room, one does not need to sweep out the dark. This policy meant that the whole pre-Edinburgh attitude of thorough sweeping was found to be unrealistic and should no longer be pursued. What was needed, said Edinburgh, was an attitude based on the awareness that "the [nonChristian] religion with which [the missionary] deals is [like Christianity] . . . an effort of fellow-men to grapple with the great problem of existence."[12] A conciliatory attitude was to be the key because, in Edinburgh's view, missionaries did not have anything to lose in so doing. Though most delegates were still uneasy with classifying primal religion as *preparatio evangelica*, they allowed that there are inherent points of contact such as the belief in God.

Edinburgh laid the foundation for inter-religious dialogue: contemptuous, vehement denunciations, and overbearing manners were largely to be avoided; vigorous opposition was to be tempered with empathetic understanding. Moreover, Edinburgh saw that African primal religionists had not manufactured a separate God of their own; theirs was just a brand of the universal God-idea.

A daring approach, which affirmed that the Holy Spirit was at work in Africa long before foreign missionaries arrived, was voiced. It stated that missionaries should rejoice in every element of "truth and goodness" that they find in the religious practice of the people among whom they serve. It acknowledged that the Holy Spirit is responsible for all truths and all goodness wherever found and however ignorant a religious devotee may be of this source. While this statement bordered on universalism and may surprise those who think that contemporary ecumenical movement has deviated from Edinburgh on inter-religious questions, it is plain that Edinburgh itself was progressive on this matter. This progressive nature of its thought is seen even more vividly when it declared that every religion exists by virtue of the truth which it proclaims rather than "the virtue of its falsehood."[13]

While some disagreed with this philosophical bent, the die had been cast. The African world, this recommendation suggested, was teaching the Evangelical world an unforgettable lesson: nobody catches a monkey in a hurry. Put differently, Edinburgh enjoined ecumenical workers to be patient in evangelizing Africa. For changing a belief-system is far more complicated and time-consuming than earlier envisaged. Or, as some delegates warned, seeds need time to take root downwards before they begin to grow upwards.

c. Concerning the crucial question of points of contact, Edinburgh was even more blunt. It argued that any difference of opinion that may exist among African respondents was apparent rather than real. For it was held by the majority of these respondents, in the research which was conducted for the Conference, that there is a modicum of truth in all religious systems, God not having left Himself without a witness in the peoples. Throughout Africa, it continued, the God idea is prevalent enough to offer point of contact. The idea of sacrifice, for example, gives a splendid opportunity for teaching the Christian idea of atonement. On the widespread belief in go-betweens or mediums, the idea of Christ could be grafted. However, sympathetic approach or abandonment of iconoclastic attitude was not to be equated with syncretism; Christianity was still absolute. How syncretism was to be avoided and "Christianity's supremacy" maintained *ad infinitum* in this fluid world was not spelt out. The ensuing discussion skirted this issue.

By skirting this issue, Edinburgh actually sent out mixed signals as far as Christian attitude to nonChristian religions was concerned. On the one hand, Edinburgh was far more positive than New York. On the other hand, like New York, Edinburgh assumed that syncretism was unacceptable in theory, though in practice it was impossible to distinguish in some African churches what was Christian and what was primal religious value. It would take the disastrous effect of the first world war and the rise and challenge of anti-Christian ideologies to force the nascent ecumenical movement to come to grips with this equivocation of its position on this matter.[14]

3. Indigenous churches at Edinburgh

At first glance it would seem that Africa would have no light to shed on the principles underlying a good relationship between church and mission. Edinburgh put such assumption to rest. It opened its data on the influence of indigenous churches and indigenous leadership with an accurate portrayal of what it had learned from contemporary African and world situation.

When the enterprise began, it was generally tantalizing to have a lop-sided view of power and influence peddling: missions could influence but not be influenced. Edinburgh found that, in actuality, this had a correlate: Africa, like other continents, was modifying Western Christianity and missions in subtle but profound ways, even though Christians remained oblivious of this modification process. In short, Edinburgh noted that, just as natural processes are constantly at work whether humans notice them or not, the African world has been impacting Christianity whether Christians like it or not.

Edinburgh believed that emergent African Christian Communities necessitated change in missiological perspective. By contrasting the past with the present, and with a narration of the different phases of Protestant mission enterprise, it called for a change in imagination and the recognition of how social existence plays a far more determining role in the making of mission policy.

Whereas, in the past, it was tempting to think that there was very little evangelical reward from missionary work in African and other mission fields, Edinburgh wanted the Church at home to see further "into the true state of the matter," namely, that the Church on the mission field was no longer a by-product of mission work; "it was itself by far the most efficient element in the Christian propaganda."[15] In order words, a new way of assessing and thinking about the Church on the mission field was necessary. This new way of assessment was to be immediately implemented throughout the mission fields.

Though it took several decades to come to this appreciation of the evangelical role the indigenous churches were, and could be playing, Edinburgh suggested that it was better to make a belated acknowledgement than to continue to ignore it. As children sometimes help to open their parents' eyes to new realities and new possibilities and unexplored options, the "younger churches" in Africa, like elsewhere, were helping their "mother churches" to see missions differently.

Why did Edinburgh say that greater appreciation be given to the evangelical role of the indigenous churches? The answer was that action speaks louder than words. The life style of Christianized Africans, being the most conspicuous, was the most important living testimony to the unchurched, and far more persuasive than abstract ministrations in preaching and teaching.

At Edinburgh, no other issue concerning the relationship of African churches and missions was seen as beckoning for more Christian cooperation than the rising influence of *Aladura* (Yoruba for prayer) or "spiritual" churches. Although Edinburgh relied, almost exclusively, on second-hand information about these indigenous churches (and so considered them as sects founded on the idea of independence from European guidance and the "self-sufficiency of the African"), it was more appreciative of their missionary role than New York. For it saw that Ethiopianism was a natural reaction, such as has been seen many times in the history of the Church, against the luxury and worldliness of the contemporary Church and in favor of a return to the simpler pattern of earlier days.

However, like New York, Edinburgh underestimated this phenomenon when, for example, it saw its rising doctrine as superficial and largely "emotional form of Christianity" and incapable of resisting the disintegrating and corrupting impact of the surrounding old order. Yet Edinburgh saw that this movement was beckoning for Christian mission cooperation, and that its radical wing was indirectly calling attention to the inadequate training and cooptation of "moderate" and "sympathetic" native leaders by the missions. Further, in areas where there was rising self-consciousness and pride in the indigenous, some African Courts were not cooperating; these scepters saw the Christian altar as counter-productive and politically inexpedient.

It was not a fitting and uplifting discovery to find that missions were talking too much about lack of sympathetic indigenous leaders when they were not doing much to produce such leaders. A serious flaw attacked was that, unlike Japan or China with a national government in charge of educational policy in which even the missionaries had to follow, Africa had each mission society largely devising its own policy and the method of implementation. The result was an educational system fraught with numerous problems typical of any makeshift and, naturally, fewer and fewer indigenous leaders, not followers, emerged from such a system.

While Edinburgh learned that nowhere else, except Africa, has experience more exclusively shown that the essential thing in education is "the personality of the teacher," it was made clear that personal examples and other character-forming influences, which make education a living thing, were not enough to produce native leaders. Too many mistakes in the choice of subject matter, unmodified procedures borrowed from Western school systems, no grounding in African sensibility and mode of thought, had combined to put a huge question mark on whether missionaries had the mind of devolution in the first place, and whether they were thinking about taking concrete action toward that end.

Edinburgh hoped that missionaries would avoid competition and concentrate on developing the indigenous church. For the want of combination was a capital defect with a heavy repair bill, the bill being, among other things, a weakened influence on government educational plans and inability to win the support of radical African nationalists.

4. Race relations at Edinburgh

On the race question, Edinburgh, like New York, did not make any special study of the matter. Nevertheless, Edinburgh, through direct and indirect reference by its Commissions to the problem, was quite aware of how native Africans were being looked down upon, and the disabilities and harsh conditions to which black Americans were subjected as they sought to labor as missionaries in Africa, not to mention their quest to become part of the mainstream of American society.

Black American presence at this Conference, though small in number, was a statement few eyes could miss. Equally difficult to overlook were newspaper headlines that announced the nascent and ugly character of the conflict as it was brooding in South and East Africa. The proceedings of the General Missionary Conference in South Africa, between 1904 and 1909, show how concerned some mission leaders were about the racial implications of the Boer/British warfare (1899-1902).[16] Additionally, delegates knew that the antagonism among nations and classes during the years prior to, and including, the Conference was often couched in racial categories.

When, then, we look at how Edinburgh treated this matter, we can scarcely fail to be struck by notable differences from New York. Whereas New York's criticism of prevailing racial assumptions was largely implicit and indirect, Edinburgh offered a sustained and open criticism of its own which attributed the root cause of the problem to economic circumstances. Whereas New York heard testimony from a few missionaries whose earlier views of Africa and Africans were undergoing changes, Edinburgh reflected more as a group and thought that the decision of "white settlers to create a white nation" and to utilize African resources as far as practicable for their sole benefit and, overagainst this, the growth and educational advancement and ambitions of the indigenes, naturally created a favorable condition "peculiarly conducive to racial antipathies, jealousies, and antagonisms."[17]

Edinburgh tried to understand why black movement for independent churches was tied to white exclusivism. Thus, unlike New York, Edinburgh did not bypass the importance of this Ethiopian movement and its effect on indigenous thought and feeling. Instead, it found that one phase of this movement was showing why, inevitably, its influence cannot be ignored in any missionary attempt at phrasing a united educational curriculum that would provide for racial co-existence and civic efficiency.

Edinburgh saw that not all forms of Ethiopianism were anti-white or anti-Christian. It found that most advocates of the movement were universalistic in doctrine and had recognized that the future of Africa is inseparably bound up with that of other continents. Though its political power was not to be exaggerated, its message was to be seen as a protest against mission status quo and all racial discrimination and a summons to more inclusive evangelical structures. As "a phase of native thought which [had] become widespread among the people from the Zambezi to Cape Town," Edinburgh said it must be taken seriously. As "a principle and as an influence on native life," Edinburgh believed it must be seen as a quest for "democracy."[18]

In the early mission days the missionary was the "overlord," directing and controlling to a great extent the life of the community in which he lived. But now, with the rise of this movement, added Edinburgh, missionary power was "passing over" to the natives. Therefore, the Conference urged missionaries to avoid further racial tensions in Africa by taking seriously the church's multi-racial origins. In short, Edinburgh saw that the new circumstance had made it impossible for the "old power to remain." The people had begun "to realise their political power"[19] and with it the new face of Christian religion in the mind of the native.

In Nyasaland (Malawi), it was reported that the movement was leaving behind "a certain impatience" among foreigners and advisers and that it had fomented a new attitude toward European authority. Occasionally suspicious and antagonistic in temper, this movement was making no sharp distinction between colonial administrators and missionaries.

In Natal, this movement was creating a national spirit within the church, and hastening the time of native self-government and beginning to alter social relations, on the one hand, between the native and the missionary and, on the other hand, between the native and the foreigner.

Seeking to educate missionaries and colonial governments as to their Christian responsibility regarding Africans and other so-called "backward races," Edinburgh issued a statement. Called "National Duties To The More Backward Races Of Mankind," the statement presumed that "only the Gospel of Christ" is able to overcome racial antipathies; and admitted that, amid the wealth produced by African dependencies, the so-called "advanced races" were showing little responsibility to the so-called "backward races," syphoning African wealth back to metropolitan centers. Low-level officials were showing this indifference in their "selfish, arrogant and callous conduct." High-level officials did not hesitate to speak of black people as if they were destined to "perpetual national servitude" and had no other purpose in life than to be hewers of wood and drawers of water for the white man.

Moreover, Edinburgh saw that dependencies and colonies inhabited by millions of black people were sometimes professedly, as well as actually, administered, not for the sole benefit of the natives, but for the aggrandizement of the colonial masters. Additionally, even where humanity and integrity tempered the behavior of the ruling power, and measures were taken to ameliorate the lot of the people, there was, not infrequently, an absence of persistent and extensive effort to help the natives and protect them from the evils of "the baser influences" of the dominant civilization.[20]

Unlike the past where a vaunted sense of race prevailed, Edinburgh, while still upholding the belief that God brought about European world dominance, introduced benevolent trusteeship as the parameter on which "enlightened Christian nations" of Europe and America should base their colonial adventures. This view would later become widespread particularly after World War I and the formation of the so-called Mandated Territories in Africa and other parts of the world. Further, although Edinburgh knew that this conviction had little influence on the conduct of these so-called "Christian nations," it desired to see them (Christian nations) dissociating themselves from all demoralizing traffic, from all selfish colonial adventures, from all exploitation of less developed cultures, and from all forms of aggression.

Edinburgh, more than New York, had an intuitive understanding for the way African mind was working and in that sense was radical, that is, not in the ordinary political sense of being "on the left," but in the original philological meaning of a concern with the roots of social difficulties. Edinburgh sought to demythologize racial differences and to bring rationality to bear on the subject. It saw that, at every turn, race relations drove back to the question of integrity and credibility of the Christian doctrine of God and creation. While it failed to fully appreciate the African past, Edinburgh admitted that African people have a future that was not only interlocked with nonAfrican peoples but also bound to have some influence on the world community. African people, Edinburgh added, mean to carve and work out their own political, religious and social history. Accordingly, the world community was asked to be prepared for the influence which Black Africa would exert on the "community of civilised nations."[21]

Edinburgh, more than New York, admitted that the so-called civilized nations were, after all, not omnipotent and that their peoples, not unlike other peoples, were just beginning to be highly conscious of human interdependence in general and Western dependence on Africa in particular. Missionaries were to be conscious of this fact and to recognize that on this matter Christians, like nonChristians, are groping for answers; and that Christians are still on earth not heaven, immature and imperfect, not mature and perfect. A statement mandated missionaries to bear in mind that the whole world was just beginning to understand that Africans have their customs and beliefs which are worthy of attention, because of their importance and potential influence on the Christian message.

At the same time, and without double talk and circumlocution, Edinburgh posited that care must be exercised by modern Christianity in resolving this colorbar. A leaf should be borrowed from early Christian expansion in which Christians were not seen as separate races but, in fact, as one—*genus tertium*, third race. Though this connoted inferiority, it was also an epitomy of the unity Christians experienced among themselves.[22] The unanswered question remained whether or not modern Christians can in fact see themselves in terms of the early Church now that Christians are found in all social strata, as opposed to the primitive times when they were largely part of the oppressed community.

Moreover, Edinburgh assumed that racism was the product of moral decline. Failing to fully probe other possible causes of racism (such as competition for scarce and finite resources), Edinburgh hoped that the problem would go away largely because of goodwill on the part of missionaries and colonial administrators. It would take the effect of the first world war to realize that goodwill alone was not enough to overcome socioeconomic exploitation on which the theories of racism and discrimination against Africans was partly, if not wholly, based.

5. Cooperation and unity at Edinburgh

In Edinburgh's hands missionary cooperation and unity became a positive concept. It ceased, at least temporarily, to connote mere comity or "missionary politeness" and was established as the sole basis for modern missions. At Edinburgh, a separate preparatory material was done by Commission VIII on this cooperation and unity question. If other Commissions saw unity in the mission field as incidental to their task, Commission VIII saw it as its sole task. Consequently, what others left implicit it made explicit. What they dealt with only indirectly, it faced squarely and directly.

To make its point, this Commission found it necessary to impress upon the delegates and their churches the importance of cooperation as raised by contemporary Africa. After sorting through the facts, it felt "that a large number of our previously accepted assumptions and preconceptions have to be very considerably modified."[23]

Statistics had shown the stark and stubborn fact that, in spite of the catchword, "evangelization of the world in this generation," Christianity was by then the religion of only a third of the human race. The ferment of governmental and commercial bureaucratic apparatuses in Africa had introduced another equation into an already complicated situation. Henceforth, because of the lure of upward mobility from messenger to clerk and interpreters in these other employment avenues, missionary societies were unable to claim to be the sole carriers of "civilization" or new social life in Africa.

Competition not only for the African soul but also his or her services was the name of the game. In such a battle, missionary propaganda, with its tragic divisions and largely reward-in-heaven teaching, could not stand a head to head confrontation with the reward-on-earth promise offered by commercial and governmental entities. Moreover, it was pointed out that the absence of united solution will further sunder the Church because, for good or ill, the globe was being reduced to a metropolitan neighborhood, ensuring that isolationism will only engender anomie in the missionary ranks and in church life.

As if Edinburgh foresaw the moratorium debate of the 1970s and the general requirement today of visa for cross-cultural evangelists, it warned that there existed the probability that doors now open may before long be closed. From that angle, divided missionary strategy with its waste of time, energy, overlapping of effort, and misdirected activity in Africa was found to be not only "foolish but criminal." The situation was grim; the issues at stake grievous. Accordingly, rethinking missions was found indispensable; and it had to be done, in spite of the cost. This cost included each mission society reconsidering its aims, its plans, and its methods in terms of the common need for unity.

For this reason, Edinburgh blasted the idea that, because the African field was so large, noncooperation should be the norm. From the standpoint of efficiency, Africa had shown that the methods by which the work had been carried out were to be "viewed with grave concern." Therefore, division among missionary forces was seen as having ultimate negative ramifications which far-outweighed and outnumbered penultimate and incidental advantages. In other words, some good lessons had come out of each-mission-to-itself approach. However, the fact remained that Christian forces were confronting their gigantic task, as the Conference added, without concerted policy, without adequate combination, and without sufficient generalship.

With a military jargon that was to gain currency in the post-Edinburgh world, this Conference was asked to confront the shameful fact that, although mission work was supposed to be a campaign of allies, many of these allies were ignorant of what the others were doing. The massiveness of African missionary problems was summoning Christian consciences to feel and exhibit in practice all the profound and fecund beauty of ecumenical aspirations. The time had come for real concrete unitive measures.

Edinburgh's unitive formulation was more dynamic than static; it was cast in terms of process rather than of structure. A cardinal point of this process was the public enunciation, for the first time, that missions must seek to cooperate with governments and that governments must make the native interest their own interest.

Yet this declaration was found to be inadequate because, unlike the Orient, particularly China and Japan (nations in which some mission societies had invested a lot of their "capital" and had reaped very little (by way of concrete converts), and civilizations in which national government could hardly be subdued without strong resistance), the sub-Sahara was different. The multiplicity of governments and varying moral commitments made the sub-continent a test case for church and mission unity. Thus the conviction was that mission/government relations could be sustained only by such united action as would draw out full support from all missions and their supporters. It was understood that, without this united action, a disorganized church, however endowed with altruism and self-abnegation cannot expect to take on a colonial government in Africa with its enormous instruments of power and control. To be sure, this was a timely warning when viewed from post-Edinburgh world events.

6. Some individual contributions at Edinburgh

At Edinburgh, several Africanists joined in making the Conference as unique as it was. Without going into the long lists of African and nonAfrican correspondents who helped in the preparatory material, let us mention some of the outstanding contributors: Dr. H. Karl Kumm of the Sudan United Mission (SUM); Dr. Eugene Stock; Dr. Julius Richter, a renowned German mission historian; the Reverend A. W. Wilkie of the Church of Scotland Mission in Calabar, Nigeria; Dr. James Stewart of Lovedale, South Africa; and Drs. John Mott and J. H. Oldham.

Of these contributions it would be impossible and unprofitable, within existing constraints, to try to sort them out one by one. The best we can do is to highlight two.

The first was by Karl Kumm. Known for his anti-Moslem posture, Kumm's contribution was mainly directed to that end. Assuming Edinburgh's overall displeasure with colonial governments' attitude toward Islam (and particularly the British Government whom delegates accused of favoring Islam and discouraging the extension of Christian Missions into Islamic territories), Kumm argued for more Christian advance. Islam, he said, was making more tremendous advance in the sub-Sahara. Kumm thought that the Moslem was advancing because of his better education and the prestige connected with his creed.

Kumm wanted Christians to take advantage of the natural barrier of the Sahara desert and avoid what he feared may have very serious consequences: the Islamization of "independent pagan tribes," meaning those African tribes which were still largely untouched either by the Cross or the Crescent.

Kumm was not only worried by the Islamic advance. He was also disturbed and puzzled by the advance of European Powers into Africa's hinterland and the fact that these Powers overtly and covertly rendered assistance to Islam. Kumm desired that Christian workers should do all they can to offset Islamic gains. He hoped that rapid social change in Africa would not adversely affect the balance of religious power in Africa.

In any case, he wanted more forceful Christian action in his time and feared that it will be an "eternal shame" on his generation if it allowed unchurched African tribes to be won over by Islam.[24] In this, Kumm was only expressing the dominant view that prevailed at Edinburgh vis-a-vis Islam or "Mohammedanism" as the Conference incorrectly called it.

Another significant contribution was made by Dr. Stewart. Through quotations from his book, *Dawn in the Dark Continent*, Stewart brought out the other side of Africa which was meant to disarm presuppositions and establish a positive attitude towards Africa. Missionaries he said had a lot to learn from Africa. A missionary who receives a purely theological training in common with the minister whose life is to be spent in a parish "is good as far as it goes." But for an African missionary, Stewart thought that such a training was "wholly defective" and "incomplete."

According to Stewart's vision, which was based on his long years in Africa, a complete and thorough missionary training should offer inter-personal skills and familiarity with the "broad lines of human development" and a willingness to avoid working at cross purposes with contemporary social forces.

Stewart cut cleanly into an area missions had neglected in the past by saying that Africa needs better missionaries, not the dregs of Western society who, displaced by economic conditions at home, offered to go to a place they would instantly be treated like "a baron" if not "a king."[25] Because the lines and methods of work followed by the different missions, prior to this Conference, were developed from experience under conditions which were very different from those that now prevail, Stewart suggested that African missionaries should be exposed to, among other things, history of missions and of religions, psychology, philosophy, sociology, and pedagogy.

Stewart also emphasized the importance of experience and gave several illustrations to elucidate that vision. Seeking to disarm criticism and dissipate wrong impressions, Stewart stated that he was not making presumptuous cavilling or seeking to find fault with existing methods of training missionaries. As a missionary veteran with several years under his belt, Stewart wished that his audience should regard his remarks as the sad cry of a man whose missionary life was coming to an end; whose life was full of wonderful opportunities; opportunities which might have been better used, and which might have been avoided had he been well-equipped, forewarned, and forearmed when his missionary career began.

Stewart emphasized the need for prompt action and better use of opportunities, and added that the African proverb, the dawn does not come twice to awake a man means that the same opportunity in exactly the same form comes only once, and that we have but one life, and that life is a short one. Stewart thought that his experience, as long as it was personal, was not of much consequence. However, seen in terms of collective Christian witness, experience becomes of measureless consequence when linked with its effect on the great question of the success of missions in Africa.

As far the training of missionaries was concerned, Stewart believed that more was necessary than a general theological education course before they are despatched to witness in a different culture. Stewart disliked the fact that Westerners who were sent to India either for administrative work or to plant trees were given a course of instruction. Unfortunately, this was not always the case when it came to those who were sent to plant Christianity in Africa or elsewhere. Stewart hoped that something concrete would be done to improve how missionaries were trained. Although he did not believe that the challenge facing the missions was insurmountable, he was optimistic that a solution would be found in post-Edinburgh days. The sad reality is that, although Edinburgh responded by naming some special courses for the training of missionaries (such as psychology and sociology),[26] this issue would remain unresolved throughout the period under survey.

Summary: A New Way To Do Missions

Finally, this must be said of the whole Conference. Edinburgh did not just list the questions; it also deliberated on them. It did not just bring a new way to *see* missions; it also brought a new way to *do* missions.

The Continuation Committee. Of the consequences of that new way, none was more outstanding and has proven to have been unmistakably unique than the appointment of a Continuation Committee. It came on June 21 when, as the Chairman of the Commission on Cooperation and Unity, Andrew Fraser, moved a resolution, which had received prior approval of the Business Committee, that a Continuation Committee of the World Missionary Conference be appointed.

This Committee was to be international and representative in character and tasked with carrying out, on the lines of the Edinburgh Conference itself, certain duties. These duties included laying sound lines for the future development of the evangelization of the world, and considering whether world missionary conferences should be repeated along Edinburgh's lines.[27]

Unquestionably, although this was a very conservative resolution carefully designed to win a unanimous support, it was also a capital and historic accomplishment. It recognized that ecclesiastical societies or churches, like states, are very jealous and protective of their independent sovereignty and autonomy. Yet what is perhaps the most important thing about it was the fact that the right of the "younger churches" to be heard and to be represented by their own people was recognized. The composition of the Continuation Committee was to reflect the balance of power among the cooperating missionary societies. Thus North America, the Continent of Europe and Britain were each to have 10 members, while one each was assigned to Africa, Australasia, China, Japan, and India.

In any case, despite the uniqueness of this resolution which, in effect, formally gave birth to the ecumenical movement, it must not be forgotten that Edinburgh was preceded by New York. There is a sense, then, that what New York sketched Edinburgh improved upon. Perhaps, nothing reveals this inter-relationship between both Conferences than the fact that the latter improved upon the former's attempt to update and restate missiological claims in conventional thought forms. Together both Conferences can be likened to tensions building up at the core of the earth and eventually causing shifts in geological structures that create new seas and continents, leaving living creatures to adapt to a new environment. The African epicenter like the others, had helped to shake the established order and had helped to bring forth a new baby or acorn.

Appropriately, the next question was whether this acorn would grow, not into the spreading oak of a Protestant Vatican which Stephen Neill[28] saw, but into anything worthwhile, given the poor record on unitive concerns which Protestants have accumulated until now. No Edinburgh delegate hazarded a guess, given the difficulties associated with predicting one's future, let alone a movement's.

Even the Chairman of the Conference, John R. Mott, known for his penetrative insight and broad ecumenical vision could, in his closing address, only dwell on the generalities, not the particularities of post-Edinburgh missions. His was an address punctuated with question marks, indicating that Edinburgh, in spite of its leaps and bounds, was, not unlike New York, the movement's *terminus a quo,* not its *terminus ad quem.* This chapter cannot more fitly close than with a few questions of his address:

> The end of the Conference is the beginning of the conquest. The end of the planning is the beginning of the doing. What shall be the issue of these memorable days? . . . Has it not tried us as though by fire? Gathered together from different nations and races and communions, have we not come to realise our oneness in Christ? . . . These and other things that press upon the whole emotional and mental nature of the delegates constitute our undoing and our peril if they issue not in performance. If these things do not move everyone of us . . . to enter with Christ into larger things, I ask reverently, what, can the living God do that will move us?[29]

NOTES

[1]Darril Hudson, *The Ecumenical Movement in World Affairs* (Washington, D.C.: National Press, 1969), p. 5.

[2]Ibid., p. 9.

[3]*World Missionary Conference, 1910*, 9 vols. (New York: Revell, 1910), vol. 1: *Report of Commission 1*, p. 1; hereafter cited as Edinburgh 1910. Some parts of this chapter have appeared in Efiong S. Utuk, "A Reassessment of the African Contribution to the Development of the Ecumenical Movement: Edinburgh 1910," *Africa Theological Journal* 18, 2 (1989): 85–104.

[4]*Edinburgh 1910, Report of Commission III*, p. *188*.

[5]Ibid., p. 381. For the entire recommendations, see pp. 364–383.

[6]Harvey Hoekstra, *The World Council of Churches and the Demise of Evangelism* (Wheaton, ILL: Tyndale, 1979); cf. Ernest Lefever, *Amsterdam to Nairobi: The World Council of Churches and the Third World* (Washington, D. C.: Georgetown University, 1979).

[7]Amjad-Ali, p. 1. Hoekstra even claims that beginning in the 1950s, WCC leaders viewed "their world somewhat differently than the leaders of the missionary movement saw theirs" Hoekstra, p. 19. This depends, in part, on one's classification of the WCC and the IMC leaders. The fact is that they were related. For instance, Oldham, Mott, Temple, and Brent were very important leaders in both the WCC and the IMC; cf. W. A. Visser 't Hooft, *The Genesis of the World Council of Churches* (Geneva, WCC, 1982), pp. 31–35 *passim*.

[8]*Edinburgh 1910, Report of Commission IV*, p. 11.

[9]Ibid., pp. 13–14; cf. Clifford Geertz, *The Interpretation Of Cultures* (New York: Basic, 1973), pp. 87–125.

[10]*Edinburgh 1910, Report of Commission IV*, p. 16.

[11]Ibid., p. 35.

[12]Ibid., p. 20.

[13]Ibid., pp. 20–21.

[14]See Lake Mohonk and Oxford Meetings in Part II.

[15]*Edinburgh 1910, Report of Commission II*, p. 2.

[16]South Africa: General Missionary Conference, 1904–1912, IMC/CBMS Archives, Box 1223, mf. 84–89.

[17]*Edinburgh 1910, Report of Commission 1*, p. 228.

[18]*Edinburgh 1910, Report of Commission III*, p. 193.

[19]This appears to be an exaggeration because, in actuality, devolution of ec-clesiastical power in mission-related churches throughout the sub-Sahara did not really and seriously begin to take effect until after the second world war.

[20]*Edinburgh 1910, Report of Commission VII*, p. 115.

[21]*Edinburgh 1910, Report of Commission VIII*, p. 6.

[22]Cf. Adolf Harnack, *The Mission and Expansion of Christianity in the First Three Centuries* (Gloucester, MASS: Peter Smith, 1972), pp. 266–278.

[23]*Edinburgh 1910, Report of Commission VIII*, p. 5.

[24]*Edinburgh 1910, Report of Commission 1*, pp. 19–20, 406–7; Kumm's vision of African missions is a theme in Jan Harm Boer, *Missionary Messengers of Libera-tion in a Colonial Context: A Case Study of the Sudan United Mission* (Amsterdam: Rodopi, 1979), pp. 125–145.

[25]On social class and early missionaries, see Max Warren, *Social history and Christian Mission* (London: SCM, 1967).

[26]*Edinburgh 1910, Report of Commission V*, pp. 110–4; James Stewart, *Dawn in the Dark Continent* (Edinburgh, Oliphant Anderson: 1903), p. 330.

[27]For other duties, see *Edinburgh 1910*, vol. 9, *History records and Addresses*, pp. 95–6.

[28]Stephen Neill, *Brothers of the Faith* (Nashville, TN: Abingdon, 1960), p. 26.

[29]*Edinburgh 1910*, vol. 9, *History records and Addresses*, pp. 347, 349.

PART II

AFRICA AND THE EMERGENCE OF
A NEW MISSIONARY PATTERN, 1911–1923

3

AFRICA AND THE FORMATION OF THE INTERNATIONAL MISSIONARY COUNCIL: LAKE MOHONK 1921

Whatever else Mott's questions accomplished at the end of the Edinburgh Conference, they were, certainly, indicators that the emerging ecumenical movement had a long way to go. Although many signs indicate that this thought was constantly present in the minds of those who planned that Conference, once the Continuation Committee was appointed, new sets of questions came to the fore: In what form or forms should the Committee pursue its work? What paradigms are there to follow? How can the spirit of Edinburgh be perpetuated and conveyed to the Church? What are the means by which it could be in the closest touch with the large body of missionary thinkers and workers throughout the world, keeping them informed of its plans and the results of its investigations, and receiving constant inspiration from the general movement of thought regarding the work of the Christian missions?

These are, to be sure, nagging questions the Committee had to ask and, in many respects, the missionary world is still asking today as the movement continues to seek a nonalienating organizational framework. Yet, current as these questions may be, it was in the years immediately following Edinburgh that they were first raised. In these years also, it became evident that, if the missionary movement was to grow in ecumenical stature, something concrete must be done to facilitate it.

This chapter analyzes how the African angle of these questions affected the preparation for, and the emergence and early growth of, the first institutional expression of ecumenical missions: the International Missionary Council.

I. PRELUDE TO THE FORMATION OF THE INTERNATIONAL MISSIONARY COUNCIL

The most important missionary gathering that claimed worldwide attention, immediately after Edinburgh 1910, was the meeting which met outside New York City:

Lake Mohonk 1921. By the time it was summoned, certain events had ensured that Africa, Christianity, and the world will never again be the same. These events were of two sources.

The first event was internal and concerned the decision of Edinburgh's Continuation Committee to embark on the publication of a missiological review, the *International Review of Missions*,[1] and the setting up of standing Committees to deal with specific issues—Committees[2] whose demise in the summer of 1914 was quickened as much by inexperience as by World War I.[3] Also, it involved the proliferation of local and regional post-Edinburgh consultations,[4] attempts at winning government sympathy for Edinburgh's vision of vigorous and balanced education of indigenous workers,[5] and area mini-conferences.[6]

The second source of events was external and concerned the rapid change of world sociopolitical order. This involved three crashing events in quick succession: the shooting down in cold blood of Russian workingmen (1905); the sailing in 1911 of a German warship into Agadir, North Africa, to demand that the German Reich be consulted concerning the future of Morocco; the beginning of the so-called war-to-end-all-wars. All these sowed the seeds of revolution of a kind the world had never seen before.

Needless to say, those who had seen Western civilization as the sole purveyor of truth and had paid every kind of tribute to it were aghast to see its moral decline. The war, one must not forget, was as much a symbol of ethnic posturing and power maneuvering as it was a war over spheres of influence in Africa. In it, curiously enough, the so-called "powerless and uncivilized" Africa was called upon to support, participate or look on, while the European peoples slaughtered one another. About a year before it ended, the Bolshevik Revolution added another countervailing force to the remaking of the political map of Europe and later the world. The tide of political power and influence which, for four centuries, had flowed steadily and uninterruptedly in one direction was no longer going to be left unchecked. The day of largely unquestioned supremacy of Western civilization with its religion and culture was about to be over, at least theoretically.

From West African colonies came insistent demand for freedom and democracy which was often talked about by colonial authorities but least practiced. Their platform was the Congress of British West Africa which met in 1915 in the very midst of the war.[7] Christendom *qua* Christendom could not ignore this tsunamic turning of the tide. It had to make a quick stock-taking to see whether it could stay in business or declare bankruptcy. Yet the blame was enough to go around. Even Africa, though a victim of the war and a central theater of the duel, could not, in the final analysis be exonerated, for by default (lagging behind in cultural advancement and political and economic power), it partially prefigured and paved the way for how the battle lines were drawn among its colonizers.

From a missiological perspective, no other person was better placed than J. H. Oldham to understand the depth of the calamity. And no other balance sheet was so eloquently and graphically drawn than his monograph which was published to undo, as much as possible, the stings of the war.[8] In it, Oldham admitted that the war was a landmark in human history, a dividing-line between two epochs. After it humanity will henceforth have a new orientation. It had made moral issues clear and conspicuous; it had shown the end of selfishness; it had brought an end to the misguided notion that the Christian Church can be indifferent to the structure of society or world sociopolitical order.

Moreover, Oldham emphasized what was obvious throughout the world, namely, that the war had overturned the established order and could not leave human thought about Christianity unchanged. With the war having shaken all things, Christian people were obliged to reexamine the foundation of their faith. According to Oldham, this enquiry was to involve establishing what the Christian Gospel really is and what it was designed to accomplish in the world.

With an analysis of his own, Oldham came to the shocking conclusion that the war was caused by individuals, classes, and nations who chose to assert themselves and their rights instead of doing their duties. This was regrettable, according to Oldham, because Christianity is a religion of sacrifice which teaches that human beings should be more concerned with what they can put into life than what they can get out of it.[9]

For the undeveloped ecumenical movement, still preparing to take off, like any unfledged bird making its maiden flight out of the mother's nest, the only thing that prevented its immediate demise or abortion was the fact that Edinburgh had met before the war. Doubtless, change in missionary claim and psyche was unavoidable. Not that missions had become moribund. What became moribund, at least in part, was the manner in which the drama of conversion and salvation was acted out in various mission stations as if every Occidental was Christian and morally better-off than the nonOccidental.

Unquestionably, the situation was unsettling and frightening for many people around the world. It was even more unsettling for post-war evangelism, given the fact that many missionaries of that generation had never seen anything even remotely akin to the calamity and tragedy of the war. Indeed many outstanding Christians wondered loud and clear. Oldham, for example, thought that the serious missiological question was not that the state of the world had proved to be so bad. The question, he declared, was why the Christian witness was "so feeble and ineffectual," given all its lofty claims and centuries of witness in the European heartland.

Oldham wanted Christian people to admit that their religion had "somehow failed" to make the impression on human minds that they, in consequence of their beliefs, were "unceasingly, unrelentingly at war" with all that was "unjust and selfish." Because of this failure, Oldham believed that the sharp lines between Christian and nonChristian ideas had become blurred; and that, regrettably, the Christian protest was "lacking in bite and sting."[10]

These were, to be sure, scathing remarks occasioned by the disturbing state of Christianity. In many parts of the Christian church, therefore, there was a deep restlessness. A longing for renewal and reform at deeper levels was expressed; dissatisfactions with traditional styles of piety and organization in the church emerged. Among laypersons and youth groups especially, there arose considerable overt as well as covert criticism. A radical action was needed to regroup the missionary forces throughout the world.

Fortunately, while many Churches were still debating behind closed doors regarding how to respond to this post-war situation, the missionary community, still largely a voluntary body, summoned several private and public meetings.

II. AFRICA AT LAKE MOHONK 1921

Lake Mohonk 1921 gathered against this backdrop. It resuscitated Edinburgh's hopes which had nearly died with the Continuation Committee as a result of the war. Attended by over 70 representatives, chosen either by election through national missionary organizations or co-option by virtue of one's interest in post-war redefinition of missions, this meeting formally inaugurated the IMC and gave the missionary movement a visible expression of united missionary action. Present were some members who were not at Edinburgh and a few who were there such as J. H. Oldham (who was named the first secretary of the new Council) and A. W. Wilkie of the Scottish Missions in Nigeria and the Gold Coast (Ghana).

Among the co-opted members were Dr. James E. K. Aggrey (1875–1927), a rising African ecumenical star who was at the time a professor at Livingstone College, North Carolina, and was named the only native African member of the Education Commissions to Africa; Dr. Robert Moton (1867–1940), a black American and principal, the Tuskegee Normal and Industrial Institute, Alabama; and Dr. Jesse Jones, a sociologist and Educational Director of the Phelps-Stokes Fund and Chairman of the Education Commissions to Africa. Conspicuous in their absence were, unfortunately, German representatives.

1. Social conditions at Lake Mohonk

At Lake Mohonk, the impact of African social conditions on the making of ecumenical mission policy took a different turn. If in the past missionaries tended to treat these social conditions as an appendix to converting individual souls, beginning at this meeting there was no doubt that the post-war situation in the world called for a new strategy. This fact was brought home by several reports which indicated that the war's effect on mission stations, particularly those which were operated by German societies, was most devastatingly felt in dependent territories in Africa.[11]

The report from Togoland and the Gold Coast, for example, indicated that all German missionaries were repatriated and their work left to wither away, though the Swiss and the Scots (led by A. W. Wilkie) came to its partial rescue. In 1915, over eighty of them were removed from the Cameroons; and it was after two years that the Paris Missionary Society seconded only two persons to preserve the preservable. In the German East Africa, the Gold Coast, and elsewhere, with the exception of South Africa where German missions continued throughout the war, the story was no less calamitous for the Protestant world mission.[12] Severe restriction was even more prevalent in Portuguese and French Africa.

This aftermath of the war and particularly the restriction placed on Germans missions made Lake Mohonk's social agenda even more difficult; and revealed the continuing tension between nationalism and internationalism in world affairs. To make matters worse, Lake Mohonk was also informed of the explosive labor situation in British East Africa, Portuguese and French Africa. Although there were variations in how these colonial governments were treating their African "subjects," a common ground for disquiet was compulsory labor. Discussion showed that this labor situation was externally generated and unforeseen, and that strong principles concerning how missionaries should react as an ecumenical and "nonpolitical" body should be formulated right away.

As there was no precedent to follow, Lake Mohonk knew that the IMC must toe a fine political line in order to preserve its political neutrality and win the confidence of its constituency, including German missionaries. Thus the meeting toyed with different labor ideas that were acceptable to colonial governments (in British East Africa, Portuguese and French Africa) and the missionary community associated with the Council. These ideas ranged from mild to strong condemnation of these colonial governments for allowing naked exploitation of African laborers.

In the end, Lake Mohonk drafted specific policies tailored to meet the differing conditions in these African territories. While these policies expressed disappointment with how the French and the Portuguese were maltreating their African "subjects," they also encouraged all colonial governments in Africa, including the British to be "humane."[13] What the Council meant by using this word "humane" is not immediately clear. Certainly, as a recurring word used in later conferences as well (see, for example, chapter 9), it did not mean giving Africans equal access to economic resources produced out of their labor. Quite frankly, at this stage, in which this international Council itself was uncertain of its very survival, ecumenical denunciation of colonialism as a perversion of Christian missions probably would have been an unwise and self-defeating political move; it would take two decades of ecumenical maturity and the second world war to hazard such a condemnation in an ecumenical conference.

Nevertheless, a burning issue to which the Council offered a response and about which it could not ignore for a long time was the condition of German missions. Given all the field reports and the discovery, to its dismay, that the Allied nations included German missionaries in their anti-German propaganda, the Council adopted a strong resolution. This resolution absolved German missions of any wrongdoing during the war. It noted that there may have been pockets of individual disloyalty among German missionaries working under the flags of other nations in Africa. However, as a rule, such acts were not in accordance with the policy of German missionary societies as a whole. Also, this resolution enunciated the view that German missions were expelled from Allied territory "due to general political considerations," not theological ones.

Some commentaries on this phase of ecumenism making, written largely from the perspective of "winners" and "losers," tend to overemphasize the good work that mission societies associated with the Allied Powers did to German missions. It is quite beyond the scope of this study to assess the ethical consequence of these commentaries. Suffice it to state that, from the perspective in which this work is written, the distinction between Allied and Axis Missions was blurred by the war. Moreover, there were neither winners nor losers at the end of the war vis-a-vis missionary work around the world; also, the one result with which missionary societies could not quarrel was the apparent fact that the ecumenical clock was turned backwards for at least several years, if not decades. Lake Mohonk's delegates were aware of this retrogression in ecumenical thought and action.

This is why these delegates were preoccupied with restoring the relative unity which prevailed among Protestant missionaries prior to the war. Certainly, this was the desired end to which the resolution on German missions was designed to accomplish. Regrettably, in its preoccupation with regaining the confidence of its missionary constituency in Europe and North America, this Council did not take up the labor situation in Africa as forcefully as native Africans would have preferred.

The reality of the situation, however, was that this Council was young and ig-norant of how to fully deal with this and other new and post-war missionary problems. Thus, it is understandable that Lake Mohonk recommended that studies be made on the actual labor situation in East and Southern Africa, hoping that a sub-sequent conference would provide a better input into the matter after these studies were done.

2. Primal religions at Lake Mohonk

On the challenge of African primal religious value and vision, Lake Mohonk found that, as a result of the war, the immediate question was no longer how missionaries should approach adherents of that religious system or, any other nonChristian religion, for that matter. The question had become whether missionaries them-selves were not in danger of losing their religious freedom, particularly in the so-called Mandated Territories in Africa. It was at once interesting and shocking to discover that the real threat to evangelism in Africa was not primal religion but the European Powers in Africa.

Beginning at Lake Mohonk, therefore, the words "toleration and nondiscrimina-tion" vis-a-vis primal religion entered into ecumenical vocabulary. This was to be expected, in view of the fact that, during the drafting of the Versailles Peace Treaty by the major combatants in the first world war, the FMCNA and the Conference of Missionary Societies in Great Britain and Ireland (CMSGBI) had, on behalf of the entire missionary movement, argued for the inclusion of a clause guaranteeing mis-sionary freedom in Africa as well as "free exercise of all forms of worship."[14]

In this, ecumenical workers were, in order to preserve their own religious freedom and access to unchurched Africans, inadvertently, beginning to protect African ancestral ways of life and worship. While this move was, in part, an attempt to ensure easy entry of Protestantism into African areas controlled by the so-called "Catholic nations" (France, Portugal, Belgium), it was also a new development in Protestant understanding of cross-cultural evangelism in Africa. For it pointed to the day when primal religionists would be fully understood and accepted as Chris-tian "allies," not "enemies."

3. Indigenous churches at Lake Mohonk

African church and mission questions also surfaced at Lake Mohonk. Recalling Edinburgh's position on indigenous churches and heightened by the war experience, Lake Mohonk assumed that the strengthening of indigenous churches is a primary aim of foreign missions, and that this unambiguous aim implies the development of responsibility and leadership in the church in the mission field. The thorny questions centered on devolution of power and control of funds; how far the native Church should be involved in mission policy-making; whether Edinburgh was not on target when it opined that church and mission were indissolubly linked; whether foreign workers should have the same or corresponding ecclesiastical status with indigenous workers; and how far new missionaries should be associated for guidance with native leaders during the first year or more of their active service.

In the course of discussion, some principles were adopted as indisputable pillars for the future. Among other things, these principles recognized the following points:

1. That there existed divergences in the policy and practice of several Churches.
2. That missions were at many different stages of development.
3. That conditions varied widely in different fields and sometimes within the same field.
4. That devolution presupposed the existence of a strong indigenous church with capable native leadership, not followership.[15]

In other words, it was found that the conditions in India, China and Japan, were dissimilar and were even more divergent from various portions of the sub-Sahara. This was another step toward acceptance of pluralism or diversity as an ecumenical parameter. However, this understanding also indicated the continuing ambiguity and uncertainty as to whether or not the evolving ecumenical movement would ever forge a united position on devolution of power from mission to church as well as a timetable for the implementation of such a united decision.[16]

4. Race relations at Lake Mohonk

Against the background of the war, Lake Mohonk faced the continuing discrimination against African people on the basis of their color. The growing racial conflict in East and Southern Africa epitomized this continuing danger. Given the relative atmosphere of toleration which prevailed at the meeting, Lake Mohonk sought to counter this conflict by initiating a post-war mission view of Africa and Africans. This attempt decried popular and mistaken racial theories and brought hope of amicable solution to the problem. For instance, Lake Mohonk directed Secretary Oldham to study all questions involved in racial relationships particularly as "these bear on missionary work." A specific question outlined for this study was the examination of the relation of the black community in America and the West Indies and their missionary link to Black Africa. This work was to be carried out in collaboration and conference with a similar study already ordered by the FMCNA.

Thus, like both New York and Edinburgh, which had recognized that race questions cannot be ignored and had, directly or indirectly, issued measured policies on this issue, Lake Mohonk attempted what delegates viewed as a post-war solution to the problem. Facing the issue head-on, Lake Mohonk decried widespread discrimination in different parts of the world and committed this ecumenical Council to an ongoing battle against all prejudice and disenfranchisement. More indicative of Lake Mohonk's "post-war temper" (and the motivation that was operative at this meeting) was the fact that the functions of this newly-founded, ecumenical Council included, inter alia, helping "to unite the Christian forces of the world in seeking justice in international and inter-racial relations."[17]

5. Cooperation and unity at Lake Mohonk

Like other questions, Lake Mohonk found that the issue of cooperation in Africa was becoming more complicated than earlier thought, because the war, in addition to the political difficulties which were associated with penetrating Africa's hinterland, had made it necessary for mission societies to enter into unwritten treaties and uneasy alliances with colonial governments in Africa. This situation was made worse by the fact that British mission societies, for example, had a relatively easy access to British Africa than to French Africa or vice versa.

Here was, clearly, an inescapable political situation for missionaries; and it was not easy to steer the IMC on its neutrality course, given the fact that (after the war and the redrawing of Africa's political map by the League of Nations), there was no adequate balance of power in Africa between Britain and the Continental Powers. In other words, beginning at Lake Mohonk, it was salient that British and American mission societies (especially the former), whether they liked it or not, clearly enjoyed a high political status, in view of the dominance of the British Empire, and the gradual but steady emergence of America as a global power, missiologically and otherwise.

Also, it was evident that, if the ecumenical movement was to stay apolitical at least overtly, mission societies from Britain and the United States (the so-called Protestant nations beside Germany) had to exercise self-control for the sake of mission unity and the growth of the IMC. It was this understanding, in addition to their exceptional diplomatic and administrative capabilities, which led to the selection of J. H. Oldham, a Scotsman, to become the first IMC scribe and John Mott, an American, its first Chairman.

Lake Mohonk's attitude towards cooperation and unity was, therefore, defined by its attitude towards African social conditions and the determination to provide a united response to those challenging conditions. To enhance unity among the Protestant forces from all Western nations, Lake Mohonk saw the restrictions in the French and Portuguese Africa as an opportunity to expand Edinburgh's spirit and to try a new approach to the training of African missionaries.

Accordingly, it directed that missions working in Angola and Mozambique should form united, representative committees for effective communication with the Portuguese government. Also, missionaries proposing to work in any Portuguese territory in Africa were to consider their preparation as incomplete, until they had added at least nine months or a year in Portugal, learning its language, securing its teaching certificates, and becoming acquainted with its ideas, customs, and colonial policies. For missionaries proposing to work in French Africa, the Paris Missionary Society was to act as the clearing house.

These requirements (knowing Portuguese language and custom and passing through a clearing house in Paris) were, for example, some of the things which were unanticipated in the early days when the Christianization of Africa began. Now, after decades of encounter with Africa and the realization that not all Western nations saw eye to eye on missiological issues in Africa (and that some of these nations had shown, through strict regulations, their unwillingness to have Protestantism in their African territories), it was easier to understand that the African mission field has helped to open new perspectives to cultural problems often ignored by missionary enthusiasts at home.

Lake Mohonk also formalized a political role for the Council's officials when it directed that these officials should communicate with authorities in Lisbon and Paris in order to safeguard Protestant access to Portuguese and French Africa and avoid future political headaches.[18] Henceforth, these officials, and Secretary Oldham in particular, made shuttling diplomacy a mainstay of the IMC's style of management.

6. Some individual contributions at Lake Mohonk

At Lake Mohonk, several leaders made brief but substantial presentations. These presentations not only contributed to the issues at hand, but also pointed to the direction these leaders wanted this young Council to go. Of these leaders, the center of attention was James Aggrey, the exuberant "African spokesman" and defender of good race relations.

Aggrey took part in the discussions, especially on church and mission relations, Christian literature in Africa and, of course, together with other members of the first

Education Commission,[19] notably Jesse Jones, presented a brief and unpublished report of the findings of that Commission.

Robert Moton, the black American, made available to the Council his educational experience as the principal of the Tuskegee Institute. Moton offered to help the IMC to transfer Tuskegee's educational principles to some African mission stations, if required.

This, being the first meeting of the Council, Secretary Oldham indicated, as forcefully as he could, the breadth and extent of his commitment to charting an ecumenical approach to African issues. He hoped that the Council as a body would be equally committed.

Chairman Mott, known for his evangelical and managerial skills, thought that the ecumenical movement had moved a step forward, in spite of its slow pace, from the time in which he closed the Edinburgh Conference with more questions than answers or solutions.

Summary

Lake Mohonk ended with appeals for cooperation and a call for the establishment of national Christian councils where none had existed. When delegates departed the comfortable landscape surrounding Lake Mohonk, "they felt secure in the knowledge that at long last an International Missionary Council existed and stood ready to serve a world-wide missionary enterprise."[20]

With the founding of this body, lingering doubts as to the indispensability of Africa in missiological "calculus" were put to rest. Indeed, because of its peculiar sociopolitical and missiological situation, particularly lack of modern educated leadership cadre, that continent in the coming years supplied most of the perplexing questions around which the missionary world rallied.[21]

In catholicity of thought and understanding of African questions, Lake Mohonk marked a significant advance.

NOTES

[1]This journal was, from the beginning, another testimony to the entry of rationalism into missiological discussion. The first editorial served notice to that effect and reads like any manual designed for efficient business management. It claimed that its purpose is to study facts and problems of missionary work and to seek to build "a science of missions." It defined "science" broadly so that both the acts of God and human actions are included in this definition. The point is that it differed from the beginning from previous missiological publications with its emphasis on thorough and fearless examination of facts, testing all missionary methods with "a view to securing highest efficiency." Notice that it adopted this perspective because of the magnitude and difficulties of the problems which Christian missions had to face. See J. H. Oldham, "Editorial Statement," *IRM* (1912): 1–2.

[2]One of these Committees oversaw educational matters and had immediate dealings with Africa. See note 5 below.

[3]For a detailed analysis of immediate, general post-Edinburgh events, see Hogg, pp. 143–167.

[4]For instance, in 1911, a conference was held in Calabar, Southeastern Nigeria, to preserve Edinburgh's gains and sensitize those who were not present at Edinburgh to its ecumenical vision. Another consultation was held at Lucknow, Northern India, to explore Christian missions in Islamic countries; see, E. M. Wherry, S. M. Zwemer, and C. G. Mylrea, eds., *Islam and Missions: Being papers read at the Second Missionary Conference on Behalf of the Mohammedan World at Lucknow, January 23–28, 1911* (New York: Revell, 1911). During the war, the FMCNA organized a conference which brought a representative group of American missionary administrators to consider what should happen in Africa after the war. A native African, Mr. Wolo of Liberia (a Harvard graduate, studying at the time at the Union Theological Seminary in New York), presented what was called "Message from a Native of Africa." Wolo's message centered on providing higher educational opportunities for native Africans. J. H. Oldham wrote to this Conference in his capacity as Secretary, Continuation Committee of Edinburgh 1910. Oldham thought that there will under any circumstance be urgent need for the North American missionary community to assume larger missionary responsibilities in Africa; see, *Christian Occupation of Africa: Proceedings of a Conference of Mission Boards engaged in work in the Continent of Africa, held in New York City, November 20, 21, and 22, 1917, Together with the Findings of the Conference* (New York: FMCNA, 1917), pp. 11–13, 113–114.

[5]Although it took over three years after the Conference, in 1914, the Continuation Committee in charge of Christian Education submitted a Memorandum on Education in West Africa to the British Colonial Secretary. In it, the Committee suggested that a Commission be appointed to see how missions and governments could collaborate on educational matters. The Committee thought that, because of increased local pressure on government to use the native resources for native education, instead of siphoning the wealth to metropolitan centers, the idea of joint education commission will meet a ready British Secretary's ear. The Secretary did not buy the idea of a Commission. Instead, he suggested that societies in each Colony could formulate proposals based on the needs of each locality and lay them before the respective Colonial Governments for consideration. A. H. L. Fraser to L. Harcourt, April 3, 1914, IMC Papers, WCC Library, Geneva; cf. Harcourt to Fraser, June 17, 1914, IMC Papers, WCC Library, Geneva.

[6]For instance, on March 17, 1920, Oldham, the IMC scribe, organized a meeting called Conference on African Education in which the idea of a united system of education in West Africa was toyed with, and arrangements were made for a British member to join a proposed Education Commission to Africa.

[7]One of their demands read thus:

> "In the demand for the franchise by the people of British West Africa, it is not to be supposed that they are asking to be allowed to copy a foreign institution. On the contrary, it is important to notice that the principle of electing representatives to local councils and bodies is inherent in all the systems of British West Africa." Cited in W. E. B. Du Bois, *The World and Africa* (Millwood, NY: Kraus-Thompson, 1976), p. 13; Lake Mohonk 1921 was aware of this development, for the *IRM* carried its story; see, "Survey of the Year 1920," *IRM* (1920): p. 31.

[8]J. H. Oldham, *The World and the Gospel* (London: United Council for Missionary Education, 1916).

[9]Ibid., pp. 1–2, 6–7.

[10]Ibid.

[11]Here we can only scratch the surface of a much more dangerous situation. For studies that have charted most of the disruptive effects of the war, see, *IRM* (1919): 433-90; cf. Rufus M. Jones, *The Church, The Gospel and War* (New York: Harper and Row, 1948); and Hogg, pp. 167–8.

[12]*Minutes of the International Missionary Council, Lake Mohonk, New York, October 1–6, 1921, p. 20;* hereafter cited as *Lake Mohonk 1921.*

[13]The Draft Mandates for East Africa and Palestine were made public at this meeting. Oldham had already published some of these Mandates in his *The Missionary Situation after the War.*

[14]*Lake Mohonk 1921*, p. 16.

[15]Ibid., pp. 48–9.

[16]Ibid., p. 47.

[17]Ibid., p. 36.

[18]Ibid., pp. 52–54.

[19]For more on this and the second Education Commission to Africa, see the next chapter.

[20]Hogg, p. 210.

[21]A formal declaration to this effect was not made until October 1929 when, at its Williamstown meeting, the IMC declared that, because of communication difficulties and the scattered existence of National Christian Councils, the duties performed by such councils in China or India were to be rendered in Africa by its secretariat; an excerpt of the statement is in appendix 3, p. 295.

4

AFRICA AND THE EXPANSION OF THE ECUMENICAL IDEA: ATLANTIC CITY 1922

Barely three months after the inauguration of the IMC, the FMCNA, a constituent member of the IMC and an emerging force in Protestant missions (whose findings from its yearly conferences, like the findings of the CMSGBI, welded a lot of influence on the proceedings of the IMC), held its twenty-ninth annual session at Atlantic City, New Jersey. Attended by 328 delegates and corresponding members and representing sixty-two societies, it met, among other things, to receive the Report of the first Education Commission to Africa and to consider the theme "The National Consciousness of the Peoples in Mission Lands and its Effects on the Development of the Church Today."

1. Social conditions at Atlantic City

Atlantic City provided a substantially new perspective on African social conditions. In light of incipient nationalism in various parts of Africa, Atlantic City called for immediate attention to "real social service" and alleviating the total needs in Africa and other parts of the world. Indeed, in a manner that may surprise those who think that evangelism means converting souls only, Atlantic City declared that, while missionary aim should always remain primarily evangelistic, what is evangelistic includes progress in forestry, agriculture, help and support to the unfortunates, education, medical care, famine relief and prevention.

This teaching was clearly a rejection of a one-dimensional approach to missions, just as previous Conferences attempted to do. The presence of some highly informed Africanists (e.g. Jesse Jones and James Aggrey) may have helped to bring about this teaching (see individual contributions at Atlantic City). However, it was, among other things, the enormity and compelling force of the African social problems that made a lasting impact and helped to force Atlantic City to adopt this balanced attitude to evangelism.

The rising nationalist tide in various parts of the world, including the sub-Sahara, with its ringing cries for self-determination in a new world order, also made an impression on Atlantic City delegates. Hence, Atlantic City was more willing than Lake Mohonk (held about a year earlier) to make social Christianity a central evangelistic ingredient in Africa, not its adjunct.[1]

2. Primal religions at Atlantic City

On the import of African primal religion, Atlantic City followed the route charted at Lake Mohonk. Since the FMCNA was among those who initiated the effort to include a religious toleration-clause in the Versailles Treaty (in order to keep all African and other borders open to all missionaries), Atlantic City's attitude towards nonChristian religions showed that missionary encounter with African primal religionists, was bearing positive fruits: better understanding and co-existence. In fact, the prevailing attitude at the Conference was that there were many other important things which required missionary attention than arguing about the evolutionary status of primal religions.

These important questions were, among others, (1) What if anti-missionary forces come to power in African nations and close their borders against missionaries? and (2) What if the new generation of African leaders are intolerant of the Christian religion? Because of these more important questions, Atlantic City spent more time strategizing on the negative consequences of nationalism than on debating the implications of syncretism.

Time continued to change how missionaries saw what can make or break ecumenical relations and mandates; caution remained a carefully guarded ecumenical ideal. Viewed from the developments in some African countries after independence in the 1960s, especially the restriction placed on foreign missionary workers, Atlantic City was really farsighted in anticipating such negative consequences of the nationalist wave.

3. Indigenous churches at Atlantic City

Atlantic City also urged missionaries to improve their attitude towards indigenous churches in Africa and elsewhere. It repeated Lake Mohonk's idea that foreign missionaries should work together with native colleagues. Also, it introduced a policy which aimed at undoing the sad fact that many foreign missionaries, including those who needed supervision, rarely served under indigenous leaders. It was said that the missionary community should do everything within its powers and as quickly as possible to overcome this sad situation or, as some delegates dubbed it, the mentality that they (Africans) always serve under us (foreign missionaries); we (foreign missionaries) rarely serve under them (Africans).

Atlantic City also probed the continuing problem of devolution. Crucial to this devolution question was how the property question should be resolved, especially given the fact that many mission societies owned property whose deeds were held in trust, tied up as memorials, and mixed up in foreign concessions. A probe of the legal aspects of this property question showed that it was not enough to say that missionaries "will give [their property] to China, or to India, or to Africa." Because there was no magic solution, some wondered how the movement eventually would get rid of "this brick and mortar."[2]

Atlantic City did not resolve this question of devolution. However, it is noteworthy because this was the first time this aspect of the question was raised in an ecumenical forum and in a very sincere manner. Compared with the way in which previous meetings (e.g. Lake Mohonk) discussed this issue, with no specific mention of the monies and deeds involved in devolution, Atlantic City's approach was a giant step forward. Members found that, as the years go by, there is much inertia "where bricks and mortar abound" and suggested that on this matter "some very definite study" should be made and concrete actions should be taken.

However, they also acknowledged that contemporary Africa needs the missionary to be at the cutting edge of nationalist aspiration and to take action to get rid of "bricks and mortar," especially in colonies such as Mozambique where the government demanded Portugueseness in everything, including language used in schools and churches.

4. Race relations at Atlantic City

On race relations, Atlantic City, perhaps because of its site, found that the state of black Americans dominated the discussion and provided illustrations for suggestions as to how this color bar can be eliminated in Africa.

A declaration which restated the historic Christian position on the catholicity and interracial character of Christianity was made. It was suggested that mission boards should send missionaries down to Tuskegee (Alabama) or Hampton (Virginia) to learn more about black development and missionary projects.[3]

This was the first time this recommendation was made in an ecumenical conference as a means of developing better interracial understanding and dialogue. However, it would not be the last. For, as we shall see when we get to Hartford 1925, it was easier said than done.

5. Cooperation and unity at Atlantic City

Atlantic City saw that Africa demanded more unitive efforts, not necessarily organic, but a practical unity of efforts and operation. While it regretted that Portuguese East Africa was still a headache, with difficulties put in the way of the work of missionaries by a colonial regime which paraded itself as Christian, Atlantic City saw such restrictions as window of opportunity for unity.

Given the growth of the League of Nations, Atlantic City was proud to remind all secular governments that the church is the precursor of internationalism and that missionaries began to work for true internationalism long before statesmen dreamed of it. This is a great and a vast movement, a statement declared, "absolutely committed to equal rights for all races, colors and classes of men, binding in a great brotherhood [and sisterhood] men and women of all nations." What better agency, the statement asked, "is there for true internationalism?"[4]

Atlantic City demonstrated its uniqueness and growing trust among mission societies through the issuing of a restatement of the aim and scope of missions, in light of prevailing world conditions. From the beginning, it declared, the missionary purpose was to make Christ known and operative among all peoples and nations. That aim, it added, must not change; but as all enterprises, however singleminded and straightforward in aim, take on new meanings in the light of new days, this extension enterprise of the Church must assume new and immense meanings and values in the 1920s.

Specifically, the statement added that "the things" the world, including the African world, demands, believes, and hopes for today are integral parts of the aims and hopes of the Church's mission of promoting and advancing God's Kingdom on earth. Listed among these cravings were the lessons derived from the Conference's theme of nationalism and missions. Others included the following points:

1. The sense of the unity of life with no water-tight or neat segmentation.
2. The power of social ideal and gospel with its call for winning the loyalty of the masses to a single educational aim.
3. The instinct of human service with its rejection of "pie-in-the-sky," cursory humanitarianism.
4. The growing mission unity with its deep and growing impatience at the weakness of competitive denominationalism and the waste of overlapping.
5. The instinct for internationalism with its recognition that no nation can walk alone and be safe or honorable.

6. The need for a new spiritual awareness with the recognition that naked materialism is insatiable and insalubrious.
7. The vision of salvation in terms of adventure with its call for sacrifice, both personal and collective.

All these new meanings of missionary aim meant that all missionary societies must unite their efforts or forfeit "all respect and credibility." They also reflected the maturation process the ecumenical movement was undergoing both in defining its self-understanding and ultimate destination as an ecclesiastical body.

6. Some individual contributions at Atlantic City

Atlantic City provided opportunity for several leaders to bring their African experience to bear on discussions and to make formative, but lasting, contributions to ecumenical thought. The first contributor to whom we must give attention was Jesse Jones, whose contribution came by way of presenting the full Report of the first Education Commission to Africa. Because the Commission was sponsored in part by the North American missionary community,[5] this Conference gave more attention to this Report than Lake Mohonk did.

Jesse Jones prefaced the Report with two impressions. The first was a whole-hearted appreciation of the spectacular spadework the missionaries were doing in Africa. The second concerned the frequent misunderstanding of that "great African continent." Unfortunately and erroneously, Jones remarked, Africa is usually called "The Dark Continent." Its proper name should, in fact, be "The Continent of Great Misunderstanding." Why did Jones say that? Four popular misunderstandings were briefly outlined and debunked at the Conference. These were:

1. *That Africa is lacking in resources and in beauty.* On this, Jones said that the Commission was highly impressed by Africa's unexplored resources of soil, minerals and waterpower. The Commission was also "charmed" by the aesthetics of many sections of the continent.

2. *That Africa is unhealthy.* This was rejected as great exaggeration. While the Commission acknowledged that there were, to be sure, dangers to natives of temperate climate in the equatorial zones, it also found that, with adequate preventive measures, these were not insurmountable.

3. *That the coming of the white man has meant the injury and oppression of the native African.* The Commission, Jones said, did find illustrations of this sad condition. However, on balance, Western incursion into the sub-continent was found to have some benefits to the local population as well. Thoughtful Africans with

whom this high-powered Commission met had realized the importance of partnership and cooperation among races for the good of all. Extreme demand for the
elimination of the white man from the continent was seen as a desire to reverse all
lessons of history which teach that every people who have successfully marched
ahead had done so with the help of other people, because the world is one and interdependent.

4. *That the African people do not give adequate promise for the future.* Jones
said that this was the most unfortunate and "unfair misunderstanding of all." His
Commission's opinion was that the African people "have remarkable possibilities."
The real task was not to have Africans over-confident and left solely to their own
struggle. With proper encouragement which abhors paternalism at the same time,
the Commission hoped that Africans will take a recognized place among "the other
peoples of the world." For this reason, Atlantic City was urged to give "increasing
recognition" to native African leaders.

In presenting the main recommendations of his Commission concerning African
education, Jones revealed the Commission's underlying, fundamental conviction
that the gospel of Jesus Christ requires the development of the mind and of the intelligence, so that those who are to present this gospel may be able to relate its implications and privileges to every phase of life. Like Edinburgh's findings, Jones
revealed that it was his Commission's belief that missionaries should not think of
education as a service to Africa as such, but as an obligation to enhance missionary
activity.

Jones outlined in a nutshell several recommendations. Among these, he underlined the following five:

1. That missions should provide for the adequate supervision of their
   educational activities, especially at the out-stations.
2. That educational organization must be planned with due regard for the
   elevation of the masses and for the development and training of
   native leaders.
3. That school activities should be more definitely related to the actual
   needs of the people.
4. That the practice of cooperation in the African mission field must be
   greatly emphasized.
5. That the workers in foreign fields must be provided with a training
   that is adequate for their varied responsibilities.

Jones asked isn't cross-cultural evangelism an important venture? Therefore, "should we not regard the activities of the missionaries as comparable in value with those of the physician or the educator or the minister in this country [USA]?"[6] Jones concluded his presentation by saying that, because Africa was undergoing rapid change, missionary preparation should also be subjected to change or modification.[7]

Another remarkable and informing contribution was made by James Aggrey. His address, which marked a high point of courageous Christian honesty and how far Africa has come, began with a polite talk designed to make the audience receptive to his supposedly outlandish view of mission at the time. Then Aggrey introduced his point of view, that of "Africa in America and Africa in Africa," expressed thanks to the missionary community for past and continuing missionary activity in Africa, and declared his qualification as a debtor to all humans, to all civilizations, to world Christianity, and to all kinds of educational programs.

Consistent with the Ethiopianist genre of prophecy of his time, that introduction ended with a punch line that saw an elective affinity between the rise of America as a world power and God's hidden purpose for "sending" more black people to that country than to England. God, Aggrey believed, meant America to play a special providential and constructive role in the history of Africa.

Then came the part he designed to "convert," modify or change residual negative opinion about Africa. It followed the main outline of the Education Commission's Report, decrying the fact that, among missionary fields, a hierarchy had developed. Prestige went to those missionaries who were working in Asian countries, for example, India or China. Or, as Aggrey put it, missionaries at the time found that it was a good status symbol even to be able to say "I have just come from Japan," whereas they were almost apologetic, if they had to say "I am just back from Africa." This hierarchy of the fields, Aggrey declared, meant that some mission boards could send anybody to Africa.

Aggrey's prescription for changing that attitude called for some white people trading places with black people just for a few days, in order to feel what black people feel and suffer as a result of such gradation of the fields and degradation of African people. To further illustrate his point, he cited the suggestion made by one paper, during the first world war, that the best punishment that should be meted out to the German Kaiser should be to arrest and bring him to the United States and "take him down South [of the United States] and let him pass for a negro."[8] Such suggestion, he added, is the attitude of some people concerning black people.

To prepare contemporary Africans for the future, Aggrey suggested to the Conference that Africa needed what he called "the choicest missionaries." For Aggrey, these missionaries were to be even stronger, meaning most broadly educated, than those who were sent to China. Why did Aggrey call for the best personnel for Africa? The answer is that, since he subscribed to the notion that the heavier the load, the stronger must be the horse, Africa, as far as he was concerned, deserved the best personnel. For, in his view, the load there was more than the load in India or Japan.[9]

Aggrey denounced as misinformed those teachings that encouraged people to believe that "God is a white man and that the evil is a black man, and that everything black is bad, whereas everything white is good."[10] Similarly, Aggrey underlined the ecumenical thrust of the Education Commissions and urged the Conference never to come to Africa emphasizing denominationalism.

In the same vein, Aggrey rejected the fact that mission education placed too much emphasis on militarism, royalty, victories on the battle field, while it gave little or no place for the farmer or those with humble stations in life. Aggrey was displeased by the fact that Western civilization looked down on Africa because it was poor and stood for peace, whereas it looked up to Japan because of its military power.

After citing his experience with some sociology students (at Columbia University where he studied and occasionally lectured), concerning giving black people opportunity to fulfill their talents and contribute to American society, Aggrey made an open-ended appeal to the Conference. "Give us [Africans]," he began, "a full rounded chance" through education, trust, and affirmation. Because many tended to emphasize the differences which characterize different peoples, Aggrey said that the missionary movement should emphasize not the differences but what all humans have in common. The sea of difference or distinction between whites and blacks, he added, should be no more.

Viewing ecumenical contribution in terms of the nativity story with the Christ-child in the manger, Aggrey declared that white folks may bring their gold, their banks, their big buildings, their sanitation, and other marvelous results of industrial technology to this manger; however, that will not be enough. Similarly, the Chinese, the Japanese, and the Indians may bring their frankincense of ceremony from the East to the Christ-child; but that, too, will not be enough.

The ecumenical gift, he said, will only be enough and complete when black people are allowed to bring their gift to the manger—"myrrh of childlike faith." Black people, Aggrey asserted, did not worry about the immaculate conception and all the technical details of biblical criticism. All they looked for was a Christ who loves all people equally and came to die for the salvation of the whole world. Africans, he said, believe in God "as a child believes."[11]

There is no question that his was a powerful appeal which sent vibrations around the Conference hall and has remained a very important appeal to this day. Obviously, the imagery of a childlike faith and rejection of criticism will not sit well with most informed Africans today. The point Aggrey was making, however, is that there cannot be world Christianity without African participation and contribution, however different and "childlike."

Aggrey also saw indigenous missionary activities as a complement to external ones. His quasi-missiology had no place for preterition which is understandable, given his Anabaptist beliefs.

On nationalism, Aggrey stole the show with a carefully articulated argument in defense of the rising nationalist tide which was sweeping the continent. He deemed it a logical consequence of Anglo-Saxon flirtation with the idea of democracy. In view of the exceeding fear expressed by many mission societies towards this "resistance" movement in Africa, particularly the call by the Pan-African movement for a reshufflement in leadership roles as the 1920s knew them, Aggrey allayed this phobia with a biological lesson with reference to the fact that heterogeneity (pluralism), not homogeneity (the melting-pot idea), will be the order in the future and that ecumenical missions must in earnest become accustomed to it.

It was difficult not to call attention to the fact that, although theoretically manumission was in effect, many black people remained in shackles of hell here on earth.

Aggrey understood nationalism to stand for self-worth and quest for recognition in the world of nations. He saw it as calling for transvaluation of values and the dominant colonial, bourgeois morality. It was not yet the time to question the idea of making the nation-state the terminal community. Instead, Aggrey, like his contemporaries, saw it as identical with leadership because those who exercised the leadership role in world politics did so in the name of a nation-state or empire to which they belonged.

Hence, Aggrey urged nonAfricans not to be afraid of Africans, for Africans are fair-minded people and would not seek to separate themselves from nonAfricans, if they create their own nation-state and are given their rightful place in the world community. Borrowing an illustration from biology where an organism is at first one-celled, then it becomes two or three-celled and so on, Aggrey thought that in the realm of race relations the whole world was fast travelling from homogeneity to heterogeneity.[12]

Moreover, Aggrey added that internationalism presupposes nationalism and that one cannot have good internationalism or ecumenism until one has good nationalism. Still, in his thought, internationalism was to supersede nationalism. Aggrey did not deny that a tide was coming. His doubts concerned rather whether, when this nationalist tide inundates African towns and villages, it will be wisely harnessed to "charge a dynamo that will cause the light to shine throughout the continent of Africa and enable it to make a contribution to the world,"[13] and whether the English speaking countries of the world will accept this nationalist challenge and know that internationalism is like a game of American football. It was a message set forth with attractiveness and compelling force and punctuated with a piece of Americana:

> A tide is certainly coming, it is rising all right; but when it has risen, the continents will not crowd together to put the white man down. If you who are up will only reach down and bring peoples up to your level, then your hand and their hands will meet. True internationalism is like a game of football. You may be the quarterback. Others will serve as halfbacks, guards or ends. When you call the signal, all will take the ball to a touchdown.[14]

After Aggrey's speech came six addresses, expounding the Conference theme of nationalism and missions. Each brought a different perspective to the subject. For instance, George B. Winston of the Methodist Episcopal Church, in an apparent reference to Aggrey's splendid performance, said that the one burning passion that possessed the soul of the man from Africa, who addressed us today, was that it should be known and understood that Africa has something to contribute.

Winston likened what was going on in the mission field to any person who has gone through the experience of Isaiah in the Bible, and is not only ready to confess with Isaiah the failings of his own people, but also begins to find those elements of worth within his people that demand recognition.

James Endicott, a Canadian Methodist, speaking on the topic "The Bearing of This National Consciousness Upon A New Missionary Apologetic," noted that nationalism is a new apologetic about which the missionary world is called to advocate. Yet he preferred to dub it not new but "additional" apologetic. The key to this understanding of mission, Endicott continued, was not to emphasize nationalism as a political movement but as an authentic spiritual movement in the life of the world.

This teaching called for a new understanding and appreciation of the real significance of nationalism as an expression of identity crisis and an attempt to recapture lost currents of the old group/ethnic life. It was recognized that for good or ill nationalism is a self-inflicted wound by the missions. For, by denationalizing individuals and conferring on them a status in which they live in two alien cultures with none to call real home (and depriving them of what Christians in the West take for granted—natural social intercourse with fellow nationals, and making them feel and become a stranger in the land of their ancestors), missionaries, inadvertently, and partly, sowed the seed of nationalist thinking.

The last keynote speaker, James H. Franklin of the American Baptist Church pointed out that the real reflex influence of nationalist movements on mission questions is the spiritual value which may be anticipated by the Christian community in North America, if they will recognize the right of Christian bodies and groups in other parts of the world to take the lead, while their own leadership role decreases accordingly.

Franklin also correctly observed that sometimes some Western Christians seem unable to believe that God does speak as directly to other people as he does to Western Christians. Franklin ended his address with the hope that "Brother Aggrey" would not misunderstand him when he says that he (Aggrey) should be an unforgettable illustration to every foreign mission board of the power of Jesus Christ to bring about new birth, and to show an ordinary African "more wisely than has been shown to the ordinary American, just how the Kingdom of God in Africa can be brought in more rapidly."[15]

This point was driven home by, and imbedded in, Mott's address "The Price Which Has To Be Paid To Ensure Fruitful International Missionary Cooperation" in which he emphasized why developments in the fields and the "coming day in Africa," as it was brought before us "impressively in this Conference,"[16] calls for a well thought out and united plan throughout the missionary world.

The Significance of Africa at Atlantic City

From the perspective of changes in the African mission field and their bearing on the policy of mission boards, Atlantic City was an important breakthrough and, some may say, a turning point, for two reasons. The first reason was the intelligent suggestion made by the Education Commission that missionaries should not pretend that their motive in education was wholly characterized by altruism. The fact of the matter was that, given the emergence of a small but vocal group of educated Africans (in different parts of the sub-Sahara, especially the coastal regions), and the direct relationship between their self-understanding and aversion to foreign domination, it was impossible to convince these nationalists that missionary activity was purely religious.

Missions, the Commissions opined, would be better off admitting that their presence in Africa was in part justified by the social and educational ministry they could offer. At issue was the philosophical justification of cross-cultural evangelism; and, for anti-missionary educated Africans, mere invocation of the biblical injunction for evangelization was seen as insufficient ground for forced denationalization and detribalization of African peoples, throwing them, for the most part, into the abyss of nonbeingness and rootlessness. Ultimately, this first Commission, like the second, saw modern education, sponsored either by the colonial government or mission societies, as an instrument of public relations and the legitimization of colonial and missionary presence in the sub-continent.[17]

The second reason why Atlantic City was significant for Africa and the ecumenical world was the noticeable presence of James Aggrey and the extensive use to which his services were put. For some Christians living in the last decade of the twentieth century, it may be very difficult to understand the impression Aggrey's presence and presentation made on the minds of Atlantic City delegates more than seven decades ago.

To appreciate the scene, one must imagine oneself in Conference Hall—a remarkable room, conducive to discussion, and crowded by missionary executives, those who had the power and responsibility for fashioning out the contour of the work in the African field. Representing different mission boards, they had come to Atlantic City from Africa, Europe, North America and Asia. Numbered among them was a man who had "rediscovered the ancient Christian virtue of hilarity" and "had more white friends" than any other black person of his time.[18]

On assembling, the Chairman of the Committee of Arrangements presented the tentative program as printed and circulated and moved for its adoption as the order of each day. After Call to Order, Opening Prayer, and Report of the Committee of Arrangement, the next item on the program was the presentation of the Report of the Education Commission by both Jesse Jones and James Aggrey.

Then came the actual presentation of the Report and Aggrey's laconic but lustrous and thunderous speech. His were not easy words; yet, his frankness inspired confidence in the African continent and its people and aroused deeper appreciation of that part of God's world. The speech was the talk of the Conference so much so that later speakers and discussants could not help interposing their prepared text with references to, or illustrations drawn from, it.

Summary

Atlantic City was an unusual Conference with unusual subjects, unusual mentality, and unusual approach to even the Conference theme which was not introduced until the afternoon of the opening day. The morning of the opening day belonged to Africa, and symbolized the increasing attention which the missionary community was giving to African problems and how these problems continued to contribute to ecumenical growth.

By probing the legal and financial aspects of the devolution question, a new international awareness was brought to this movement regarding how to structure future trust deeds, and how to provide an orderly transfer of wealth from one nation to another, and from one missionary group to another.

The Conference showed that when old worlds are burned up, when half-worlds are discarded, when new worlds begin slowly to emerge, there comes a vividness and immediacy in the appreciation of that which was once prematurely written off: Black Africa.

NOTES

[1]*Foreign Missions Conference of North America. Being Report of the Twenty-ninth Conference of Foreign Mission Boards in Canada and the United States at the Vernon Room, Haddon Hall, Atlantic City, New Jersey, January 11–13, 1922* (New York: FMCNA, 1922), p. 37; hereafter cited as *Atlantic City 1922.*

[2]Ibid., pp. 119–120.

[3]Ibid., p. 119.

[4]Ibid., p. 38.

[5]This Report was, of course, the same thing that Lake Mohonk heard from this Commission, though it appears it was given in full here for the first time. Lake Mohonk's minutes only has a passing reference to it. Beside the North American missionary community with work in Africa, the study owed its origin to two other groups, the Phelps-Stokes Fund (whose founder had specifically asked that the Fund be used for the education of black people both in Africa and the United States), the end of World War I, and the provision of "Mandatories" for the so-called backward people under the League of Nations. This drew the attention of "publicists in Europe and America" to the vital need of pre-empting violent inter-racial friction by adopting wise educational policies in Africa.

[6]*Atlantic City 1922*, p. 175.

[7]The full report of this first Commission is titled *Education in Africa: A Study of West, South and Equatorial Africa* (New York: Phelps-Stokes Fund, 1922).

[8]*Atlantic City 1922*, pp. 176–7.

[9]Ibid., p. 177. Actually, Aggrey misjudged the load in the East. Whether he did it deliberately is hard to say. Perhaps, the point he was making had to do with cost-benefit-analysis reasoning, given that Western missions poured much more energy, resources, and time into the conversion of the East than Africa.

[10]Ibid.

[11]Ibid., pp. 179–80. Sometimes, it is not easy to understand whether he is metaphorical or literalistic; cf. the following statement, found in a different context, but accentuating the same theme of opportunity and contribution:

> "The debt we Africans owe Christian missionaries is incalculable. And when Christianity comes to need us we will rally to her banner of the Cross even more willingly than we fought on many a battlefield to save many flags of many nations [reference to the first world war]. We will rush even more quickly to her

aid than we hastened by forced marches to help save Judaism for the Jews. We, too, have our contributions to make that may be valuable in His eyes." J. E. Kwegyir Aggrey, "The Native Students of Africa," *Student World* XVI, 2 (1923): 70.

[12]*Atlantic City 1922*, p. 133. See also the next note.

[13]Ibid. Aggrey's speeches or discourses were always full of anecdotes and similes. For example, he illustrated the type of internationalism he had in mind with his recent experience at Lake Mohonk 1921 where he coopted some Westerners into a Committee of non-Westerners and worked with them. Then he recited a poem, adding that the kind of world he hopes for will belong neither to white people nor black people alone.

[14]Ibid. Notice that Aggrey did not imply that Westerners must always be the quarterbacks or the ones who should always give the signal. Africans, he believed, are equally endowed with leadership qualities and equally capable of playing the role of a quarterback. A generous English biographer writes that Westerners who met him could not help but like him. For he did not appeal to their reason or emotion but presented himself as a model for white/black cooperation. Aggrey, he said, had a wonderful power over both white and black audiences; and he never failed to drive his points home. Aggrey's familiar illustration for good race relations was the piano which needs both black and white keys to produce harmonious music. See Edwin W. Smith, *Aggrey Of Africa: A Study in Black and White* (New York: Doubleday, 1929).

[15]*Atlantic City 1922*, pp. 135–136.

[16]Ibid. This was, again, an apparent reference to Aggrey. Mott had a profound interest in enlisting Africans as missionaries and he relied a lot on persuasion and study reports to push his ecumenical vision.

[17]In a letter marked confidential to Colonial Governor Guggisberg in Accra, Ghana, on November 20, 1920, several months before the Report was made public, Jones, the Commission Chairman, admitted that he hoped that the effect of his commission's study of education in Africa will be to center the thought of Government and missionary boards on adaptation of education so that they can win the masses. Frankly, he suggested that in order to win the support of the natives it was critical to begin to select some natives "one from each of the large language groups— probably totalling six" and sent to America for studies and experience at Hampton and Tuskegee and their local out-schools. Thomas Jesse Jones to Governor Guggisberg, IMC/CBMS Archives, Box 263, mf. 2.

[18]Smith, *Aggrey*, pp. 5–7.

5

AFRICA AND THE STRENGTHENING OF THE ROOTS OF THE INTERNATIONAL MISSIONARY COUNCIL: OXFORD 1923

Eighteen months after Atlantic City, the second organizational meeting of the IMC was held at Oxford, England. This, being the second year of its life, it was found essential to immediately tackle Lake Mohonk's unfinished business and to give further clarification to Atlantic City's statement on missionary aim and scope.

The list of delegates shows that numerous delegates were old faces on the ecumenical scene. However, there were also new faces, including Dr. Henri Anet of the Belgian Protestant Missions in the Congo (Zaire), J. J. Willis, the Anglican Bishop of Uganda, the Reverend A. R. Stonelake, Secretary of the Congo General Conference of Protestant Missionaries.[1]

1. Social conditions at Oxford

Of the African questions that brought restlessness—and succor—to Oxford, social conditions were high on the agenda. Considered first was how the continuing changes in social relations in Africa had a bearing on the policy of mission boards and on the qualifications and training of missionaries. Oxford looked into various proposals on African education, including the recommendations made by the first Education Commission and briefly presented by Jesse Jones and James Aggrey at Atlantic City.

Without waiting for the second Commission, which was on its way to East African cities and mission stations, to present its Report,[2] Oxford suggested that mission boards should place the first Report within the reach of all missionaries and of the members of their home committees concerned with Africa; and that area conferences should be held "so as to concert plans and united action wherever desirable."[3]

An important development which came to have a lasting effect on how missionaries approached African education was announced by Secretary Oldham. This concerned the fact that the British Government, after receiving representations from the British missionary community, had decided to form the Advisory Committee on Native Education in Tropical Africa (ACNETA), with representatives from civil, commercial, and missionary interests. While this body was to advise British colonial governments in Africa on education, it had the effect of forcing colonial governments in the French and Portuguese territories in Africa to set up similar Committees and some standards in their colonial school systems.

2. Primal religions at Oxford

At Oxford, African primal religion became an indirect ally of Christianity, receiving even more respect and commendation. Since the Council was still preoccupied with gaining official toleration of religious freedom and worship in Africa, there was no longer any need to condemn primal religionists even before their religious beliefs were better known. More than Lake Mohonk, Oxford realized that the real religious challenge to Protestant Christianity in Africa was civil in nature—governmental propaganda with its self-glorification and deification of the colonial order as the best possible world for Africans.

Similarly, it was salient that the ethos of the African public square still had more impact on African Christianity than the civilization that was growing around the "mission house."[4] Oxford continued Edinburgh's legacy of seeking to understand native religious and ethical assumptions and advising ecumenical workers to study and adapt them in the emergent church communities.

3. Indigenous churches at Oxford

On the challenge posed by changes in the African field, resulting from the growth of the indigenous church, Oxford made a brief study of the issue. Recognizing that it could not make a pronouncement on it, the Council referred the matter to its secretaries with a view to a further study of the whole subject to be carried out on lines approved by the national organizations. Since, as at 1923, there was no national Christian Council in Africa controlled by native Africans, this action meant that the issue could not be resolved in Africa until such organizations were put in place and national leaders were produced in good number.

Oxford recognized that native leadership included men as well as women. However, the attempt to actually produce such indigenous androgynous leadership continued to be plagued by differing understanding of the meaning of indigenous leadership.

4. Race relations at Oxford

The task of reeducating the public as well as the worldwide church on the true state of race relations consumed part of Oxford's time. Because, on this race question, the Council was under severe post-war pressure, it deliberated extensively on this subject and has the distinction of being the first IMC meeting which resolved that an interracial missionary band should be created to diffuse mounting criticism of some mission societies and their racial policy. Although this idea of an interracial missionary band was not necessarily new, given the fact that earlier Conferences paved the way for such thinking, Oxford provided the opportunity for this plan to be openly discussed.

Yet when one looks carefully at Oxford's deliberations, one sees that the fuel or impetus for bringing this plan to the conference floor came from various directions. These directions were, among others, an appeal from a Conference of African and black American students affiliated with the Student Christian Movement (SCM),[5] the Committee appointed by the FMCNA to study the advisability of employing black American and American-trained Africans as missionaries in Africa, and this Council's earlier request (at Lake Mohonk) of Secretary Oldham and his associates to continue to study this thorny subject of Christianity and racial relations.

During the debate on how this Council should encourage interracial bands, an African student, Kamba Simango, was called into the meeting to give a brief address on the subject under consideration. African and black American students also addressed an appeal to the WSCF which in the previous year (1922) had invited Willis J. King, a black American professor at Gammon Theological Seminary, Atlanta, Georgia, to address its Peking Conference.

The appeal contained the African view that the IMC should follow the WSCF's example of inviting African students to representation in it. The appeal also commended the Federation for recognizing that the African was a member of the human family not its "missing link."[6]

Oxford did not pass a resolution on the general problem of race relations, given the Council's earlier decision to study the matter before a resolution could be made. However, in view of the heavy pressure on the Council to support missionary societies controlled by whites to send black Americans as missionaries to Africa, Oxford made a carefully worded resolution.

What were the main points of this resolution? Let us look at the resolution a little bit more closely. There were three major parts.

The first part of the resolution said that the Council was in support of the idea of allowing black Americans to evangelize and educate the peoples of Africa and elsewhere. This preamble of the resolution merely stated the obvious. For some black Americans had already created their own independent mission societies and were already planting churches in Africa wherever they had the least opportunity; what they mostly required was more opportunities to express this missionary commitment.

The second part of the resolution declared that a special approach should be used in selecting potential black American missionaries. This aspect of the resolution created a double standard for the selection and training of missionaries, especially because it suggested that black Americans were not reliable as foreign missionaries and politically immature. Moreover, the resolution failed to require white missionaries to pass through the same rigorous examination which was required of black missionaries.

Why did Oxford choose to create this double standard at this stage of the making of ecumenical mandates? We would never know for certain what transpired in the minds of the Council members. This is one thing of which we can be certain: politics and concern for the immediate had a major role to play in the making of this collective decision.

Why was this the case? Documents show that Council members were more interested in maintaining a better relationship with colonial governments in Africa than with the black American community. This was the case particularly because these colonial governments dreaded like a plague the presence of some black American missionaries in Southern Africa in particular, fearing that they would ferment political unrest and give them troubles more than their unjust colonial system was able to handle at the time.

The resolution also specifically said that black Americans should pass a special "fitness test" designed to establish what the Council called "scrupulous loyalty" to the governing colonial power in Africa. Thus black Americans were required not only to show their missionary zeal and responsibility prior to being accepted by the mission boards controlled by white individuals and churches. They were also required to meet a certain ideological frame of mind—maintaining the status quo and calling foreign oppression part of God's master design for Africa.

The third part of the resolution expected white missionaries to extend to their black colleagues help, cooperation and sympathy. It also indicated that the process should be gradual with a few black missionaries used as test cases. It hoped that after the first group of black missionaries had proved "their fitness" colonial governments would open the doors more widely. Finally, it indicated that there were "social difficulties" which must be taken into account in the implementation of this resolution. This implied that the resolution was in fact, toothless, given the fact that it was not going to be widely implemented by many white mission societies in view of these so-called "social difficulties."

Still, the resolution was a landmark resolution which influenced how later Conferences saw the matter throughout this colonial era. One may disagree with the resolution's general conservative leanings and calculation. However, one would do well to remember that the Council was young, immature, and politically inexperienced; and that on some matters the Council tended to follow the beliefs of its major supporters[7] as in this instance. Regrettably, on this matter, while those who paid the piper dictated the tune, the integrity of the Council itself suffered in the long run, because Oxford showed an apparent unwillingness to call a spade a spade.

5. Cooperation and unity at Oxford

Oxford found that Africa continued to offer unfamiliar routes to mission unity as well as mission cooperation with governments. High on this unfamiliar list was a draft collection of Treaties, Acts and Regulations relating to missionary freedom in African and other territories. This was presented to the meeting by Secretary Oldham.[8] Contemporary and indicative of the flimsy state of missions in Africa, these documents exemplified in a concrete fashion the red tape which missions, beginning in the 1920s, had to pass through in Africa.

A continuing problem was how to forge a united position on continuing anti-Protestant policies pursued at Belgian, French and Portuguese territories in Africa. Oxford, like Lake Mohonk, found that the ecumenical movement had neither the physical nor the political power to fight these colonial governments; and that its only power was moral in character. Accordingly, societies were advised to comply with the wishes of those colonial governments, though, depending on the issue in question, appeals to higher authorities (home governments) could be made by the IMC with no guarantee of success.

Oxford also tackled the question of missionary cooperation in view of doctrinal differences. At Lake Mohonk, during the founding of the IMC, doctrinal issues were carefully avoided in order to secure widespread unity for the new organization. Now, at Oxford, due to increasing separatist activities by some denominational mission groups, the question could no longer be avoided.

After much deliberations, Oxford felt that, at this stage of ecumenism making, the IMC had no jurisdiction on matters touching denominational doctrines, since few affiliated denominations and societies could stand the Council poking into the merits and demerits of their doctrinal opinions.

A resolution reaffirming the nonpartisanship of the Council was submitted and carried by a rising vote. In it, emphasis was laid on those articles of faith enhancing broad agreement among Christians (common loyalty to Christ as epitomized by the confessions of St. Peter, "Thou art the Christ, the Son of the Living God," and of St. Thomas, "My Lord and my God"), and on nontheological, nondoctrinal acts requiring immediate cooperation—translation of Scriptures, production and dissemination of Christian literature, conduction of schools, combating social evils such as narcotics and the liquor traffic.

6. Some individual contributions at Oxford

Some contributions which had reference to Africa were made by the Council's Associate Secretary, A. L. Warnshuis, who prepared the paper which led to the Council's recognition of the fact that colonial governments in Africa could not be wished away; they were to be influenced.

Dr. Allegret of the Paris Missionary Society presented a French view of the question of mission freedom in Africa and how that had a bearing on indigenous people and religion. Being a member of the "minority church" in a nation which considered itself as Catholic, Allegret stood for more freedom. He did not like to contemplate what would become of Protestant missions in Africa, if Catholic France continued its overbearing policy on Protestant missions in its African territory.

Chairman John Mott was relentless on insisting that national and regional Christian councils be established in Africa. Mott realized that the continuing rivalry among the Colonial Powers was not helpful to the ecumenical movement. Mott hoped that the Council would keep to Lake Mohonk's decision to arrange for a series of national and regional conferences in order to enhance more unity and overcome nationalism.

Summary

Finally, in view of the fact that the awakening peoples of Asia and Africa were now weighing in the balance the claims of Christ upon their allegiance, the Council also resolved to institute "Special World-Wide Effort of Prayer," instructing its officers to arrange better ways for common training grounds in the fields. It was, indeed, a Council deeply conscious of the fragility of its premises engendered by the theological divide between fundamentalists and non-fundamentalists, on the one hand, and, on the other, modernists (exemplified by the Scopes trial in Tennessee) and traditionalists seeking to restore Christianity to what they felt was its lost purity.[9]

While Oxford made several disclaimers, sharp questions hitherto brushed aside and considered marginal—even by Lake Mohonk—made their way into the very center of its deliberations. It was asked whether ecumenical missions is possible without uniformity of creeds.[10] Some wondered whether the IMC was not constituting a "super-board," just as the WCC is today being dubbed a "super-church." Others wondered the practicability and appropriateness of cooperation in face of credal diversity.[11]

At this point in time, where the conflict between nationalistic, divisive tendencies vis-a-vis international and ecumenical sentiments was quite real and dangerous, mission questions from Africa and elsewhere helped to enable the Protestant forces to stay united[12] and the IMC to find itself. Oxford's carefully crafted resolution, "Missionary Co-operation in View of Doctrinal Differences" did not hide this fact.[13] It averted turbulence, at least temporarily, by appealing to the common loyalty which all missions owe to the Nazarene—the embodiment and guarantor of co-operation.

Yet this theological resource was to be complemented and solidified by the more tangible evidences of union schools, hospitals, and other humanitarian programs in Africa and elsewhere. It was an acknowledgement that the roots of the IMC were still insecure, a situation which required a special meeting to resolve some lingering organizational issues at Atlantic City in 1925.

EXCURSUS: A SPECIAL MEETING TO DEEPEN THE ROOTS OF THE IMC

As soon as the Oxford meeting was over, attempts were made to further deepen the claims of the IMC. In these years of turbulence very little was left to chance. The marching words at both the London and New York Offices of the IMC were organization and planning, perfect variables for routinization and bureaucratization of any new movement. The opportunity came at a special meeting held at Atlantic City in 1925.

Here gathered were members of the Committee of the Council, "the small inner circle which conducted interim business"[14] whose task was further definition of the necessity of the Council itself. While it can be said that, at Oxford, those who questioned the Council's functions were in part "outsiders," the same cannot be said about what transpired at this special meeting; for here the leading spokespersons for a clearer job description for this Council were "insiders" and specifically, its secretaries, Oldham and Warnshuis.

Between 1923 and 1925, the two secretaries strongly wondered the good of the organization, in view of the fact that there was overlapping between its envisaged functions and the functions of the national mission agencies. In a private memorandum to the two most powerful IMC member-bodies, the FMCNA and the Conference of British Missionary Societies (CBMS), Oldham and Warnshuis admitted that, in these early years of its formation, the IMC amounted "practically to nothing more than a conference held every two years."[15]

One reason for this powerlessness and ineffectiveness of the IMC was because, in actuality, it was not the IMC secretariat which looked after, say the orphaned German missions, which Lake Mohonk thought it should. Instead, it was other European mission agencies which took over direct care of German missions in different parts of Africa. For example, the Paris Missionary Society took care of German missionaries in French Africa. Also, most of the negotiations to allow the return of these orphaned missionaries to British Africa after the first world war were carried out, not directly by the IMC, but indirectly by the CBMS.

Such a situation was not seen as particularly helpful to this young body. Hence, as soon as this meeting was opened for business, the first questions were directed to structural matters: "Is international missionary co-operation as now conducted absolutely necessary?" If so "Why?" and "To what end?"[16] To the first question the reply was a quick yes. But to the second "positive answers came more slowly."[17] Debates were necessary and also exhausting.

With no prototype to turn to, this Special Committee had to think on its feet in order to rescue the Council from heading down the path of a confederation with no power, let alone will. Its resolutions pointed to what Oldham and his associates had envisaged, namely, that the Council's sphere of influence must be limited to bearing witness to the universality of Christian fellowship and in keeping missions up to date with the forces shaping the lives of people whom missions serve.

With a resolution this special meeting settled, once and for all, the recurring question as to whether the Council had come to stay and was necessary. Even in the best of circumstances, the resolution said that Protestants could not do without a Council like the IMC.[18] Specifically, what brought about this affirmation was, predictably, the many and varied issues of race relations, religious liberty, indigenous churches, opium and liquor traffic, Christian education and literature. The formation of national councils in Africa was to be a priority, while those already formed in other continents were to be strengthened and encouraged.

A special feature of this meeting was the recognition that Africa was no longer wholly enigmatic but in fact an unsung source of Western wealth and power. Accordingly, the meeting endorsed the decision (first made at Oxford) that the Council's general sessions, for example, Lake Mohonk, and Oxford, be supplemented by area conferences and "international conferences having a strictly limited purpose and dealing with a particular subject,"[19] for instance, modern education in Africa.

This also meant a recognition of the fact that "there are some things which the Council must attempt to do at all costs."[20] In this, the Committee produced an understanding that the times required a "strong forward [ecumenical] movement"[21] and capped one era and ushered in the next: The Gospel of Education.

NOTES

[1]*Minutes of the International Missionary Council, Oxford, England, July 9–16, 1923* (London: Edinburgh House, [1923]), p. 8; hereafter cited as *Oxford 1923*.

[2]This second Commission was sent in 1923; see also chapter 6 note 2.

[3]*Oxford 1923*, p. 30.

[4]For more on the theme of civilization around the mission house, see, for example, J. F. Ade Ajayi, *Christian Missions in Nigeria 1841–1891: The Making Of A New Elite* (Evanston: Northwestern University, 1969), pp. 126–166.

[5]*Oxford 1923*, p. 14. See Willis J. King, "The Federation and the Negro Students of the World," *Student World* (July 1922): 85–92.

[6]For more description of the appeal, see Willis J. King, "The African Students Conference," *Student World* (April 1923): 48–50. This issue of the journal was devoted to the contributions of black people to Christianity and a synopsis of the African Student Union. The editorial, probably written by John R. Mott, the editor, did not fail to mention that it was the presence and able leadership of the African representatives at Peking 1922,

> "which made visible and audible the fact that the time had come to give larger attention to the claims and problems of Negro students throughout the world and to afford them fuller opportunities to make their unique contribution in the common united endeavour." John R. Mott, "Editorial," *Student World* (April 1923): 42.

[7]*Oxford 1923*, pp. 35–6. On efforts to strengthen the Council, see the next section in this chapter.

[8]This was later published under the title *Treaties, Acts & Regulations Relating To Missionary Freedom* (1923).

[9]A leading thinker of this school was J. Gresham Machen; see his work, *Christianity and Liberalism* (Grand Rapids, MI: Eerdmans, 1923).

[10]See Robert E. Speer, "Is Identity Of Doctrinal Opinion Necessary to Continued Missionary Cooperation?" *IRM* XII (1923): 497–504.

[11]E. J. Palmer, "The Practicability of Missionary Cooperation in Face of Doctrinal Differences," *IRM* XII (1923): 505–514.

[12]This is not to ignore that in America in particular some groups, such as the Bible Union of China, viewed any unitive move by the IMC with suspicion or that they stopped taking groups which preached the social gospel, such as the National

Christian Council in the USA, as signals that the *parousia* was eminent. On the contrary, it is to emphasize that foreign missions remained a major plus to Protestant unity in these years of turbulence.

[13]*Oxford 1923*, pp. 36–38.

[14]Hogg, p. 216.

[15]Memorandum from Warnshuis and Oldham to Maclennan and Turner, IMC Papers, WCC Library, Geneva. Maclennan was the secretary of the CBMS, while Turner was the secretary of the FMCNA. There is no date; Hogg thought that it should be dated between 1922 and 1923; Hogg, p. 412.

[16]These questions were raised in a special paper prepared by the secretaries and in consultation with Chairman John Mott. J. H. Oldham, "International Missionary Cooperation. A Statement of Fundamental Questions of Policy for consideration by the Committee of the International Missionary Council, January 11–15, 1925," pp. 4–5.

[17]Hogg, pp. 218–9.

[18]*IMC Committee Minutes, Atlantic City, 1925* (New York: IMC, 1925), p. 4, 22–3.

[19]Ibid.

[20]Ibid., pp. 5–6.

[21]Ibid., pp. 6–7, 23–24.

PART III

AFRICA, MODERN EDUCATION, AND THE GROWTH OF THE ECUMENICAL MIND, 1924–1926

6

AFRICA AND THE GOSPEL OF EDUCATION:
HIGH LEIGH 1924

Strictly speaking, when the Committee of the IMC recognized that the Council's general sessions required supplementation by international conferences "having a strictly limited purpose" and subject, it was simply giving an explicit approval to what the Council's staff were already doing. Indeed, among the things which provided the rationale for institutionalizing area or limited-purpose conferences was the invaluable insight gained from High Leigh (Hoddesdon, England) in 1924. Thus, although in theory this proclamation took place in 1925, in practice it reminisced High Leigh's accomplishment which took place the previous year.

The Conferences discussed in this and the next three chapters are, therefore, not extended footnotes to past meetings. Instead, they are united, first, by the immediate results which followed this proclamation and its growth and outworking in the years 1924–1926; and, second, by the fact that these years saw the emergence of what I call the gospel of education or the new mission.

A less-known Conference, High Leigh 1924 was the first international conference organized under the auspices of the IMC and solely devoted to the particular subject of Africa. Called the "Conference On Christian Missions In Tropical Africa," it was held in Britain (September 8–13) because, among other reasons, it attracted immediate world attention, given the fact that after the war, Britain was the dominant colonial power in Africa—and the world.[1]

We have seen that the first Report of the African Education Commission (1920-21), which covered the missionary situation mostly in West and Equatorial Africa, was received both at Atlantic City 1922 and Oxford 1923, as priceless information. On November 21, 1923, a second Commission was sent to East and South Africa.[2] Like the first, this second Commission's findings were no less revealing and startling. Unlike the first, however, these second findings were not yet fully publicized either within or without the missionary community. Moreover, because neither Oxford nor Atlantic City gave the first Report the exhaustive attention or time for which it called, the IMC staff summoned the High Leigh meeting. These two voluminous documents contained what some observers such as Oldham characterized as "the Christian opportunity in Africa."[3]

Accordingly, the circular announcing the meeting was devoid of diplomatic niceties.[4] In pungent language, it invited member societies to send representatives to High Leigh. Questions affecting the future of Christian missions in Africa in the 1920s, it warned, entertained no waste of time. Upfront it slated as the priority question the necessity of considering the full implications of the Commissions' Reports and problems connected with Christianizing Africa.

High Leigh opened on September 8 and regulars such as the CMS, the Baptist Missionary Society (BMS), and the Society for the Propagation of the Gospel (SPG) signed in. Among the irregulars who were represented were the SUM, the Qua Iboe Mission (QIM), the Regions Beyond Missionary Society (RBMU), and the Protestant Missionary Society (PMS) with C. P. Groves, author of *The Planting of Christianity in Africa* as one of its two representatives.

The Bremen Missionary Society sent a native African worker, the Reverend Robert D. Baeta, an emerging defender of church unity. Also present were those categorized as visitors such as Max Yergan (1893-1976), a black American who was working with the South African YMCA, and others (James Aggrey, Jesse Jones, A. G. Fraser, Principal of Government College, Achimota, Ghana, and Dr. Garfield Williams of the CMS, among others) who were mainly members of the two Education Commissions.

Other delegates were Ruth Rouse of the WSCF, Major H. Vischer, Secretary of the ACNETA, and Lord Frederick Lugard, ex-Nigerian Colonial Governor. North America was represented by seven Societies and the Kennedy School of Missions, while from the Continent came the German, Swiss, Belgian and Swedish Societies.[5] Of the German delegates, the most notable was Professor Westermann, a linguist from Berlin. In all, over seventy delegates took part in the meeting.

1. Social conditions at High Leigh

At High Leigh, it was impossible to miss the fact that African social conditions were having a determining effect on how mission thinking was developing. This was because the Reports of the Education Commissions on which the discussion was based were very thorough and objective in their findings and recommendations. While the second Commission found variation in African social conditions in East and Southern Africa (as opposed to the findings of the first Commission in West Africa), both Commissions' recommendations emphasized a need that was common to all regions of the sub-continent, and aimed at sustaining the emerging new social order in Africa.

This need and central recommendation was, in a word, the elevation of education as the sole aim of missionary enterprise, and in particular the involvement of the masses in this gospel of education.

It is important to note here that this central recommendation by the Commissions carried with it the need for a radical change in missionary understanding of education as an adjunct of evangelization. Given the fact that the Commissions were appointed by political, commercial, and missionary groups, and given the fact that these Commissioners were highly respected individuals on both sides of the Atlantic Ocean (Western Europe and America), the Reports with their recommendations carried the ecumenical and international weight and respect which was probably impossible to achieve in any other way.

This is, to be sure, one reason why this Conference generated so much media interest (see summary of High Leigh below) to the extent that even missionary societies which were officially and doctrinally unaffiliated with, and opposed to, the IMC attended the meeting. Also, the time was ripe for the Commissions' recommendations to be enthusiastically embraced by some colonial governments in Africa. Moreover, some missionary societies also saw these recommendations as a golden opportunity to work with colonial governments in order to gain substantial financial support for mission schools; hence, the unusual presence of many missionary societies at High Leigh with fields in Africa, including those who had serious doubts about deviating from traditional understanding of evangelization and making education the sole aim of missionary presence in Africa.

It is in this light that we must understand High Leigh's preoccupation with redefining *what* missionaries were supposed to do rather than *how* they were to implement this new gospel of education. For, in the view of these high-powered Commissions, missionaries were already acquainted with the altruistic motive of their presence in Africa. What was not widely known by the missions, as indicated by the Commissions, was the fact that the altruistic motive had become highly tainted by Western collective self-interest, symbolized by colonial regimes in Africa.

Since missionaries as a rule could not in practice separate themselves from their homelands, and since in general it was becoming very difficult for Africans to distinguish the missionary from the colonizer, these Commissions, with their emphasis on education, provided the missionary movement an external validation and a new powerful argument for their presence in Africa. At the same time, this emphasis on modern education also made it easier for colonial governments to become interested in spending African tax money on native education, given the fact that many of these governments were, for many years, hesitant to commit themselves to providing adequate modern education in their African territories.

Doubtless, this was a classic example of the politics of the moment and a social policy initiated and formulated, not by bona fide government officials or missionaries, but by a committee of outsiders whose nonpartisan and international status was believed to be capable of diffusing some of the perplexing problems of the period, and winning the support of native, commercial, missionary, and governmental groups.

As a comprehensive and sound interpretation of what the Commissions saw as the new missionary objective (in a rapidly changing world in which the IMC had little or no control), High Leigh was unable to fault this new interpretation. While it was an interpretation done largely by outsiders (and, therefore, found easier to soften, if not dispense with, the traditional missionary motive of converting individuals), reading through the minutes of this meeting, one gets the impression that, even before this meeting started, many delegates had already decided to support this new understanding of mission as the gospel of education, despite its liberal tendencies. Indeed, ensuing discussion showed that the problem was how to translate this new and high view of social Christianity into discharged duty. For delegates did not only adopt the Reports. They also endorsed the Commissions' vision and program for attacking all industrial, social, and economic problems in Africa.

This program attached greater importance to the masses' participation in education and economic activities. For, as the delegates reasoned, African masses are also carriers of civilization and their social state the benchmark for evaluating the progress of African societies. This understanding of the masses was, of course, inspired by the Commissions' Reports as well as personal testimonies from those who attended the meeting. For example, the Bishop of Uganda, J. J. Willis, spoke about the deep participation and contribution of the masses in his episcopate. In 1923, Willis recalled that the masses paid eight thousand British pounds for education. African masses, Willis added, from the earliest days when new congregations were organized in different parts of Africa, including Uganda, had contributed enormously to the growth of the church. Other speakers confirmed that the issue was not whether the masses were participating in education. It was, rather, whether or not the missionary community was ready to harness more fully that participation.

Given the enthusiastic mood in which High Leigh embraced this gospel of education as it affected all social conditions and the masses in Africa, one must not think that High Leigh voted to overturn all past educational policies. The fact is that the objective for this new social and educational program was to be guided by evolutionary fervor not revolutionary ones. Subjects taught were to be colored by the simple language and atmosphere of local life. It was admitted that every subject cannot be placed first on the page; and that special attention should be given to the education of women as a social group as well as using their education as a step to reaching children while they were impressionable. Teaching modern agricultural techniques, for example, was to be tied to the local idea that agriculture is not only a physical profession but also a mental and spiritual one.

The cost of this program, in terms of finance, labor or equipment, was not specified. Instead, High Leigh hoped that proper and efficient planning, including the establishment of union schools, would make the program workable. In practice, this program, after High Leigh, meant the recruitment of literally hundreds of Western teachers to work in Africa as missionaries in order to implement this decision. However, the decisive thing which kept the program going was not the specialists who were recruited but indigenous support generated by local obsession with modern education and willingness to pay the necessary taxes to support it.

This endorsement of mass education also led High Leigh to adopt the Commissions' strong suggestion that education should be conducted in the vernacular. At Lake Mohonk, it was found that missionaries frequently succumbed to governmental enticement to produce, through the school system, natives who preferred foreign languages to native ones. High Leigh mandated that the native tongue must be the language of church and school life so that the future of Christianity can be guaranteed in Black Africa.[6]

Unquestionably, this unanimous position on the use of vernacular in African schools was nothing new. However, in view of the fact that the Commissions' Reports (on which this educational understanding was based) presupposed immediate missionary-cum-colonial governments alliance on educational matters in Africa, one must understand that this emphasis on the vernacular was directed more to those colonial governments (e.g. French and Portuguese) which did not want local language to be used as a means of instruction in their African territories than to all mission societies. Also, this directive served to remind contemporary missionary workers that Christianity must not remain "a bourgeois religion" in Black Africa, as in St. Augustine's North Africa, fit for Westernized Africans but denied the rhymes, puns, and riddles of the masses' verbal fireworks.

2. Primal religions at High Leigh

The same unwavering attitude which characterized High Leigh's position on the impact of African social conditions defined its position on African primal religions vis-a-vis Christianity. Because the Commissions had made it crystal clear that primal religions will not be immediately crushed as some missionaries had hoped, High Leigh, more than Lake Mohonk and Oxford, found it easier to continue the positive attitude which began in part at Edinburgh.

For High Leigh, this positive attitude meant that missionaries were free to make full appropriation of local religious ideas to explain Christianity. The symbolism of the family, which is more inclusive and coextensive than the individual, was to be tapped for missionary work. The indigenous idea of God and reverence for the surrounding world (environment) was to be utilized in the evangelical process. Initiation rites which taught group solidarity, etiquettes which encouraged decorum were to be baptized into the Christian system. The belief behind the various African rituals were to be probed, and thoughts were to be turned more to what made Africans value not only that which lives within humans, but also that which exists among them.

Because this understanding was clearly a repetition of Edinburgh's position, delegates were unhappy at the slow pace at which past decisions on primal religions were being carried out in mission stations. For it appeared to some delegates (for example, J. Outmann of the Leipzig Missionary Society) that there was some inconsistency in how past Conference decisions were being implemented in some mission stations. This was an acknowledgement on the part of some delegates of one of the ongoing problems in this new movement, namely, inadequate ability to fully implement conference decisions.

Delegates were consoled by the fact that the IMC was not the only international organization with implementation difficulties. For it was pointed out that the Life and Work Movement, the nonmissionary wing of the ecumenical movement, was also having difficulties in practicalizing its vision of the post-war world. It was this realization that some past decisions were not being implemented, as quickly as they were meant to be, which led High Leigh to underline what past Conferences had only implied in some of their statements, namely, a slow but steady approach to dealing with African missionary problems.

This endorsement of gradualism, over against overturning everything with a tincture of the past, logically led High Leigh to advocate some of the permanent values in primal religion such as filial piety and a dominating sense of community. This new evangelical attitude meant respecting the processes of nature and the several generations that are required to outgrow superstitions—assuming one ever does. This gradualist teaching was, quite frankly, a remarkable missionary concession to the persistence and thriving of primal religions in Africa, despite past and continuing missionary attempt to downgrade and uproot them.

This concession meant that in general missionary societies (particularly among the members of the IMC) began to emphasize consolidation of old churches rather than planting new ones, indoor activities rather than outdoor activities. In other words, High Leigh wanted missionaries to begin to teach and equip the converts already won instead of continuing to plant new churches when it was impossible to cope with the ones already planted, in terms of providing them adequate catechistical instruction sufficient to make them become mature Christians.

In effect, High Leigh said that in the past missions went to Africa "to break up paganism, arrest Islam" and establish churches. Henceforth, it added, the emphasis must be on consolidating the position gained and undoing past mistakes. Here one finds that modern sociology, through the Education Commissions' Reports, continued to find its way into ecumenical discussions and position on primal religions. If previous Conferences, including Lake Mohonk and Oxford, were ambiguous in their mandates vis-a-vis primal religions, High Leigh was patently straightforward and unambiguous. With this position, High Leigh urged missionaries to abandon the old image that Africa is a stagnant and impoverished backwater, and mandated missionaries to embrace primal religion as a sympathetic faith to Christianity.

3. Indigenous churches at High Leigh

At High Leigh, mission thinkers were more aware of the importance of indigenous churches in Africa than previous Conferences. Largely influenced by the Education Commissions' highly critical reference to continuing missionary underestimation of the genius of these churches, High Leigh found that these *Aladura* or Independent churches were spreading faster than the so-called mission-related churches. Realizing how the Kimbanguist Church, for example, was growing, in spite of the Belgian Government's attempt to silence it, by incarcerating its leader, Simon Kimbangu (1889–1951), High Leigh gave thought to the implication of the heightened presence of such churches.

Times had changed. Unlike past Conferences, including New York and Edinburgh, where negative pronouncements on these indigenous churches outnumbered positive ones, High Leigh's view was clearly positive. At the very least, this was a reflection of change in the political, ecclesiastical, and economic circumstances of the sub-continent. As a consequence, it was clear that increased indigenous participation in missiological affairs would mean a corresponding reduction or diminution of the sway of the foreign missionary and boards.

In discussing the challenge of these churches, High Leigh took the unusual step of regretting past missionaries mistakes, especially concerning the fact that some missionaries tended to talk about Africa's social improvement as if they did all the work for the natives. This came as the Education Commissions made public the fact that there were many social development programs embarked upon by individuals, native churches, and improvement associations on their own. Cited were, among other things, the South African interracial committees, Joint Native Councils, and the Kenyan Tax-Payers Association.

Some of these nonmissionary, locally inspired groups (tired of, and impatient with, the glacial pace of officialdom), had embraced measures designed to hasten franchise and suffrage. Discovering these groups, throwing missionary support on them, and encouraging them to participate in the new holistic educational system was seen as a task for the 1920s and beyond. In this sense, far more than what Edinburgh could have imagined, High Leigh accorded more respect to aboriginal educational and socializing patterns and commercial forces which were equally shaping and remaking Africa.

High Leigh sought to initiate a concrete plan to quicken the creation of native leadership in mission-related churches. Although by the standard of the Independent churches (e.g. the Kimbanguist Church in Zaire, and the Prophets Harris and Garrick Movements in West Africa), this idea was at least two decades late, High Leigh still found it to be an explosive topic. In addition to this, there were expressions of doubts as to whether all the missions and their workers could be persuaded to accept the Education Commissions' Reports with their sweeping call for multiplying the ranks of native transmitters.

This was believed to be an important question, in view of the fact that, in order to get the native to believe in this new gospel, missionaries themselves first had to believe in it. The delicate ecumenical task, then, was to create a vital fellowship by insisting on more power to the converts, without thrusting societies who refused to see the changed African circumstances outside the IMC's sphere of influence. Also, a plan of action was approved in order to address the transition problems associated with making modern education the central theme for contemporary African missions (see transition to gospel of education below, pp. 115–117).

4. Race relations at High Leigh

High Leigh's thinking on race relations was at once an expansion of past thought on the subject and a reflection of the findings of the Education Commissions. The Commissions had found that throughout the African regions they visited the natives were very willing to cooperate with foreigners; and that the practice of racial discrimination was, unfortunately, initiated by the foreigners who continued, even after the first world war, to see themselves as more civilized and physically and mentally superior to the natives.

High Leigh, following previous Conferences, realized that the missionary community must continue to fight against both overt and covert racism; and that, if nothing concrete was done to implement the Commissions' call for increased educational opportunity for the natives, no one should later say that both the missionary community and the colonial governments were not given sufficient warning. Calling racism an anti-thesis of all that Christ stands for, High Leigh called on all mission societies working in Africa to rededicate themselves towards eradicating all forms of racism.

The problem, however, was that racism was already getting beyond missionary control, especially as policies which fostered racial separation were being pursued both covertly and overtly in South and East Africa, despite several attempts by the IMC officials to influence British policies in those areas. Moreover, the realization by the colonial authorities that the missionary community was largely limited to "pious" pronouncements on the issue did not help the missionary cause very much.

This notwithstanding, High Leigh had its high moment on this issue when delegates received the recommendations of the long-awaited ecumenical study on racism, titled *Christianity and the Race Problem*. A piece that showed how thought is conditioned by prevailing mood and intellectual conventions,[7] High Leigh's delegates employed its recommendations to blast those views that believed that capacity coincided with the color line. Agreeing with the Education Commissions on several race-related issues, the book made it compellingly clear that, on this matter of racism, European and other civilizations, in spite of their glories, were still impoverished.

High Leigh found that there was very little it could add to the book's cogent arguments against racism in church and society. Thus delegates resolved to make the book's conclusions available to all mission societies and to admonish missionary workers not to relent in their struggle against discrimination. They also agreed that this was a crucial political and moral problem with which the Church must grapple and find ways in which all people can live together in peace and harmony. The guiding thought was the idea of common creatureliness inspired by an unending struggle against natural and human obstacles that prevent the realization of a nonalienating, nondiscriminatory world.

5. Cooperation and unity at High Leigh

At High Leigh, mission and unity question was kept alive and given a new urgency and direction by the decision of the Conference to adopt, through a special and unexpected resolution, the thinking of the Education Commissions as the basis of a new understanding of missionary duty in Africa: the gospel of education. Drafted by Jesse Jones, the Memorandum summarized the thought of the Commissions and reflected High Leigh's consensus on most of the Commissions' recommendations, ranging from Christian attitude towards primal religion to combating racism.

While attempts were made to qualify this gospel, it was self-evident that the main thrust of this gospel was accepted and that something unusual had taken place at High

Leigh. For, although this resolution came as a surprise (in view of the fact that the Call to the Conference insisted that there would be no attempt to "pass any resolutions"[8]), High Leigh knew exactly that, by endorsing the memorandum with its single-minded commitment to, and call for, sound education, it was refocusing mission aim in Africa. Here is the resolution:

> The Conference has had under careful consideration a Memorandum . . . on *An Educational Policy for African Colonies*. Without endorsing every detail of this Memorandum, nor its particular order of emphasis with its main conclusions the Conference finds itself in entire agreement. The Conference recommends to all the missionary boards represented the careful study of the Memorandum, and requests the boards to transmit Dr. Jones' proposals to their missionaries working in Africa, and to urge their consideration as the basis of a general educational system for Africa.[9]

Emphasizing better educational system in Africa as an end in itself, Jones' Memorandum, through this resolution, gave rise to the need for more unity among cooperating mission boards as well as a need to seek a working relationship, if not an alliance, with colonial governments in Africa. The presence of high-powered British Government representatives—Lord Lugard and Major Vischer—afforded a rare opportunity to discuss how this new "alliance" could be struck.

Understandably, the first debatable point was whether government and missions can agree on one aim in education. It was suggested that for both to agree the aim must be religiously neutral, say, for instance, the formation of character. Plato, Aristotle, Mazzini, and other educational philosophers were appealed to during the search for such a common definition of aim. It was the state's interest to secure a system of education which would lead to the formation of public spirit and strong moral character. Because building such a system of education needed a religious foundation, this aim met an enthusiastic response from the missionary representatives.

The quagmire was method of cooperation, given the obvious divergence between the premises on which both government and missionary societies based their presence in Africa. Since in principle, both parties had agreed that they were operating on the same wave length on some matters (as it was put, "for the sake of Africa"), mutualism was seen as the way out. This mutualism was particularly inevitable because the mission school system, with its meager financial base, badly required the infusion of African tax money (which was controlled by colonial governments) for it to meet contemporary educational demands; and colonial governments in order to show that they were becoming interested in public education, badly needed the existing school system owned and operated by missions.

Moreover, for the one, a new prestige and credibility was gained by this agreement; for the other, immediate access to educational infrastructure was made possible, eliminating more years, if not decades, of the usual slow planning process associated with many a bureaucracy, including government. Both parties recognized that they were about to enter into a difficult period of transition and experimentation and that the success of the new scheme largely depended on the response of the native population, particularly how they perceived and interpreted this intimate mission/government affair.

High Leigh recognized the importance of the new era into which the IMC with its constituency was entering and knew that it was rewriting missionary aim in Africa. For this reason, before looking into some outstanding individual contributions, we must briefly pause to look at what was being proposed to actualize this "new gospel."

Mission Transition to the Era of the Gospel of Education

Deliberately reserved for the last day of the meeting, the first transition question concerned logistics. Or, as some delegates understood it, the issue had shifted from theory to practice and from the question of redefining the objective of Christian education to whether or not missions were committed to first-class education and first-class missionary preparation. In this respect, the conferees agreed that the standard of missionary training and Christian character expected of missionaries was infinitely higher than the one called for by the Education Commissions. Nevertheless, these Commissions' findings were held as "a reproach and a challenge to [existing] missionary schools"[10] and how the training of new missionaries was being conducted.

Missionary boards were urged to pay particular attention to the training of first-class workers in order to meet the new conception of educational missions. It was hoped that the contemporary missionaries, while they, like the contemporary soldiers, possess much more paraphernalia of equipment, but are certainly not romantic figures as their predecessors, would still be possessed with the spirit that bears essential Christian qualities of compassion, love, and dedication.

Another transition question concerned how missionaries would be able to develop in Africans a positive concept of African culture, after decades of condemning that same culture. Tied to this was the problem of trust and convincing the missionary, on the one hand, and the natives, on the other hand, of the value in this new teaching. For the missionary, High Leigh suggested that more is needed than just telling him or her "physician heal yourself." A frantic campaign to change attitudes and to win acceptance to the new system was endorsed.

For the natives, the force of the difficulty was recognized and seen as particularly cumbersome, given past snobbish missionary teachings against indigenous customs. Past mistakes had come back to haunt this movement and delegates knew that foreign personnel were largely handicapped and limited in whatever schemes of self-worth they may promote to win most natives to this new religio-educational emphasis. Indeed, it was doubtful that this ecumenical body would be able to reverse the damage done by past negative characterization of African culture.

The other burning and transition issue concerned how the home church and cooperating boards could be persuaded to support this whole new package of the gospel of education. Two practical steps, both involving public relations campaign, were suggested to ensure good results.

The first step involved informing missionary constituencies and supporters of the real nature of the work which missions were doing in Africa as at 1924. Plenty of home supporters, it was observed, still thought that all African missionaries were doing pioneering work. Moreover they thought of the missionary as the pale man in black clothes beneath the African palm tree preaching sermons carefully prepared in England, They were to be told that such an era was long gone. Pioneering days were over; consolidation days had begun.

The second step involved enlightening and informing Christian workers in the field of this new educational ideal. Confirmed in the idea of progress and the maxim that everything can be done better than it is being done, High Leigh thought that many missionaries would be better persuaded by fellow missionaries who had already embraced the new educational philosophy than by a commission of outsiders.[11] In other words, since the Education Reports called for a change in the understanding of all phases of missionary work, and expected missions to admit the failure of some aspects of their educational work, it was felt that missionaries who had already subscribed to the gospel of education as a nonpartisan instrument should lead the way to "convert" the unconvinced brethren and colleagues.

Of the ideal missionary fit for the new gospel, it was admitted that no training ground was available by then which could produce in a single missionary the reasoning of a theologian, the firmness of a pedagogue, the patience of a farmer, the strictness of a sanitarian, and the tact of a diplomat and many more in one training course. This realization necessitated urgent measures to plan new training courses and opportunities to equip new missionary recruits so that they would be better qualified than their predecessors and specialized in different fields of education and other aspects of foreign service.

This was an interesting transition decision because it meant, at least in theory, the arrival of the day which James Aggrey and others hoped to see in Africa: the day in which better qualified missionaries were to be sent to Africa and the construction of better plans to build better training facilities in Africa for native and foreign missionary personnel.

6. Some individual contributions at High Leigh

High Leigh featured numerous and remarkable contributors who brought their growing experience and special knowledge of Africa to bear on the Conference deliberation.

Dr. Garfield Williams, speaking not as a CMS missionary, but as a British member of the second Education Commission, told the Conference that there is more in Africa than meets the eye, and that ecumenical missions must stop at nothing in promoting the gospel of education in Africa. Noting that Africans everywhere were demanding an education which will enable them to adjust to their new environment, Williams said that missionaries must learn to deal with the concrete situation in concrete terms. Additionally, missionaries were to learn how to respond to concrete needs and be willing to take new risks by experimenting with new ways of meeting the social needs of the natives.

Linguist Westermann espoused an educational angle that emphasized the importance of the African's past and native languages. Westermann avowed that the denationalization of the African was no longer necessary; that Africans had a right to keep their language and systems of thought; and that missionaries should keep them from becoming strangers in their own land. Language, Westermann asserted, was the ticket to the soul of any people.

In this respect, missionaries were to understand that they have come to Africa as strangers with a strange message, and that, even if they speak the same language (as with the educated native), there is a fundamental gulf always in thought. Consequently, Westermann emphasized that missionaries should use *all* the powers within them to enter into the mind of the African, since the most adequate expression of the soul of a people is its language. Westermann also added that ecumenical workers should take note of how language can shape a people and help to build a lasting and prosperous civilization.

Then, without hesitation, Westermann said that the experience of the English people in Germany with their numerous English churches in German cities witnessed to the desire of people to hear the gospel in their own language. Similarly, what is good for the goose is good for the gander. As in Europe where education is guided by pedagogy and children are not taught in a foreign language that would ensure their despising what should be dearest to them—the tongue of the mother, the African, Westermann emphasized, deserves linguistic principles which preserve traditional permanent values and mode of life.

This teaching was the death knell to the notion that God cannot speak African languages, especially in territories where colonial governments prosecuted, with a religious zeal, the Europeanization of the territory under their tutelage. "Some of the African languages,"argued Westermann, "will rank among the literary languages of the world."[12] These languages and customs, he added, are the soil of the African mind. Thus, they should not be forced to abandon their customs and arts, if these are not "contradictory" to the gospel.

Moreover, Westermann thought that missionary respect for aboriginal customs will correspondingly lead to respect for the missionary religion. How, he asked, can Africans respect the Christian message when Christians do not respect African customs? If Christians respect African customs, Westermann believed, the enduring benefit will be, not the rejection of the Christian religion, but a corresponding respect for it. For the community will benefit more from one who has learned to respect the ancestral way of life than from the radical who wants to throw away all aspects of the African's past.

Edwin W. Smith, now working in Southern Africa, seized upon this idea of mutual respect and gave it another sharper dimension for the envisaged educational system. He lamented that the present system was only a veneer. The new gospel, he added, should incorporate all facets of the Christian presence in Africa. Cutting the African from his past was no education, since he was being squeezed into the Western mold. Naturalism (meaning letting Africans to develop according to the laws of their own nature), was to be the new policy with a heavy emphasis on adaptation of education and sublimation of the African's past.

Max Yergan brought a black American perspective to High Leigh's deliberations. Yergan urged missionaries to realize that Africa has been waiting for too long for the new emphasis on mass education. It was his opinion that white missionaries were late in reacting to some changes in African societies. He wondered what would have been the rallying point for the new emphasis without the Reports of the Education Commissions. Yergan promised to coopt more native and black American students to join in implementing the new gospel of education. An article in the *Student World*, shortly after the meeting, confirmed his commitment to the ecumenical world as well as his understanding of race relations.[13]

E. W. Thompson, the West African Secretary of the WMMS, spoke on "the Requirements in regard to Personnel and Training for giving Effect to this Programme of the Gospel of education." Thompson posited that the machinery of cooperation with government cannot uphold mission education unless the missionaries—themselves the backbone and defense of missionary education—are well-equipped. Borrowing his metaphor from the Old Testament prophets, he said that ecumenical peace will not be found by calling the missionary educational system "the temple of the Lord" which shall not be destroyed. For a prophet may arise to say that all human temples, including missionary educational system, must be destroyed. Oldham, the diplomat-secretary, recognized the meaning of this prophetic talk. He knew that a growing ecumenical body must be prepared to try to reconcile opposing views—even when they are clearly irreconcilable. He knew that within the ranks of missionary board members, those who could pull the string and make something happen in the field, there remained lingering doubts as to whether native Africans would like to cooperate to implement this new program.

Fortunately, for Oldham and his secretarial associates, who organized this meeting, a man named Aggrey had already proven himself to be an inheritor of many legacies and cultures. To Aggrey, another emerging "moderate" voice (Robert Baeta, from the Ghanaian/Togolese border region) was added and tasked with a presentation on how native Africans were viewing the missionary situation vis-a-vis the new emphasis on education.

Baeta's address was not meant to be scholarly or theoretical as such. His presence, like that of Aggrey, was meant to lend credence to the necessity of the new gospel. So, as the Conference minute secretary tartly recorded the presentation, Baeta told his history, recalling the poverty of the early missionary beginnings at Keta, Ghana, his three-year studies (1897–1900) in Wittenberg under the auspices of the Bremen Mission, and his work in Togoland and the Gold Coast under the German, British, and French flags.

The Mission, Baeta said, was slow to make use of native helpers. Two men were ordained in 1909 and three the following year. On the eve of the first world war, when foreign missionaries had to leave, two additional native pastors were ordained to carry forward the evangelical torch. Baeta spoke of the evils of the division of the field into French and British sections—a situation complicated by the war—and hoped that it would soon be possible to allow communication between the French (Togo) and British (Ghana) spheres.

Also revealed was the extraordinary manner in which native workers, only seventeen in number, kept sacrificing in order to keep the church alive, despite the war situation. The priesthood of all believers was not merely a doctrine. It was cardinally practiced so that adequate pastoral work could be done; members assisted in looking after the women and children and visited one another.

Then Baeta said what the supporters of the new gospel of education presumably wanted to hear. Although the natives were equal to the task, the Togolese Church did not want to be abandoned in mid-stream as German missionaries, forced by the war, had to do. He alluded to the problems associated with either untimely withdrawal of foreign aid or persistent foreign hegemony. The Togolese Church had taken practical self-support measures. Still, they needed the presence of fraternal helpers. Baeta said that the Church was going on with more energy than before. Ironically, the war situation increased rather than decreased their faith. Baeta indicated that his Church would be glad to welcome the Germans back because the responsibility of evangelistic expansion needed every hand it could get. A particular need was "lady missionaries" and teachers for the women and children.

Another speaker to whom we must make reference is James Aggrey. Aggrey's presentation at this meeting was nothing new to those who knew him prior to this forum; it was mostly a crystallization of growing convictions and, in many respects, an amplification of Baeta's. The only thing he had to do differently was to recognize that he was speaking to an audience that numbered, among its members, some movers and shakers of African political events of the time.

So Aggrey made it a principled defiance of the notion of cautious benevolent trusteeship. Paternalism in church just as in state policy, he asserted, is inadmissible. The people of Togo and other African ecclesial communities, Aggrey observed, were living proofs that Africans are taking their share in evangelizing their continent. Mass movement into the church, he suggested, presupposes strong native heralds who, like in the old social order, would, with the evangelical gong or percussion instrument in their hands, assemble the people at the village square and march them into the church community. If Africa is to be saved, he added, it must be done by such heralds. To avoid hindrances either politically motivated or otherwise, Aggrey declared, "you [missionaries] can get us [Africans] to do the things you have to do now. If you do not do this it will check the work."[14]

Aggrey had much to say on the use of the vernacular in evangelism. Through serving on the Education Commissions, he found that the actual prevailing policy on native language was that, in some stations, the rule was "native language and nothing else" while in others it was "foreign language and nothing else." Actually, he said, the next generation of Africans will need both native and foreign languages, a point which goes without saying in contemporary Africa but which ought not to go without consideration as we look into the future of human existence.

Aggrey suggested to High Leigh the importance of recognizing the value of the indigenous institutions as one way to gain unalloyed native trust. The natives, he said, did not feel like they belong in the new regime. What they remembered was largely their destroyed and neglected past. Mission societies, he added, were not mindful of the fact that the confidence of the African people, like that of any people, cannot be won *a priori*; good public relation tactics, sound psychology and anthropology were needed to win them over to the church community.

Aggrey also said that it was important for missionaries to realize that *how* they presented the gospel message to Africans was as important as *what* that gospel had to say to Africans. He was concerned that even after the disaster of the first world war, some missionaries were still presenting the gospel to Africans from the point of view that everything Western was inherently superior to everything African.

It was Aggrey's staunch belief that the missions had no other alternative but to embark on the new educational project. He asserted that, if they failed to do it, colonial governments, because of internal pressure, will do it. A church and state perpetually divided on racial lines will be the result. Aggrey, understandably, like his contemporaries, saw Christianity as the panacea for everything. This is why he thought that missionaries should ensure that Africans receive missionary education so that racial antipathy would be overcome. For he feared that any education not tempered with religion would not do the job. Africans, opined Aggrey, desire to be partners in a new missiological and world order.

With those words still ringing in the ears of the delegates, High Leigh jumped into an unusual debate for and against repeating a similar conference on Africa. Then they took time to do what the IMC officials had hoped would be rewarding to all participants: one by one disclosure of lessons from, or benefits of, the five-day deliberations. Documents show that many delegates testified to coming to grips with the diversity of opinion that existed on practically all the issues which were tackled. Others gained insight from these shades of opinions.

Summary

Judged by the purpose for which it was set—giving African missionaries, who were in many instances isolated in their work, an opportunity of coming into contact with missionaries in other societies and from other fields, and of discussing with them matters of common interest—this Conference marked another definite advance in ecumenical missions. Practically all were in favor of a similar conference at frequent intervals. Both the Religious and Secular Press hailed it as an exceptional and important development. A correspondent of the *Church Times* of London summed it this way:

Here we were, nearly all from Africa, all trying to understand
Africa and the African; all grappling with, and groping for light
on, the problems of that continent, and all full of that love for and
devotion to the country and its people that perhaps only those who
have lived in Africa can understand.[15]

High Leigh was another testimony to the growing and profound effect of changing
African circumstances on missionary work. For the first time, it was openly acknowledged that public opinion, both at home and abroad, can have an effect on the
how and *when* of foreign missions. Some asked how did we get to such a state of ignorance of the need for better educational program for so long? It is bad enough,
said others, for the general public to live in ignorance, but for the church, which
prides itself on educated clergy and laity, to fall into the same pattern is an affront
to all that Jesus stood for and taught about evangelizing all the nations.

One cannot help being struck by the realistic portraits of Africa that prevailed
at High Leigh. Instead of settling down to believe that the colonial era would last
forever, High Leigh delegates were concerned about post-colonial church life. The
challenge of qualitative education, the necessity for quick action, the realization that
even after the war racism did not recede, the knowledge that African life was not
solely dependent on what missions did or did not do, the profound social and
economic changes combined to make High Leigh thoroughly preoccupied. Its view
of African culture indicated that the ecumenical movement was becoming self-con-
fident and had its own sense of Africa's destination, a view which seems paternalis-
tic and conservative in retrospect, but which was capable of opening up intriguing
horizons to this growing movement.[16]

High Leigh saw more ecumenical rationalization not less. It wrote the epitaph
of the old missionary educational system and sketched the master-plan for the gospel
of social development and education.

NOTES

[1]International Conference on Christian Mission in Africa, High Leigh, Hoddesdon, September 8–13, 1924, IMC Paper, WCC Library, Geneva; hereafter cited as High Leigh 1924.

[2]Like the first Commission, government, missions and other interested parties joined hand to sponsor it in order to ameliorate conditions, knowing that the war, which later engulfed the leading nations, was sparked at the little-known town of Sarajevo.

> "So[, claimed the report,] both altruism and self-interest combine in making it seem desirable that everything possible should be done to remove possible causes of serious friction or danger even in a continent so 'remote' from the great political capitals of the world as Africa." *Education In East Africa: Study of East, Central and South Africa by the second African Education Commission* (Phelps-Stokes Fund, 1924), p. xiii. Incidentally, a similar commission was sent to China.

[3]Indeed, Oldham published an essay with that title. In it, he argued that the Educational Reports presented not only an immeasurable opportunity to Christian missions, but also an opportunity to make a momentous choice: standing aside from the influences which are making themselves felt in the life of the peoples of Africa or dedicating themselves afresh to the gospel of education. "The Christian Opportunity In Africa," *IRM* (April 1925): 173–187.

[4]Several correspondences, dating back to 1922, were made between the IMC secretariat and key African missionary figures who were imbued with the spirit of Edinburgh. These correspondences solicited advise and counsel as to which meeting should first be held, regional or international. After many persuasions, this international meeting was secured. See, for examples, A. W. Wilkie to Oldham, May 6th, 1923, IMC Papers, WCC Library, Geneva; and Emory Ross to Oldham, 1923, IMC Papers, WCC Library, Geneva.

[5]This was a unique, post-war ecumenical fellowship and opportunity, for it marked the first time many German societies returned to the movement after the war—a point many delegates commented on. It should be noted that, at Oxford, the mood was really subdued when the miserable condition of German missions was brought to the attention of the meeting. Here, at High Leigh, delegates hoped that restriction on one part of the ecumenical body would be a thing of the past. It was

never to be. For more on Oxford 1923, see chapter 5. For future developments, see chapter 12.

[6]Professor Westermann recalled that, when, during the first world war Christianity stayed alive in German mission stations in Africa, it was because of the vernacular Bible.

[7]This book was published by the SCM about four months (May, 1924) before High Leigh met. Its conclusion, in the words of a reviewer, was presented:

> "not as a prejudice, but as the inevitable inference from careful
> observations. Its importance is both apparent and immense, for
> it means that racial antagonism is not grounded in human nature
> but in conventions of thought and conduct, so that by a change in
> those conventions it could be removed." W. Manchester, Bishop
> of Manchester, "Christian Statesmanship," *IRM* (1924): 449-54.

[8]Call To The Conference: High Leigh 1924, IMC Papers, WCC Library, Geneva.

[9]High Leigh 1924.

[10]Ibid.

[11]This was a reference to the fact that most members of the Education Commissions were not "missionaries" per se. Less than two years later, the meaning of missions was changed to incorporate whatever all foreigners did in Africa; see chapter 9, Le Zoute 1926.

[12]High Leigh 1924.

[13]Max Yergan, "The Significance of the High Leigh Meeting to Negro Students," *Student World* XVII (October 1924): 168-69.

[14]High Leigh 1924.

[15]*London Church Times*, 19th September 1924.

[16]Some of the papers of this Conference were published in volume 14 of *IRM* (1925).

7

AFRICAN WOMEN AND ECUMENICAL MANDATES: LONDON 1925

Shortly after High Leigh, the increasing role African questions continued to play in forging ecumenical response to missions was also epitomized by another lesser-known conference in 1925. This was the Conference On The Education Of African Women which was held on July 21 at the Church Missionary House, Salisbury Square, London.[1] A one-day assembly, it kept this ecumenical train in Britain for nearly another year; and drew its inspiration from High Leigh which, as we have found, had accepted the Education Commissions' position that issues concerning the education of African women as well as their role in the emerging new Africa required more than cursory attention.

In addition to missionaries from different parts of the sub-Sahara (thirteen societies in number), except the Wesleyans, there were present at least three members of the Education Commissions, Major and Mrs. Vischer, Drs. Garfield Williams and James Aggrey. Others included A. G. Fraser, Miss Burstall, a member of the ACNETA at the British Colonial Office and Miss Shaw, an educationalist in East Africa. Secretary Oldham chaired the meeting.

Being the first of its kind and a sensitive subject at the time, just as it is today (given the presence of substantial opposition to coeducation and ordination of women[2] by some missionary societies), the Conference had no fixed agenda. Conscious of this opposition, the IMC office, which planned the meeting, thought that, in order to have broad and wide representation and participation, the objective of the meeting was to be deliberately left open and partially vague.

Accordingly, the invitation letter to this Conference declared in general terms that the meeting would aim at providing an opportunity for the interchange of ideas on the kind of education which will help all African women, the difficulties to be encountered, and the means of overcoming them in the hope that, as a result of such interchange of views, lines of action may emerge which will be followed up with advantage.[3]

1. Social conditions at London

At London, African social conditions were discussed, understandably, with particular attention to how they affected the African woman. It was found that, because women have an important role to play in African society, more attention should be paid to their education. For example, the growth of industrialization throughout all the old and new African cities was seen as having more devastating impact on women more than men. Special mention was made of the larger responsibility thrust on women, particularly near the mining towns in South Africa where men were gone for a greater part of the year, leaving women and children poorly cared for.

The meeting found that, although increasingly these women were being given added responsibilities in the emerging new Africa, they were not being provided with education as nearly as men. Questioned were three ideas. First, the popular idea that a separate educational philosophy for women must be devised. Second, the idea that separate and unequal institutions must be operated for the sole purpose of training women. Third, the contradictory idea that, because the economic future of the continent preeminently depended on the woman, she must be encouraged to cultivate food crops instead of cash crops such as cotton and coffee.

Discussion showed that these ideas must be repudiated and that the IMC should advocate equal opportunity in education with special attention given to the fact that some Africans, including African women themselves, were expressing misgivings concerning exposing girls to Western education, not to mention adult women. Delegates also agreed that there was no use in boys reaching a higher education standard than girls or vice versa; like the eponymous Adam and Eve, they were to be brought up together without sexual discrimination.

In other words, coeducation (Aggrey), rather than separate and unequal education was to be encouraged. Missions were to make deliberate attempts to reverse their conservative educational attitudes which resulted in a disparity between the number of men and women who were being educated. While delegates were determined to advance the status of African women, they failed to fully appreciate the fact that these women would have been more receptive to the gospel, if the mission boards were able to assign more women missionaries to Africa. It would take more than a decade of this gospel of education to address this gender gap in the missionary ranks and African communities.

2. Primal religions at London

Ordinarily past conferences, for the most part, focused on the role African men played in traditional religion and its effect on their participation in evangelistic efforts. London, true to its agenda, devoted much time to examining the African woman's attitude towards primal religion and how that affected the spread of Christianity in Africa. It was found that, contrary to popular thought, some African women occupied important positions in the traditional religious hierarchy. For example, in some communities, there were women who performed critical religious functions as native doctors and seers. More important, it was learned that women tended to be more devoted to traditional religion; and that it was likely that they would, if converted, carry over to Christianity their deep sense of cultural and religious devotion and enthusiasm.

To ensure a better evangelistic communication with women, London suggested that missionaries should devote more time to understanding the roles played by women in traditional rituals, feasts and ceremonies. For, by having a better understanding of how different communities designated certain religious functions to women, it was argued that ecumenical workers would be able to present the gospel as a better option to traditional religious practices.

London also recognized that in some communities women were vehemently opposed to evangelistic efforts because they saw Christianity as alien and otherworldly, seeking to deprive them of the meager gains they had won within the old social system. Missionaries were to be careful with how they presented the gospel to women because their acceptance or rejection of Christianity had a domino effect on how others (especially children) may be attracted to, or even distracted from, the church.

A protracted religious and ethical issue which remained unsolved was whether African girls who became Christian should ignore circumcision as a rite of passage and polygamy as an option for marriage. London was divided on this issue. Some noted that this custom assumed that women were property to be bought and sold at will by men; and that the circumcision procedure was dangerous and excruciatingly painful and humiliating. Others argued that, because missionaries were no longer interested in condemning African culture, female circumcision and plural marriages should be allowed to continue, because it was long valued by traditional African culture.

It is interesting that this debate focused more on African culture vis-a-vis Western ideas of dignity and self-worth as understood in twentieth-century America and Western Europe, not the Dark and Middle Ages Europe. Clearly, here was an issue which could only be resolved by Africans themselves; and its solution depended, not on too many external rules and prohibitions, but on the enduring effect of evolution and the rise of a new generation of African young adults and Christians imbued with a new attitude, a new consciousness, and a new value system.

3. Indigenous churches at London

The subject of women leadership in church and state was voiced. However, in view of the fact that leadership presupposed modern education credentials, discussion centered more on where the financial support for preparing such leadership will come from. Given that, against all odds, parents preferred to train boys more than girls, London called for behavioral modification or changed mentality regarding the education of women.

London believed that the proper place to begin to change such a mentality was the Christian community rather than the traditional African society at large. This was so, in particular, because Mrs. McGregor Ross of Kenya disclosed that some missions spent three times as much on educating boys than on educating girls. Clearly, this disclosure enabled the ecumenical movement to see that it was no use focusing all the criticism on traditional African culture for the subordinate role assigned to women in family life. The church, delegates acknowledged, was also guilty of subordinating women to second class membership, given that women were allowed to contribute their time and money to the church, but were seldom elected church deacons; they were allowed to sing in the choir, but were not allowed to become pastors.

In a statement that was at once a telling criticism of early missionary practice and an indicator of future trends, London urged that missionaries should take this point to heart and should realize that money is nearly always forthcoming for leadership program for men and very rarely for women. All missionaries were urged to use their influence, whenever possible, on church councils to secure a more equal distribution of educational resources. Missions, it was said, are not likely to provide sufficiently for education of women until there are at least two women on every "committee that deals with money."

Though this money talk was a sad commentary on how some, if not many, mission boards operated, it was also an indication that some problems can be corrected, if there is a change in policy as well as sympathetic people on these boards. Here was a clear indication that even in the church one need not take some things for granted; and that this growing ecumenical body must represent the voiceless and the poorest of the poor among whom numbered thousands of African women and children.

4. Race relations at London

On the issue of race discrimination, London was particularly concerned about its psychological and social effects on women. Knowing that as mothers or would-be mothers, women stood to influence the attitude of many African children, London urged missionaries working in areas where there were overt racial conflicts to be extremely sensitive to how women were treated. London discussed the South African situation in particular but found that ecumenical hands were tied in that it could only react to governmental race policy based on earlier ecumenical statements on this issue. While no unique or unusual mandate came out of London's discussion of this issue, it saw that women, particularly in Southern Africa, were victims of double jeopardy, not given equal educational opportunity and being discriminated against by the old and new Africa.

To remove that jeopardy was seen as an ecumenical task which was to involve not only foreign missionaries but also African men and women whose view of gender was in part responsible for the ongoing discrimination of women. This was an interesting ecumenical development because, for once, it was recognized that foreigners do not have the answer to all African problems and that Africans themselves must on their own or in participation with others, seek solutions to their cultural problems.

5. Cooperation and unity at London

London, like its predecessors, was conscious of the fact that cooperation within and outside the church was indispensable, if African women were to be supported and encouraged to make it in the emerging new Africa. Because of the multiplicity of the problems plaguing African women, delegates insisted that missionaries should endeavor to make a very real and determined effort to view the many needs in terms of the sub-continent and in their proper perspective.

Delegates agreed that African mission societies "are in their youth" and that cooperation with government and commercial houses was indispensable. All societies were urged to cooperate in setting up training centers for women. It was said that missionaries cannot pursue a solitary way with any hope of safety and success without a strong support from native women—and men.

There was a real sincere determination on the part of some delegates to make issues concerning women central in future ecumenical conferences. Regrettably, after decades of missionary neglect and unequal education, nothing could be quickly done to remove the disparity which existed for decades between the number of educated African boys and girls. This disparity has continued to show its statistical significance decades after many African nations became independent; and has helped to perpetuate social inequality and imbalance in all these new states. Needless to say that it has also helped to inspire the formation of feminist groups dedicated to removing old and new discriminations against African women and girls, though these groups are not as radical as they really should be.

6. Some individual contributions at London

Of the several presentations which enabled London to probe the issues facing African women, we must look first at Mabel Shaw's. Based on her ten years' "imperfect experience" of a school village in Northern Rhodesia (Zimbabwe), the thrust of her address was the enormous impact that the African woman can have in the new educational missions and the problems associated with overcoming the traditional subservient role to which tradition assigned her in the scheme of things.

Miss Shaw enumerated the difficulty of having regular classes for women, since their days were well filled. Often, she said, these women were in their farms till long after midday and when they came home household chores and fatigue took their toll. An unfaltering faith with patience was necessary to help these women. Miss Shaw disclosed that, when she first arrived in Zimbabwe, she was "almost entirely ignorant" of all the gender roles in African society. She saw only the surface of things, though she dimly knew that there were deep forces underlying every behavior and custom. African girls considered her a stranger, while older women considered her a child. She was confused and unable to cut through the social barrier which separated her from the natives; and so she had to wait, not daring to seek entrance or force herself in before the door was opened for her.

After that experience, she began to see things differently, particularly the fact that the inexperienced missionary must, like the convert, grow slowly into maturity. As far as she was concerned no scheme of education, however sound and comprehensive, was going to uplift the African girl unless it was imparted by ecumenical workers who had won her trust, knew her role expectation inside out, and did not shrink from it. Miss Shaw's emphasis was on gradual steps, not leaps, teachers, not things taught.[4]

Shortly after Miss Shaw's, the representative of the British Colonial Office and the ACNETA, Miss Burstall, took the podium. A teacher with forty years of experience, she quickly called the delegates' attention to the diffidence that characterized her presentation, noting that being an expert in British education did not qualify her as an expert in African education.

Ironically, her observation exposed the haphazard manner in which membership in the ACNETA was chosen (without any native representative) and expressed a rising willingness to confess that Western knowledge, like all knowledge, was after all culture-bound. Hers was another indication of the changing Western image of Africa and the influence her firsthand encounter with Africa had on her consciousness and action.

A nonmissionary, she was among the first colonial officials to criticize the notion that African people do not like to work, and that they preferred literary to industrial education.[5] She confessed that the more she learned about African people, the more she realized how much alike they are to British people. In the Manchester High School, where she was headmistress for many years, she found that when she introduced house-craft, students showed a preference for literary education and a dislike of industrial training. She thought that probably the problem was inherently associated with the class structure and reward system in each society. For people showed a dislike for industrial education largely because industrial workers were poorly paid and were not given the kind of social status and privileges sufficient to create widespread interest in technical and industrial education.

Miss Burstall charged the Conference to see this problem not as an African problem but as a universal problem. Because some missionaries and colonial officers themselves did not indicate by their actions that industrial education was a societal necessity, Miss Burstall said that they should share the blame for not making industrial and technical education attractive to all Africans, not to mention African women.

In a view that may surprise some today, she did not boldly endorse all the three R's for African women. She gave reading a strong recommendation, presumably, because reading was a requirement for being a good Christian; writing received an unenthusiastic endorsement; and, for arithmetic she reserved her "extremely skeptical" view, wondering what good that will do to a practical people. Against this, Miss Burstall ventured to suggest what she called the three H's: "hygiene, vital to the future of the race; house-craft adapted to African conditions; and handwork." She would rather have these women cultivate their extraordinary gifts of music, poetry and proverbs than waste time studying "history that means dates [and] geography that means lists."[6] Then, in one sentence, she, unfortunately, dismissed the idea that the African woman needs geography. For Miss Burstall, hygiene and housecraft were much more vital matters.

Miss Burstall agreed that teachers were part of the problem. To inspire good recruits, she noted that the ACNETA[7] was overseeing sounding the call for teachers and encouraging some to consider educating African women. She wished that the public, particularly, the Church public, as she called it, would overcome apathy and inertia and begin to know what the success of missions in Africa would mean to the whole world.

Then Miss Burstall announced what took some delegates by surprise: the issuance of a Government White Paper on education. With a provision for the education of women, this White Paper laid down principles which called for urgent great care and a very great deal of expert advice. Also, it urged that education be conducted in the vernacular, especially in the early grades.

Miss Burstall concluded with history's lessons for contemporary missions and a piece of evolutionism by recalling the great part played by women in the early history of mission work in England. She cited as an example the influence of the Christian wife over Edward of Northumberland and mentioned countless other women who encouraged their sons to read. Unfortunately, she realized that most English women in the Dark Ages, like contemporary African women, did not encourage their daughters to read. She hoped that contemporary missions would not make the same mistake but would take courage and find a way to provide equal educational opportunity for all, including women and children.

In the interest of the future, and because of their role in procreation and socialization, education of women was seen as indispensable in the task of Christianizing the continent. Speakers after speakers took this for granted. James Aggrey hazarded a controversial proverb which, in essence, said that, if he had his way and could only educate one sex, he would educate women and girls and leave men and boys alone, given that to educate a boy or a man is to educate an individual and to educate a girl or a woman is to educate a family.[8]

Aggrey also took the Conference by storm in his denunciation of the idea of separate education. As one of the brains behind the Conference's advocacy of coeducation, Aggrey declared that he believed in coeducation with the proper kind of teacher because "it makes for progress." Aggrey chided those who advocated the opposite view. "In Africa," Aggrey declared, "you say that our ideas are not the same as the ideas here [in the West]. How are our ideas to be the same if the boys and girls are kept separate?"[9] Looking ahead to future generations, Aggrey, in the words of the scribe who minuted the discussion, "felt strongly" that the church will not be able to turn back the evolutionary clock and eliminate the gender gap, if it failed to situate the gospel of education for men and women on an equal and strong footing.

To Aggrey, it boiled down to the kind of cultural legacy the missions wanted to leave behind in Africa. Apples can only beget apples, not grapes. Therefore, he argued that, if Africa must have a culture where all sexes would be equal both sexes should be trained together. Consequently, Aggrey added that it was no use for missionaries to tell Africans not to do this or that. It was Aggrey's conviction that Africans should be compelled to do the right rather than the wrong; and the right in this case was coeducation. In this, Aggrey's overriding concern was to show that any idea that verged on separate education will, in the long run, prove disadvantageous and catastrophic.

Recalling the view he expressed at High Leigh concerning the either/or approach to native languages, Aggrey ventured the opinion that he would like to see the schools in the whole sub-continent use both foreign and native languages for educational and business purposes. Aggrey noted that East Africa was emphasizing native languages whereas West Africa was emphasizing European languages. His assessment of this divergent approach to languages was that both were at once wrong and right. The two regions, he suggested, should "take lessons from [each] other"[10] in order to grow ecumenically and not be left behind in the future.

On the issue of school inspection, Aggrey agreed that the missions must create their own corp of inspectors. Yet he differed from others who clamored for only foreign inspectors. Educate the native, he insisted, to help in this job. Wondering how many women missionaries were thinking of educating the native women to stand side by side with them in their work, Aggrey thought that missions were not only to educate African women. They were also to groom a substantial number of them into leaders without waiting for several generations to pass. Quoting a successful experiment launched by the CMS in Kenya to give women leadership positions in church and society, Aggrey said that, for effective results to be achieved on this matter, missionary societies should not leave anything to chance. On the contrary, he urged them to create the proper environment to enhance the possibility of arriving at the desired results or goals, irrespective of how long it will take to achieve those ends.

Further, Aggrey enjoined that foreign missionaries must think of training the native women just as they were beginning to do with men. At the same time, he saw missionary training as both-sided: ordinary training in metropolitan centers was to be complemented with another training in Africa as well as the possession of an open mind by all missionaries before they went to Africa. For, as he said, "all that is good is not on this side [Western society] and all that is bad is not on the other side [African society]. There is something good on both."[11] Aggrey concluded by saying that as far as the Church is concerned "what Africa is going to insist on is not denominationalism but Christianity," a statement which brought an angry letter to Oldham immediately after the Conference, wondering what Aggrey meant by Christianity not denominationalism.[12]

Garfield Williams wanted to see what he called the ground-floor of education— the system of sub-standard mission schools—eliminated. Colonial governments in Africa, he said, based on his contact with many of them as a member of the Education Commissions, simply wrote off such schools, not only because their standard were below official expectation, but also because they could not afford the enormous numbers of inspectors required for effective management.

Williams was also one of the speakers who insisted that technical education would only work in Africa, if the missionaries who were sent to Africa were themselves convinced believers in technical education, agriculture, and scientific experimentation. He insisted that the Reports of the Education Commissions must serve as the basis for educating African women as well as men; and that schools must be made a community center in which parents, teachers, and administrators work together for the good of all.

Oldham's last word as the Chair was apt and instructive. It consisted of extensive utilization of the New Testament imperatives and admonishments. Let us face it frankly, Oldham began. Christian missions, he added, are at the beginning of this subject, not the end. However, he considered it a very important subject because, in his view, Africa's future heavily depended to some extent on how missionaries dealt with this question. Oldham thought that there were two immediate tasks to be accomplished.

The first task concerned the fact that missionary societies had to "carry on propaganda," that is, influence public opinion at home and abroad. Though this word has a negative connotation today, Oldham employed it positively to distinguish missionary motive in Africa from the motive of imperial powers, particularly Britain. Colonial governments, he said, were in Africa for the raw materials not the people. For the ordinary Briton, Oldham harbored no uncertainty that his or her interest in Africa was in the fact "that it produce[d] cotton and sisal and coffee and other things required here [in Britain]."[13] For this reason, Oldham believed that only by a constant propaganda will the truth be recognized that in the long run, from every standpoint, the future of the African continent depends on human beings, preeminently on the woman.

The second task was a corollary of the first and concerned the missions being prepared to bring about "a revolution in the normal attitude" of Western people towards African problems. What that meant was clear-cut as far as Oldham was concerned. It meant that, because the burden rested to a large extent on missionary societies, missionaries had to rise to these responsibilities in ways they had never dreamt of. Also, it meant that the extent of their power to influence public opinion and the policies of *Pax Britannica* depended very largely on the degree to which they understood the realities which were brought out in this Conference.

Summary

London 1925 met at a time when the gospel of education was gaining ascendancy. While it made no resolutions, it contributed through its discussion and brainstorming to the growth of the ecumenical mind. Because of this meeting, African missionaries were not only to preach about education in the sense the Conference talked about as a matter of missionary opportunity. They were also to "demonstrate it by doing it."

Equally important was the necessity for a conscious effort to strengthen ecumenical missions through shared educational projects dedicated to enhancing the status of the African woman. The Conference asked that all missionaries should hold together and maintain contacts. It was recognized that on this subject missionary forces must find new ways to join forces with other elements, namely, commercial and colonial officials.

This was an indirect reference to another important conference (Le Zoute 1926) which was more than one year away. However, because American mission boards were planning an anniversary conference and a preparation meeting for Le Zoute, a direct and open invitation was made to all delegates to attend Hartford 1925 which was only three months away.

All delegates were to return home or to their mission stations with the knowledge that they must continue in the coming months and years to work at this problem so that united, both in thought and practice, they would grow in insight and understanding of the whole problem and become more effective in grappling with it.

NOTES

[1]Conference on Education of African Women, London, July 1925, IMC Papers, WCC Library, Geneva; hereafter cited as London 1925.

[2]This is an angle which is frequently glossed over in emerging critiques of mission education of women.

[3]Oldham to Board Secretaries, July 11, 1925, IMC Papers, WCC Library, Geneva.

[4]London 1925, IMC Papers, WCC Library, Geneva. This address was later published in *IRM*; see Mabel Shaw, "A School Village in Northern Rhodesia," *IRM* IV (1925): 523–36. A fuller account of her experience in East Africa was given to the second Education Commission to Africa; see, *Education in East Africa*, pp. 344–346.

[5]This view of the African's attitude to work expressed in 1925 should be contrasted with the one expressed by Andrew Fraser, who, as Chairman of the Continuation Committee of the World Missionary Conference, wrote in 1914 that the instinct to work will come hardly to a race to whom making a living has never entailed much serious work; see, Andrew Fraser, Memorandum on African Education To British Foreign Secretary, February 27, 1914, IMC Papers, WCC Library, Geneva.

[6]London 1925, IMC Papers, WCC Library, Geneva.

[7]The massive papers of the ACNETA constitute a sizeable proportion of IMC/CBMS Archives.

[8]London 1925, IMC Papers, WCC Library, Geneva.

[9]Ibid.

[10]The gravity of this situation is now becoming plainer in that, while a great part of East and Southern Africa is able to speak or understand Swahili, most West African communities and nations can only use either English or French as lingua franca. From ecumenical perspective, the saddest consequence of this situation is being played out in the AACC where French and English are used as official languages not any indigenous African language as such.

[11]London 1925, IMC Papers, WCC Library, Geneva.

[12]In an attempt to explain and clarify the misunderstanding, Oldham wrote that Aggrey did not mean to undercut the need for denominations. From his experience, Oldham wrote, nine of ten Chinese, Indians, or Africans tended to say they were not interested in Western denominationalism but in ecumenism; see, Oldham to Stacy Waddy, July 24, 1925, IMC Papers, WCC Library, Geneva.

[13]London 1925, IMC Papers, WCC Library, Geneva.

8

AFRICA AND THE NEW MISSION MANDATE: HARTFORD 1925

High Leigh and London were succeeded by Hartford, another Conference which, from a balanced perspective, made 1925 a crowded year for ecumenical advance.[1] Like the others, its aim was not to recapture a generation long past or parade past missionary achievements at the expense of immediate pressing needs. Contrariwise, it was a Conference organized to counter the embarrassing fact that the American missionary community and its supporters, in spite of Atlantic City 1922, were still ignorant of the full content of the Reports of the Education Commissions, and that they had left largely unexamined the other pressing questions which contemporary Africa was raising.

Held for many days (October 20 to November 1) to indicate the importance which was attached to the meeting and the gradual but steady emergence of America as a global missionary force, this Conference brought together 109 delegates. Like High Leigh, these delegates were consciously chosen to convey the message that mission societies alone were incapable of addressing the challenges of modern Africa.

A government official, H. L. Shants of the U. S. Department of Agriculture, was invited. Other advisory experts were J. H. Dillard of the Jeanes Foundation, E. C. Sage of the General Education Board, Professor Mabel Carney of Columbia Teachers College and 11 other educators. Present also were 22 missionary administrators, 40 missionaries, and 9 would-be missionaries. Three familiar faces—Oldham, Westermann, and Jones—were also present.[2]

1. Social conditions at Hartford

Hartford's understanding of mission was severely impacted by African social conditions. This influence was first explained by President W. Douglas Mackenzie of the Hartford Seminary Foundation who, in his opening address, outlined why he thought it was appropriate to hold the Conference at Hartford. The son of a famous

African pioneer, Mackenzie, in a manner that betrayed his American apocalyptic vision, hoped that surveying African conditions will cause "a fresh thrill" all over the African field; and that conferees would see the unusual providential opportunity granted to missionaries to "uplift" and transform Africa.

A symposium on "Problems of Sanitation and Public Health" dominated the social question. Tackled first was sleeping sickness and its treatment. Dr. Louise Pierce of the Rockefeller Institute (now University), New York, described the various degrees of prevalence of this disease in different parts of Africa and reviewed the many experiments in its treatment. It went without saying that a united effort by various governments was seen as the only way to deal with the disease. It was Hartford's opinion that the disease could be controlled, if governments, firms and missions united in dealing with it, treating groups of people on a large scale.

Hartford found that, in proposing how ecumenical missionaries should deal with public health and sanitation, the health situation in the black American community was to serve as a reference point. Because lessons generated by this American experience were thought to have bearing on the public health challenges in Black Africa, considerable pains were taken to point out those lessons which were to be replicated in that sub-continent. Among these lessons were the necessity for rest, recreation, fresh air and nutrition, public awareness campaigns and year-round health courses.

It is hard to imagine that, while these health measures may seem quite obvious to some contemporary eyes, they were not that obvious in 1925. Ensuing discussion saw a coterie of missionaries who advocated instant application of those lessons in Africa. Hartford suggested that new missionary recruits be equipped to inculcate sanitation into church life and school curriculum. Further, more partnership with, and involvement of, the masses was suggested as one way to achieve a high degree of success in all forms of health care delivery.

A high point of this discussion came when attention was drawn to the fact that, while "Sanitation and Public Health in Africa" was the theme under consideration, other mission fields were interested in public health. The Council on Public Health Education in China was cited as an example. Hartford thought that, if a continent-wide council composed of medical missionaries of different missionary boards was organized in Africa, the attack on this and other diseases will be much more forceful and full of excellent results.

Hartford also faced the challenge of 'African industrial and mining centers and the opportunities they presented for evangelism. Hartford rightly saw that there was nothing unique about African urban life. Thus it was observed that, except for its unplanned growth, chaotic, and nightmarish condition, the process of urbanization of Africa was in line with the urban trend of the world. Also, it was remarked that African cities were beginning to value machinery, increasing individualism, and rebellion against established authorities. Hartford wanted ecumenical workers to see these cities, like all cities, as morally neutral, leaving human beings only to worry about their propensity for categorization and pigeonholing.

In this understanding, "cities can be and are centers of either for the contamination of humanity or for the dissemination of the forces of righteousness."[3] As in High Leigh and London, it was stated that the wives of the working men in these cities furnished a very special problem, because, compared with village life, they had less social control and readily got into trouble. In this sense, industrial civilization was seen as producing its own worldview and ethos which frequently made a mockery of the old and the nonindustrialized. Additionally, Christianity was seen as difficult to maintain in its purity, because employers were deliberately making it hard for Christian working men to practice their faith.

The state of agriculture in Africa also had an impact on Hartford's social thinking. Led by botanist H. L. Shantz, a member of the second Education Commission, Hartford was told that agricultural missions must be based on fact, not fiction. For instance, missionaries needed to know that Africa is about four times as large as the United States, that the world was only beginning to know the "country [sic] scientifically,"[4] that one half of the continent was like western Texas with natives who have remarkable skill in adapting agricultural methods to the various types of land and climate. For they are natural agriculturalists.

Hartford urged that, in order to deal with the African farmer, Western organizations seeking to provide assistance needed to study indigenous African agricultural methods. These may seem slouchy, it was remarked, "but usually are not so." Careful study had shown that the African has a way, even if it is not the best way, of dealing with soil renewal. Hartford suggested that Western methods may not necessarily be improvement on the African's. Deep plowing, for instance, was seen as not advisable in some parts of Black Africa.

Hartford heard that a way must be found to displace the African belief in magic as the important means of stimulating and ensuring good harvest and experimentation of new planting techniques with the natives. This, necessarily, recalled the need for agricultural missionaries and opened another chapter of the need for specialized training. Hartford called for a school of agriculture which should be combined with industrial training and thus provide a broader education. The debate which ensued on farm machinery and its use in Africa brought differing opinions. Some thought that simple types of machinery were needed. Others rejected the notion of machinery outright. However, all endorsed the importance of fertilizers.

A mental task associated with that endorsement of fertilizer concerned how to convince the African farmer that fertilization will result in relatively large crops, instead of making weeds grow faster as some believed. A work-ethic, consistent with the new emphasis on agriculture, was to be encouraged. To achieve this puritanical commitment to work, Hartford thought that missionaries themselves must honor farming and look at it as a natural task not a job to which only the peasants are consigned.

In this Conference modern agricultural techniques were presented as if they have no bad consequences to nature and human beings. Moreover, in view of the weak state of agricultural research, and the continuing dominant belief that whatever was good in the metropolitan centers was necessarily good for Africa, the negative consequences of chemical use probably did not cross many minds. Here we must remember that the intention or motive behind all this was to help Africa; therefore, as far as many missionaries and agricultural experts were not yet aware of the darkside of these chemicals, the end, apparently and arguably, justified the means.

2. Primal religions at Hartford

At Hartford, African cultural and religious values affected ecumenical warrants for missions. This effect was made more pervasive by the presence of many educationalists and linguists. Rejecting the superficiality of the gilded age of missions, Hartford shifted the question from whether African primal religions have any permanent value to whether missionaries were aware of their big debt to pre-existing African civilization and value system.

In seeking to evangelize through church and school, Hartford asked missionaries to raise questions which many had, consciously or unconsciously, avoided in the past. These included questions of social and religious bonds and the vital factors in aboriginal African social cohesion. This meant exploring the meaning to Africans of birth, family, death, and rebirth or reincarnation, and determining how etiology affected how they saw Christ as the mediator. Missionaries were to identify those elements of social cohesion which proved to be strong enough to withstand this foreign influence. They were to know what kinds of new socio-religious forms came into existence in native society, for example, nuclear family and monogamous marriages.

Here, Hartford's overall aim was to make missionaries to recognize that Africans were undergoing an unprecedented rate of social change; to take steps to help the natives to create new social and religious bonds and replace those which were breaking down; and to avoid the dangers associated with a rapid change in their life systems. By the same token, missionaries were to be aware that tribal life in

Africa was not specifically African, but a common evolutionary stage of human development which the so-called higher civilization had without conception left behind to develop new forms, perhaps, because they found sib or clan life to be incompatible with "higher" forms of civilization.

Accordingly, missionaries were to face the fact that some forms of clan organization will disappear in Africa (just as it disappeared in some other parts of the world), when the weight of the new order renders the maintenance of sib life impossible and exorbitant, and any attempt to cling to it artificial and medicine after death. On the other hand, certain primordial bonds in clan life may prove vital enough to survive within the new order. All this meant that the ongoing changes in Africa, while far more intensive, were not to be characterized as specifically African, but human. This was an interesting sociological understanding of religious and social life in Africa, far more realistic than how the London delegates saw it, especially in seeing some aspects of African culture as a phase in social evolution rather than anything specifically African.

Therefore, one should not be surprised to learn that Hartford wanted all missionaries to understand that the human problem in Africa called for increased knowledge—and a systematic one for that matter—on the part of all those who have gained in one way or another from that continent. For, nothing was plainer, to Hartford's delegates, than the fact that what was particularly needed in African ecumenical work was an objective based on the history and past development of the African people and involving an intelligent conception of their needs.

Apparently Hartford, like High Leigh and London, was evolutionary in thinking. Whether delegates were really down-to-earth about evolutionism is hard to determine. What is crystal clear is that Hartford advised missionaries to seek to understand the viewpoint of the preliterate African. For example, it was said that, if missionaries are to work with the African, they must try to understand why the African does what he or she does. For only this kind of understanding can begin an evolution upward.

Consequently, delegates pleaded for a process of building upon the African culture, music and religion and saw that in Africa are groups at all stages of evolution and in them people of every stage of growth. Here was another indisputable attempt to undo past misunderstanding of primal culture and religion, and in embracing evolutionism as it did, however piecemeal, Hartford was sounding just the American version of the same gospel of new understanding of the African. Also, it was exceptionally conscious of its language vis-a-vis primal religions in particular and African culture in general. Phrases such as paganism, animism, and heathenism were not used. Salient was the fact that past concerns about syncretism were put in the backburner; emerging was American pragmatism at its best.

3. Indigenous churches at Hartford

Hartford blended its anthropology of native religion with its sociological understanding of native leadership-needs in church and civil life. Moving beyond High Leigh and London, Hartford passed on a distinctive lesson by asking missionaries to ascertain that the Christianization of Africa did not mean the African loss of his or her inner equilibrium without viable new connections to restore him or her to sanity.

While how this disequilibrium was to be avoided was not dealt with, Hartford's theories made two other things increasingly acceptable: the fact that the progress of the new order in Africa will involve an unending struggle, conducted with all the resources of science, missions, and native ingenuity against natural and social hurdles; and the fact that what used to be called "primitive man" was not that "primitive" in his power to resist appropriation and refusal to be dissected, analyzed, and fitted into prefabricated schemes designed for him by others.

Hartford understood that, because indigenous churches in Africa exemplified varying degrees of immaturity, it was imperative for the ecumenical movement to allow them to create their own self-understanding and identity and be given ample opportunity to grow into full maturity. Meeting in a country where black churches were increasingly part of the cultural landscape and the dominant institution for black self-expression, Hartford's delegates understood, far more than the Conferences which were held in European cities, that indigenous leadership was tantamount to church growth and expansion of Christianity to remote places in Africa where no foreigner could afford to go. It was understood that native control of churches, unquestionably, meant rapid church growth; therefore, Hartford urged cooperating societies to implement devolution schemes in Africa as suggested or implied in past Conferences.

4. Race relations at Hartford

At Hartford, calls for a better understanding of the human race and a better treatment of African people were heard loud and clear. Hartford said that the continuing discrimination against Africans was sharpening the missionaries' ethical duty, and they were to perform that duty by making all European nations, with colonial ties to Africa, realize that all policies of discrimination and deprivation needed immediate change. As part of its retooling effort on this question, Hartford thought that it was necessary to underscore the idea of "human family" which was, by the 1920s, not a new vocabulary in the thought of the time.

Yet packaged in a new way, this idea of human family meant the recognition that the dominant forms of civilization (British, French, Portuguese, Belgian) in Africa were, without exception, expressions of foreign civilization, with accompanying strong consciousness of superiority and a natural wish to ensure that the cultural ideals of their foreign origin should form the basis of the new order in Africa. Granted that this view may to a certain extent be justified, Hartford deemed it in danger of overlooking the fact that Africans, unindustrialized, though many were and are, have their social individuality and a mental culture of their own which is, not unlike other peoples', the direct creation and expression of their soul.

Additionally, Hartford saw that the low-state of Africa's cultural achievement should not constitute the basis for horrendous discrimination against its people. For discrimination against one part of the human family was tantamount to indirect discrimination against the whole human family. Realizing that many people (including, especially, many members of the educated class throughout the world), were simply misinformed about Africans, Hartford thought that the gospel of education should be expanded to include re-educating those who were simply misinformed about Africa and Africans.

Hartford also required that the most fundamental feature of education be the preparing of the native African for "effective life within his native environment and on the basis of his own race qualities and genius."[5] If, in the past, some missionaries tended, consciously or unconsciously, to Europeanize Africa, new awareness quickened by contemporary social sciences, and ecumenical willingness to use these sciences, helped Hartford to denounce such attitudes, and to advocate better race relations.

In view of the violent history of race relations in America, Hartford found that social conditions in America would affect conditions in the sub-Sahara. For this reason, Hartford was dismayed that many European missionaries instead of many white American missionaries were more anxious to visit black institutions and churches in America. Many white American missionaries, it was observed, had gone from Alabama to Africa without setting foot in Tuskegee.[6] Hence, it was asked, how can there be a change in Africa without a change in the American society? Here, indeed, Hartford was putting its finger on the real world in which many American missions continued to operate: racial lines. Many were disheartened, because, despite past ecumenical directives on this matter, particularly Oxford's, many interracial missionary bands were not yet in operation.

It is important to recognize that there were many reasons why many white American missionaries had gone from Alabama to Africa without "setting foot in

Tuskegee." For one thing, some had avoided Tuskegee because it was the conventional thing to do. Certainly, others did so in part because they were largely misinformed about black institutions in America. Psychologically, prestige was more in Africa than at home, for Jesus' saying that a prophet has no honor in his own country was as true then as it is true today. Sociologically, deep-seated racial suspicion was still not overcome, for America, as a nation, was still held captive by segregation doctrines which governed all aspects of life in that country from birth to death.

On this question Hartford, realizing that white and black missionaries and church leaders in America were themselves products of social segregation policies, knew that the missionary community should not pretend to be in the foreign (African) field what it was not in the home field. Thus, the Conference relied rather heavily on personal testimonies from those black and white missionaries who were bold enough to go against the tide in American society and speak of their interracial experience for the benefit of other conferees. Many spoke of how they became acquainted with black missionary initiatives and how they began to appreciate what black Americans were doing. A clear and good example was given by James L. Sibley, once an educational official in North Carolina. At Hampton, he said, could be found all kinds of training ranging from the purely educational to the cultural. Hampton, he confirmed, had many excellent group of black teachers, well trained and enthusiastic to show what black people can do in all spheres of human endeavor.[7]

In the same vein, Westermann, the Berliner, said that his recent visit to Southern schools in America gave him a new idea of what black people can do and can be, and of what can be "accomplished by the close, faithful, unselfish cooperation of whites and blacks."[8] It takes two to tangle, Hartford suggested. So mutualism must supplant separate, black and white mission development and relations, otherwise their separate work would be "almost negligible."

It is in this spirit of continuing attempt to overcome the racial divide in Protestant mission enterprise that we must understand Hartford's declaration that white American missionaries must first demonstrate their interest in Africa by becoming acquainted with black people and institutions in America. Whereas ordinarily a furlough year could be spent in the comfort and protection of a college and seminary campus, Hartford suggested that the world of black people and other institutions, encouraging interracial cooperation in America, should become at least in part one way to spend such a vacation.

For example it was suggested that white missionaries should devote part of their furlough to visiting the Southern States where most blacks lived. A possible tour could take a missionary from Harlem in New York City to Hampton Institute and Howard University, two predominantly black institutions. Another tour could lead one from Atlanta (to study the work of its interracial mission and school system) to Tuskegee to see the great educational and industrial plant there, made famous by the great black educator, Booker T. Washington (1856–1915). It was believed that such tours could be "intensely profitable" in terms of improving race relations and exposing white America to the other America—black, poor, enslaved, and still struggling for full emancipation.

5. Cooperation and unity at Hartford

Hartford's theoretical suggestions on unity and cooperation in the African field were made possible by Africanists who knew what they were talking about. By listening to the presentations made by these Africanists, the Conference came to the conclusion that cooperation and unity should mean working along *with*, not *for* somebody else. This was a distinctive understanding of ecumenics which pointed to the day when the whole world would be seen in reality as the mission field just as Edinburgh had foreseen fifteen years earlier; and that ecumenism was indeed something the church must accomplish for its own sake not for somebody else.

Hartford suggested to missionary boards that they should tap the experience and "wise methods" of the General Education Board which was founded by the Rockefellers to be of service to the Southern States in America. Attention was called to the fact that it took over six decades for some missions to attain the new ecumenical attitude of today, and that more conscious effort must be put in enhancing unity in the field. Despite denominational differences, it was thought that, if missionaries would simply preach Christ, not denominations, cooperation would be easy. Also present were views which obscured, rather than revealed, the true character of the real facts of church disunity. For instance, it was suggested that Liberalism and overemphasis on new methods not "vision for souls" brought about disunity. Others, seeing themselves as Conservatives, imperceptively advanced sin as the sole cause of friction among missionaries and churches.

It cannot be denied, however, that in this Conference, like other post-war ones, sensitive thinkers were asking whether older mission visions were still tenable and whether modernist missiologists, in an attempt to accommodate Christian missions to the consciousness of modern humanity, were not wedding Christianity to modernism very uncritically, and with little or no "dowry." The fact is that at Hartford there were to be found sincere men and women who were honestly trying to make sense in our modern world of doctrines defined in earlier centuries and in entirely different circumstances.

Thus, despite the tension and the fear that soul-winning was in danger of being eclipsed, the new fact of the time was that missiology was undergoing a course cor-

rection not, as some would have it, an outright repudiation of everything conservative. Invariably, a significant development was the recognition that there exists the
world of the African which the Church cannot completely control but which, through
unitive action, it can influence in a meaningful way.

6. Some individual contributions at Hartford

At Hartford, several figures made unassailable contributions. J. H. Oldham's set
the tone and backdrop for the contributors. Addressing "The Present Situation in
Africa," Oldham wanted North Americans, just like the Europeans, to be familiar
with the dominating factors which were overtaking Christian mission plans and
uprooting Christian communities as quickly as they were being built. These factors
were chiefly nonmissionary, official, commercial, and native in character.

The thrust of the address was not novel. Yet, it evidenced Oldham's continuing reflection on these challenges. Africa, he said, so long isolated is now in the full
current of human life with immeasurable potentialities and pressing problems. The
attempt to erect a bustling civilization on the slow growing one had created serious
economic complications. Politically, this recreation process raised the question as
to which group shall govern, a racial question as to which shall lead, and a cultural
question whether the new shall supplant the old. Oldham was sad that America,
which should have been at the forefront of combating these questions, was itself, still
largely indifferent to racism against blacks. Still, Oldham thought that, in the solutions of these problems, American sympathy, ideas and wealth will have a share.

Oldham knew that the missionary enterprise was a positive force in Africa.
However, he refused to belabor the point, adding instead that while mission influences in Africa were relatively stationary, nonmissionary forces were marching ahead
"absolutely transforming native life."

On Oldham's account three facts or issues stood out. The first fact was that
Europe's economic interest in Africa was not ancillary but primary. The second fact
was that missions would not drive away the European Powers from Africa, even if
they could. What they could do was akin to the view expressed at High Leigh: a
conscious galvanization or enlargement of the force of public vision and opinion so
that Western nations would come to see why in Africa human and moral viewpoint
should prevail over the purely economic. The third fact was that the outcome of
such missionary influence on public opinion was not expected in any way to be fruit-
less or hopeless at all.

Oldham's reason for this optimism was apparently the result of his experience
in the ACNETA. He had discovered that after the first world war, not all government officials were disposed to think of European presence in Africa in purely and

only economic terms; broadminded officials could be made to "agree that human beings are more important than the piling up of wealth."[9] In this respect, Oldham thought that the establishment of the ACNETA, with the responsibility of thinking about human interests in Africa, was a "noteworthy fact."

Equally noteworthy was the rapid development of government schools (e.g. Achimota College, Ghana), based on what Oldham termed a broad and "generous" attitude and in accordance with educational ideals which met with hearty approval by the missions. Oldham expressed the fear that these government schools may put mission schools out of business, if the latter are not of first rate quality.

Oldham wanted Americans to be happy that one of their own, Jesse Jones, was among those spearheading the new gospel of education and that the Reports of the Education Commissions were receiving raving reviews and acceptance in missionary and government circles. Indeed, said Oldham, one governor of East Africa had remarked, at a British Government dinner party in honor of Jones, that the Commission Report for East Africa was his "Bible of African education."

From this perspective, Oldham granted that this Hartford meeting was important not only because it was held in North America but also because of its African theme and the fact that the Conference attacked African problems "in the right way." Oldham also looked forward to another world Conference on Africa, Le Zoute 1926 (see next chapter). Whereas in the previous Conference, London 1925, Oldham did not speak openly about the proposed Le Zoute Conference, here at Hartford, it was a different ball game.

Since it appeared that all signs pointed to a very successful world Conference on a grand and unusual scale, Oldham spoke with more enthusiasm. Le Zoute seemed to him as a divine leading, because colonial governments were expected to send representatives. Also, with some hesitation the way had become very clear as all boards and interests in Africa, North America, the Continent, and Britain had enthusiastically agreed to pray and plan for this great Conference (Le Zoute).

Oldham hoped that Le Zoute will provide the needed vision and unity so that missions can interpret African questions in a better way to home churches and to public opinion. Oldham spoke of the difficulties of setting up a program, given that subjects are, necessarily, approached from so many viewpoints to the extent that a discussion is apt to bring out differences rather than to promote unity. He was convinced that Africa is not an area to be covered, but a new group of forces molding human life to which missions must relate themselves.

Oldham wanted Hartford delegates to see that the problems facing Africa to be tabled at Le Zoute was not merely European in origin. The difficulty, he added, was not merely a problem of black against white. Asia, for example, had brought more additional problems to Africa both from the religious inroad of Islam and Hindu migration, particularly into Kenya Colony. For this reason, Oldham believed that the agenda for the Le Zoute meeting would be far-reaching and all missionaries should be prepared for it. For it was possible for the Le Zoute meeting to become a turning point in the making of ecumenical mandates as far as Africa was concerned.

Another presentation was made by Jesse Jones. Jones introduced a discussion on "Educational Objectives and Adaptations in Africa." This came straight from a chapter of his Commissions' Reports. Education, in Jones' conception, was the whole approach (spiritually, physically, mentally and otherwise) to a complete training and making of a person. Jones alluded to how modern psychology had driven educationalists to the people themselves to discover how to approach them with care and wisdom.

Jones wanted the missionaries not to see education merely as a transfer of data from one hardware to another, nor the accumulation of "write-protected" or unchangeable knowledge, but the assimilation of the right and amenable data. Consequently, he wanted those who sought to educate the African community to have in mind four things: its health, its ability to utilize the resources, human or material which it possesses, its means of preserving and transmitting its own best heritage through its home life, and its recreation. Tough-minded, hard-working, and possessed of a sympathetic understanding of the psychology of the African life, Jones advocated the teaching of history, geography and other studies in African schools, for, in his view, these subjects were useful in imparting historical knowledge of other peoples who have developed in these four ways.

Recalling Atlantic City and High Leigh, this shrewd and substantial Jones let it be known that this practical education, if it be so called, will not hinder or dim the revealing of Jesus Christ in power and life, instead, it promised to provide a direct opening of "the way for such a revelation." Jones also indicated his unwavering concern for the education of women and girls. He mentioned the handicaps under which many African women suffered. Yet he believed that their place was still in the home and that they should be so trained as "home makers." He did not see coeducation becoming an immediate part of African educational landscape, though he thought that the education of girls should parallel that of boys.

One Mrs. Donohugh also thought that the girls should be sent back to their villages and not allowed to migrate to the cities. For this reason, Mrs. Donohugh believed that it was important to determine just what girls should be taught in order to stem their influx into cities. In Natal, the situation was found to be exceptionally good for the training of women, for as Miss Caroline Frost recounted, women graduates of schools could go far and wide as teachers. Besides, they were, like many other foreign missionaries, excellent voluntary evangelistic workers and church builders in their own way.

Looked at in another light, the discussion on this topic turned out to be in part a referendum on how missionaries exercised patience in dealing with their African converts. For example, Mrs. Ivy Craig of Rhodesia wondered whether patience on the part of missionaries was not becoming difficult to exercise. Why talk about African women, she asked, as if they are untouchables and unimpressionable? "They," she said, are "quite teachable." The question was whether there remained missionaries who possessed "sufficient patience."[10]

William Aery presented a synopsis of his work at the Hampton Normal and Agricultural Institute, Virginia. He urged the ecumenical community to be mindful of the role played by special black institutions of higher learning. Hampton, said Aery, aimed at an education which was suitable for useful living and retained no student who refused to work hard. Its guiding principle was that black people demanded and deserved "an outlet for innate abilities."

President John Hope (1868–1936) of Morehouse College, Atlanta, made an open invitation to any and all guests to drop in freely and see his College. He offered to show any guest not only the College but also other interesting plants in the city of Atlanta. Black people in America, he correctly saw, with a population of more than 12 million, were "in danger of group selfishness and narrowness," particularly because, although they had "plenty of heroism," they had "too little opportunity to show it in service."[11] This brought to the fore the continuing limited opportunity black Americans had as missionaries in Africa, despite the resolution on this matter at Oxford 1923.

Hope urged that black Americans be enlisted for service in Africa. Hope made a passionate appeal for the understanding of Africa in its resources, its natural groupings, its great religious divisions, its racial distinctions and various cultures. Moreover, Hope wanted missionaries to understand Africans not as dead wood but as a people pulsing with life.

Westermann presented a paper that dealt with the persistence of tribal sensibilities, in spite of missionary work. Westermann began by referring to governmental attempts to stamp out the activities of a murderous secret society in West Africa. At the trial, it was shown that one member had been thoroughly educated in England, but that what he had gained had not rubbed out his old beliefs. To understand incidents like this, Westermann opined that missionaries must, first of all, try to understand the old inner life of the African whose secret only the vernacular could divulge. For the vernacular allows the African to reveal his real genius, his good sense, his artistry and his wise use of the principles of life.

Westermann wanted missionaries to see the vitality which may belong to Black African languages and cultural life. He thought that the Berbers offered a clear example of a people who have persisted for over four thousand years, in spite of various foreign yokes from the Phoenicians to the Arabs.

Westermann capped his presentation by disclosing that the IMC and many non-missionary bodies were planning to establish the International Institute of African Languages and Cultures[12] in order, among other things, to provide governmental and missiological clients technical information regarding African languages and cultures.

Dr. Mackenzie used the book of Ephesians to give a theological summation of Hartford's deliberations. He told Hartford that this book was a statement of the genius of Christianity and its supreme glory. Mackenzie, while clearly upbeat in his hermeneutics, was equally dialectical. He spoke of Pauline great antitheses in Ephesians, eternity and time, heaven and earth, holiness and sin, the salvation of the individual and the salvation of the race as embodied in Christ. The theme of the epistle, he believed, is what God is making of human nature, of the mystery of His will and purpose. To know the will of God in history, he asserted, is to understand all history. Yet he saw that these lofty ideas led to a practical end. This end concerned the practical questions of "social life with its industrial problems, its families, its laborers." The implication was undeniable:

> The questions we have asked about Africa are the questions
> which Paul asked of himself, how Christianity was to enter the
> life of that day, remaking human nature, moulding men and
> families and communities in accordance with the new ideal.[13]

Summary

Overall, despite its inability to conform collective vision to its individual ideals, Hartford closed on the positive note of intercession. An exhibit was made of the standard books and bibliography on Africa prepared solely for the Conference. With this, the FMCNA's Committee on Africa was trying as much as possible to introduce many people to the real life conditions in Africa, instead of hear-say.

Hartford reflected, for the most part, the ambiguities and popular ideas (equal and individual rights, freedom of belief and expression, etc.) which constitute life in America. It knew that the socioeconomic reality in American society was completely different from those popular ideas as they exist in the ideal state. This is why, as an ecumenical gathering, Hartford sought to break away from those national ideals and spoke of the gospel in universals which needed concretization.

For this reason, it was made explicitly clear that Africans are anxious to have missionaries tie up what they say to practice and not speak in abstract terms; and that they looked forward to the time when they will obtain relief from their difficulties and a field for the unhindered cultivation and untrammelled development of their peculiar gifts as a people.

With this understanding, Hartford added another point on the ecumenical scoreboard, and reminded the IMC that the new mission mandate and, therefore, its real challenge, increasingly, was no longer imagination but praxis.

NOTES

[1]Africa Conference (FMCNA), Held October 20–November 1, 1925, at Hartford, Connecticut, IMC Papers, WCC Library, Geneva; hereafter cited as Hartford 1925.

[2]Ibid.

[3]Ibid.

[4]Ibid. This geography lesson was valued very highly because many North Americans had a shallow knowledge of Africa as a continent, not a country. Unfortunately, after nearly seven decades, North Americans still are not at home with the geography of Africa. A lot still remains to be done in this regard.

[5]Hartford 1925, IMC Papers, WCC Library, Geneva.

[6]Ibid.

[7]Ibid.

[8]Ibid.

[9]Ibid.

[10]Ibid.

[11]Ibid.

[12]This Institute was later established on June 29, 1926 at the University of London. Many individuals and groups in Africa were involved in its formation, providing help which only the natives could provide in terms of idioms and syntax.

[13]Hartford 1925, IMC Papers, WCC Library, Geneva.

9

THE NEW AFRICA AND THE NEW MISSION:
LE ZOUTE 1926

Meanwhile, in New York City and London, final preparations were being made for another conference on Africa and ecumenical way-station—Le Zoute 1926. After more than two years of behind-the-scene arrangements, all roadways and waterways led to this resort town by the North Sea; and all eyes now were, not on who would show up, but on who would dare to decline his or her invitation to this momentous and exclusive gathering.

We have already drawn attention to how London and Hartford looked forward to this Conference. In this chapter we examine how it brought tremendous growth, progress, and public confidence to the IMC, and how it gave to the ecumenical world deeper missiological insight and mandates from 1926 onwards.

A proper place to begin our examination of the Le Zoute Conference is to recognize that its title was not the Christian *missions* in Africa, but the Christian *mission* in Africa. This title was deliberately chosen to indicate that faith must adjust to the brute empirical realities of modern Africa, and that all foreigners and natives in Africa have something to do which bears significance beyond the merely temporal and mundane. More important, Le Zoute aimed at "educating" all foreigners in Africa that they cannot exploit the continent without thinking about its impact on the natives, and that a united program for remaking Africa was necessary for the good of all.

So Le Zoute set a very high goal for itself and aimed at taming elements of collective egoism through bringing them under the dominion of conscience, or, in the words of its organizers, "under the dominion of Christ, so that all individual, social and national life may be in harmony with the Will of God."[1] Not only did this avowed goal presage how innovative the organizers of the Conference wanted it to be, it also indicated how they wanted it, so badly, to create an international impression that the IMC meant business with influencing world politics in Africa. Accordingly, this bold moral aim influenced the choice of its membership; and, because the meeting was billed as a capital one for the IMC and the world, we must take a closer look at the composition of this membership.

Thirteen nonAfrican nations were represented: America, Belgium, Brazil, Denmark, Finland, France, Germany, Britain, Norway, Holland, Portugal, Sweden, and Switzerland. Nearly all African territories sent representatives. Among the notable "sons of the soil," we must mention N. S. J. Ballanta, a prominent figure, who was making headlines with his research in African music; N. T. Clerk, Synod Clerk of the Scottish Mission in the Gold Coast; John Dube, founder and principal of the Ohlange Institution in Natal and editor of the local newspaper; N. D. Oyerinde of the Nigerian Baptist Convention; and Z. R. Mahabane, President of the African National Congress in South Africa.[2] From America came over fifty-eight delegates. These included two black Americans who had also attended the Hartford Conference, Max Yergan and John Hope.

Although the majority of the delegates were appointed by seventy missionary societies and other organizations, the spotlight was on the forty-three nonmissionary members. Called consultants, they were mainly men and women with life-long colonial and other nonmissionary interests in Africa. Among these were Dr. Broden, Director of the Brussels School of Tropical Medicine; General De Meulemeester, ex-Governor of Belgian Congo; M. Louis Franck, ex-Colonial Minister of Belgium; the Governor of Ruanda-Urundi and Madame Mazorati; S. E. Senhor d'Oliviera, the Portuguese Minister at Brussels; Professor Westermann, now Director, International Institute of African Languages and Cultures; and Professor Julius Richter, Berlin University.

Among the American consultants were Jesse Jones who, through the Education Commissions to Africa, helped to bring this Conference about. Others were J. H. Dillard and E. C. Sage, experienced educationalists; Canon Phelps Stokes, President of the Fund that bore the name of his family; and Professor R. L. Buell of Harvard University, a researcher into land and labor questions in Africa.

In the band of British consultants, Lord Frederick Lugard and his wife were pre-eminent figures. With them came Edward Garraway, former Resident Commissioner of Basutoland; E. B. Denham, Colonial Secretary for Kenya Colony; Major Hanns Vischer, Secretary of the ACNETA; W. T. Welsh, Chief Magistrate of the Transkei; Dr. J. L. Gilks, Director of Medical and Sanitary Service in Kenya. The leading consultants from South Africa were Dr. C. T. Loram, an educationalist and one of the Commissioners for Native Affairs, and Professor W. M. Macmillan of Witwatersrand University, an authority on land questions. Also in attendance were prominent women delegates and consultative members. Numbered among them were physicians, Mrs. Donald Fraser, Catherine Mabie, and Louise Pearce of the

Rockefeller Institute. Others were educationalists, Misses Whitelaw and A. M. E. Exley, and Mrs. Parker Crane. At the background were, of course, the planners-in-chief, Oldham (who appropriately chaired the business committee) and his colleague, Warnshuis. In all, delegates numbered 221.

Doubtless, this was an impressive assembly of influential missionary and governmental dignitaries of the time. On this, many observers were right when they observed that never before, perhaps, has such a mass of ripe experience been concentrated for a week (September 14th to 21st) upon the consideration of the Christian mission in Africa.

However, it was one thing to bring important figures together in this Conference and quite another to benefit from their presence. To say this is another way of posing the question, how did this Conference grapple with African questions?[3]

1. Social conditions at Le Zoute

With regard to the challenge of African social conditions, Le Zoute deepened the views expressed at previous Conferences, and displayed a willingness to declare, more openly and forthrightly, that the findings of the Education Commissions had made the debate over the correlation between evangelism and social action superfluous. Thus, like Hartford, which had a broad understanding of evangelism, Le Zoute situated social action and evangelism on equal footing and saw them as indissolubly linked biblical motifs. In fact, in view of the presence of nonmissionary figures, Le Zoute had no other alternative except to affirm both motifs and all Western activities in Africa as leading to one and the same aim: Christian mission. Forced by the need for social development, health, school, land, and labor questions, Le Zoute boldly faced this issue and, thus, moved the IMC a step forward on social Christianity even before Jerusalem 1928.

To be sure, as no conference on Africa in the 1920s was thought complete without economic discourse and, in view of the presence of men and women who were not only colonial policy makers but also doers themselves, Le Zoute devoted an unusual time to socioeconomic questions so much so that it had to be defended in the official report which was later widely distributed. Why was this necessary and how come missionary leaders did not fear, as some contemporary Christians would do, that non-theological questions were diverting their attention from the so-called purely evangelical task of the church—converting souls?

The answer is found in Le Zoute's belief that the problems of an economic kind, which arose from Western invasion of Africa, were so perplexing and influential that they challenged consideration wherever and whenever people met to discuss the development of the continent. Moreover, because the Conference was also concerned with justice issues, the omission of economic questions, it was believed, would stultify the program of any conference summoned to discuss Christian expansion in Africa. Although, understandably, there were some missionaries outside the IMC community who advocated anti-social Christianity and had attacked this view of missions, Le Zoute did not offer any apology for the amount of time it devoted to economic questions. For, in its view, no apology was necessary, irrespective of what critics had to say.

Naturally, the motivation which was operative at Le Zoute, particularly on this economic question, was not to drive the Europeans away from Africa. For, even before this Conference took place, the partition of Africa was a fait accompli and delegates (such as Oldham who had been ringing this economic bell at every conference stop he made) knew that Europeans in general went to Africa to seek homes and a livelihood, and, in the case of companies, enriching their shareholders, not the natives and laborers. Also, Le Zoute knew that, having staked their claim of one part of Africa or the other, Colonial Powers were not about to simply pack and go home, without a substantial payoff for their adventure in Africa. Therefore, Le Zoute merely sought to find ways to balance what it perceived as native interest with European interest; and, specifically, to remind colonial authorities that the League of Nations' Mandate had a dual clause: the right for the strong to rule the weak and the former's ethical debt to the latter, though the extent of this debt was not explicitly stated.

In these years, working for justice was a question of becoming actively involved in conferences or of persuading governments to adopt so-called "humane" policies. Attempts at removing the social structures which encouraged poverty and dependence were still few and far between. Similarly, witnessing to a simpler lifestyle in metropolitan centers in order to help in raising the standard of life in African colonies was not taken seriously. The sad part continued to be the fact that, despite Le Zoute's expression of concern, no strong anti-colonial ethic evolved, even within the missionary ranks, to question the morality on which the League of Nations' Mandate was based.

Obviously, this may sound horrible to the contemporary African that those who made the rules and decided what was ethical included the same people who stood to profit most from such arrangement. However, this is the fact Le Zoute had to confront; and this is the reality with which it had to work, and the backdrop against which pronouncements on social questions were made.

Le Zoute's economic faith as expressed by its resolution on this matter recognized that the future of the world is bound up with the moral, physical, and intellectual development of the African peoples. It mandated that missionaries and colonial governments must accept the integrative and central role that land plays in Africa. It urged colonial governments to see that, in addition to making land available to foreigners, the natives should have clearly protected deeds and tenure to their lands. It admitted that the incursion of acquisitive capitalism into Africa's hinterland "may prejudice the healthy growth of native communities" and rejected all forced labor for private enterprise. However, a variance was allowed on forced labor because of national or public interest based especially on the following reasons:

1. Outbreak of epidemics, floods and other national emergencies.
2. Communal labor required of all members of a particular group or sex and sanctioned by appropriate code of Native Law and Custom.

That it was a resolution which took into account the varied conditions in the continent, including the growing gentrification of some African communities, was never disputable. It also reflected the viewpoint, which prevailed during the discussion, that of guaranteeing the natives access to their land and, at the same time, making it easier for foreign entrepreneurs to have access to this highly indispensable and valuable asset.

2. Primal religions at Le Zoute

Le Zoute's view of African primal, cultural and religious values was a crystallization of the conclusions reached at High Leigh, London, and Hartford. Indeed, one need not probe too deeply to find that it abandoned the old missionary hope of a total sweep of the old order. It was also evident, more than ever before, that missiological thinking vis-a-vis Africa was becoming a creation of the African circumstance than its creator.

For example, in view of the continuing back-to-culture movement and renewed speed with which the indigenous churches adopted primal religious values for Christian worship, Le Zoute had no choice but to declare that native ethics could not be separated from native religious practices. Therefore, to condemn native religious orientation was tantamount to condemning the people themselves and planting a rootless Christianity. Moreover, in view of its emphasis on the new—new relationship between Westerners and Africans, new understanding of Africa's past and present, new understanding of missions as all-embracing, Le Zoute mandated that everything "good" done in Africa by all Westerners must be understood as part of the Christian missionary experience.

Also, nothing revealed the impact of the African situation on the character of this new teaching and mandate than Le Zoute's conception of all religions as belief systems which embrace the ends of all good and right endeavors. By this idea of the good and the right, Le Zoute meant the positive roles played by many foreigners (including doctors, traders, colonial administrators, linguists, teachers, employers, and missionaries) in the task of "remaking" Africa. All these professionals were to see their presence in Africa as part of the missionary business of giving African life a new lease and constructive unity. And all of them, whether or not they saw themselves as "missionaries" were to be regarded, beginning at Le Zoute, as missionaries. For, as the Conference claimed, they were all engaged in different facets of the Christian *mission*.[4]

Also evident was a frantic attempt to move beyond a mere sociological and anthropological appreciation of Africa's past, and to use this past as a means of creating a new consciousness in which Westerners would readily see the common humanity which binds them with Africans, rather than the difference in material development which tends to divide them.

For example, a statement admitted that Europeans and Americans have their own social heritage just as the Africans have theirs; but for various reasons there are differences in heritage. Africans, like other peoples, see the world with different eyes, interpret facts in a different way, not because their mind is constituted disparately from the European or American mind, but because of environmental factors brought to bear on the individual whether by deliberate socialization instruction of their elders or the unconscious influence of the group to which they belong, no matter how this group is designated—clan, tribe, or nation.

Another statement which borrowed heavily from contemporary phenomenology of religion, was made:

> Spirituality asks for our reverence wherever we may encounter it. Light is light, whether it be the morning starlight or pagan piety or the sunshine of Christian piety; the Light of the World, whether as bright and Morning Star in pagan darkness, or as the Dayspring in our Christian revelation, manifests Himself to His World, and demands our reverence, however dim some particular manifestations of Himself among our primitive peoples may seem to us to be.[5]

In other words, Le Zoute clearly took for granted that, while missionaries should be concerned about syncretism, it was time to recognize that this was no longer the paramount problem. Indeed, one can argue that some delegates in fact promoted universalism, given the tacit suggestion that there was nothing essentially different between the idea of revelation in Christian teaching and the idea of go-betweens in primal religion. A paper on "The Value of the African's Past" may have helped to prepare the ground for such a novel teaching about Africa; certainly, it helped to create a new appreciation of that continent.[6]

Beyond this appreciation, Le Zoute consciously sought to relate Christianity to African customs and values. However, as the delegates found out the hard way, diversity of opinion on this issue was still unavoidable. Thus, there was one party which defended unrestricted baptism of everything African into the new religion. And there were those who argued the opposite and rejected any blanket identification of primal religions with Christianity.

Yet this was not a racial issue. On all sides of the spectrum were to be found all races, "modernists" and "conservatives" arguing among themselves. For example, Z. R. Mahabane wanted tolerance and Dr. S. M. Zwemer, the Islamic expert, wanted the Conference to learn from the Islamic law of contraries and proceed with caution. In the end, some delegates realized that even the Bible occasionally undergoes revision and that, because modern missionaries have gained a fuller acquaintance with African life than their predecessors could have, they should be free to revise former decisions in the light of new knowledge and better understanding. The report of the Conference shows that "modernists" for lack of better word, won the debate.

Two arguments seemed to have influenced the resolution on this question. The first argument suggested that contemporary missionaries should not be tied to old rigid positions vis-a-vis primal religions simply because of loyalty to their predecessors who had taken those positions in greater ignorance. The second argument suggested that, because of cultural and religious pluralism, there was no need to think that African values are necessarily wrong because they happen to differ from some Western customs.

Le Zoute's position on this question, then, sought to avoid making rules that would end up creating *artificial* sins. The principle it advocated was embodied in a resolution called "Suggestions on Evangelism" in which it stated that "everything good in the African's heritage should be conserved, enriched and ennobled by contact with the spirit of Christ."[7] This implied that everything "bad" should be condemned and abandoned. Although the resolution left a wide margin for future interpretation of what is "right" and, therefore, more in tune with the Christian ideal, Le Zoute was convinced that monogamy should be the basis of Christian family life in Africa as elsewhere. This meant that official policy or mandate did not condone polygamy as advocated by primal religion and tradition.

The resolution also mandated that a high standard of discipline should be maintained in the church; and that discipline should be understood in terms of promoting edification not destruction. Finally, it expressed the hope that, ultimately, African Christians will be responsible for building a corpus of Christian custom based on their understanding and genius. This was a discernible difference from London and High Leigh where it appeared that those Conferences forgot how limited they could legislate morality in a fluid and changing African situation.

Despite the fact that this pronouncement made no mention of the differing opinions among delegates on the value of Africa's past and primal religious values, it should not be accused of indifference or inconsistency. For, on this matter, Le Zoute, like Edinburgh or even its immediate predecessor, Hartford, could not have issued a straightforward, unambiguous resolution, in light of the complexity of the problem.

To be sure, Le Zoute's hope that African Christians would have the ultimate power to determine the body of Christian custom in Africa[8] must be understood along with another framework expressed, first at Edinburgh, that no complete break with the past is possible; and that to require of Africans to do overnight what Europeans have done after centuries of thought and struggle, was to create an unnecessary stumbling-block, jeopardy, and false expectation. This understanding showed the premium the movement continued to attach to getting to know Africa better and how experience continued to shape and reshape conciliar ecumenical mandates.

3. Indigenous churches at Le Zoute

Beside pressing economic and religious questions, Le Zoute did what no other Conference had attempted in regard to indigenous African leadership in church and national life: bringing together differing national, governmental, and missionary views of how to produce indigenous leaders through an affirmative educational program. Philosophically, its resolution on this matter was a remarkable achievement, in view of the composition of the delegates. This resolution, based on the Reports of the Education Commissions (and largely an affirmation of the position adopted over a two-year period at High Leigh, London, and Hartford), equated the provision of modern secular education with evangelism.

Looked at from the perspective of past Conferences, this resolution merely brought to a wider audience the idea that the word, evangelization, had a new meaning: secular education. Or, as I prefer to call it, gospel of education or the new mission. The resolution saw Christlikeness as the supreme moral and educational achievement, and the patterning of school curriculum after that ideal the aim of modern education for leadership and life in Africa. It deliberately and formally gave birth to an important policy the missionary organizers of the meeting had hoped the Conference would achieve: convincing all colonial governments in Africa to see that providing education to citizens was the proper function of government.[9]

The resolution also reaffirmed that education for leadership must include women, and assumed that the indigenous system of education was not without permanent values after all. It synthesized the old and the new, agricultural and industrial, training and skill, religion and science, Christian gospel and Western civilization. It reaffirmed the conviction present in all the preceding Conferences that Africa will best be evangelized by its sons and daughters; and that it was "of the utmost importance" for missionary societies to "search out and train" such indigenous leaders. Further, it set one end for everything done by missionary and nonmissionary forces in Africa: uniting Africa to the whole world.

This understanding that both missionary and nonmissionary forces (e.g. colonial governments) had similar interests in Africa was, though utilitarian, an extreme definition of evangelism. However, it clearly fitted well with the theme of the Conference—Christian *mission*, not Christian *missions* in Africa; and made no attempt to conceal the marriage of convenience which had taken place between colonial governments and mission societies. This was the first time this new definition of mission was openly put forth; and symbolized, in a questionable manner, the extent the IMC was willing to go in order to achieve unity in the African mission field.

In any case, the resolution concluded with one of Paul's mystical, educational hopes, and an admission of human inadequacy and readiness to keep learning, until everyone is matured and equipped with the stature of the fullness of Christ. This was a smart use of Pauline thought to justify a conscious political decision, a decision which did not escape criticism of the IMC for, supposedly, selling out and compromising the transformative aspect of Christian evangelism.[10]

Yet the resolution, despite its attempt to emphasize the significance of the indigenous churches, failed sharply to give those churches the recognition they merited, given what they were doing to expand Christianity. It is also significant that delegates embarked on this discussion on the role of indigenous churches as a long-term plan, expecting foreign missionaries and colonial officials to direct African affairs for the foreseeable future. Instead of seeking a quicker avenue to let go of the indigenous churches, and move ahead to propagate the Gospel in regions where the church did not exist, some missionary delegates acted, for the most part, as if they wanted to create in the sub-Sahara a situation in which church and state would be inseparably linked like in pre-Enlightenment Europe. The result was more not less imperialism (as far as political matters were concerned) and more not less paternalism (as far as ecclesiastical matters were concerned) in the years after this important conference.

It would take the effect of the second world war and increasing African and non-African protest, within and outside the churches, for a proper and better recognition to be given to the concept of the African Church and its selfhood. By that time, the missionary community would act as a people under siege, because of the war situation and the inevitability of devolution whether or not the indigenous leaders were adequately prepared.[11]

A crucial question which must be raised here before examining how Le Zoute viewed race relations is this: Why did the missionary community feel that this Conference was the right place to declare that whatever every foreigner did in Africa was part of the Christian mission? Although the business of reading human intentions is slippery at best, it is clear that one possible answer to this question is the simple fact that the missionary community was in desperate need for financial and moral support from colonial governments.

The complexity of the missionary task in Africa, especially after the Reports of the Education Commissions and the designation of education as the new mission in Africa, meant that missionary dependence on voluntary financial support was no longer enough; and that they must look for alternative means to support their enterprise in order to raise educational standards in their school systems and deliver better health care in their medical facilities. For clearly the new mission implied the erection of new and better buildings, writing and publication of suitable and locally inspired books, and hiring of teachers and inspectors. All these, in addition to intangible necessities, required immediate financial commitment, not bonds, credit cards, or endless talk (see appendix 1, p. 278).

Was there any other funding source to carry out such a new and bold understanding of missions? Obviously, there were other sources to which they could have turned such as individual Churches. However, the most enduring and best source was the colonial governments whose support was tantamount to local taxation, a revenue source which could only be tapped by governments. Thus, it is clear that, although alliance with colonial governments degenerated into more and more paternalism and imperialism in church and state, the missionary aim, as far as it lends itself to empirical deduction, was to win native support through their pocketbooks.

From this perspective, this Conference probably took what was the most logical, though not moral, step when it equated colonialism with missions. It is also understandable why missionary achievement in Africa or elsewhere should never be considered a one-sided affair, with the foreigner getting all the credit, while the native receives little or no credit at all. For, without the taxes and levies which the natives paid, willingly or unwillingly, the story of the African impact on ecumenical mandates, at this point in time, would have been entirely different.

4. Race relations at Le Zoute

Le Zoute also found that it could not escape the problem of color-bar. Speaker after speaker, all of whom held "progressive" racial views, admonished the IMC to take drastic action before the conflict got out of hand. On this issue, it was quite a sorry sight to see that many nations and mission societies were inclined to say one thing and do another. The following two familiar aspects of the issue were of interest to Le Zoute:

1. Allowing black Americans freedom to conduct missions in Africa as they wished.
2. Finding ways to resolve the South African problem.

Concerning the first aspect of the issue, a resolution in its favor was passed after several appeals were made by some Africans and nonAfricans.

It is interesting to compare this resolution with the one adopted at Oxford 1923. Le Zoute's did not differ substantially from Oxford's.[12] However, it is fair to say that it was more diplomatic in language and, consequently, not without prohibitive demands on black Americans. Thus, on the one hand, it lauded the whole desire on the part of black Americans to go and missionize Africa. On the other hand, it yielded to governmental pressure by requiring that they should enter Africa under the auspices of "responsible societies," meaning those societies whose loyalty to the Colonial Powers in Africa was largely unquestionable.

Still, while Oxford's sought to disguise its politics and was in part euphemistic, Le Zoute's was largely straightforward in its motive, though some may disagree with it. Article three, for example, openly said that colonial "governments should be supported" in their stringent rules banning some black Americans from Africa. Also, some delegates must have known that to suggest that missionary societies must seek to send only black American men and women with a fine spirit of cooperation and able "to meet the same tests as white missionaries" effectively blocked any large scale implementation of this resolution. For this suggestion was a code word which ensured that only the so-called nonradical black Americans were sent to Africa as missionaries. Moreover, the basis for distinguishing radical and nonradical black Americans and who among them should be declared *persona non grata* was, by no means, objective or free of politics.[13]

In any case, Le Zoute showed no readiness to remove all obstacles which made it extremely difficult for black Americans to go to Africa as missionaries. The resolution, therefore, lacked forthrightness on this matter and suggested that God was on the side of gradualism, not revolution; and that the ecumenical movement should settle for something less than ideal when the issue concerned its relationship to indigenous and black American churches.

The situation in South Africa brought much anguish; and many delegates recognized that here the Conference was in a quandary. However, this was the first time a sustained effort was made to hear all sides of the issue as fully as possible in an ecumenical forum. Le Zoute passed a separate resolution, expressing solidarity with the people in that land. This resolution expressed the conviction that the welfare and prosperity of both blacks and whites was inseparably bound up with the advancement of the whole region, not separate development. What the resolution failed to include, however, was the fact that some delegates saw the situation, clearly, as an unparalleled problem for Christianity.

Le Zoute recognized that the situation was compounded by rational and irrational forces. For white and black alike were being driven blindly by forces which they did not sufficiently understand, and were ill-equipped to intelligently control. Some said that improvement, not solution, would come about only through increasing mastery of these forces; and that the attempt to master them will need to be made on a grand scale, that is, in terms of the whole sub-continent and with the labor of thousands of patient workers.

It was recognized that the problem would not be solved overnight; the essential thing was to make a start. All yearned for the day when the Dutch, African and British will live in perfect harmony. At the same time, it was also recognized that mere preaching of common humanity and denunciation of one party or another was not enough. Action was the need of the hour; and such an action was to be designed to remove the conditions which made it absolutely and practically impossible for different peoples to live in harmony in that part of the world.

Amid all the complexity of the situation and diversity of viewpoints, all agreed that the fundamental interests of both races are one and prayed for easy adjustments. Ironically, the resolution was silent on the nontheological factors that had conditioned and gave birth to the situation, even though delegates knew and heard that these conditions were the determining variables or causes of the friction. As this was the first time a sustained effort was made to hear all sides of the issue as fully as possible in an ecumenical forum,[14] it is understandable, why Le Zoute sought the middle ground, even though it meant being silent on some of the real causes of the problem.

5. Cooperation and unity at Le Zoute

Le Zoute's discussion of the issue of mission and unity also pushed forward the idea of international missionary cooperation. Perhaps, as a compensation for its ambiguous direction on the Christian/primal religionist encounter, Le Zoute made bold attempts on questions of unity. In view of the presence of powerful nonChristian and secular influences in Africa, Le Zoute emphasized the importance of the laboratory type of cooperation instead of the lecture room type. This meant both the older and emerging African churches cooperating with their Western "parents," and missions and other para-church organizations joining hands with governments.

Le Zoute, not unlike High Leigh, did not give sufficient thought to the fact that mission/government alliance was potentially dangerous for missions. For, in view of its quest to make manifest what was latent, namely, that the world is interdependent and that social justice is indivisible, it was willing to strike any alliance. Indeed, plans were made to improve past uneasy relations with government. For, in the mind of Le Zoute's organizers and delegates, the tremendous new forces which had come into existence in Africa (though silent in their workings and often scarcely perceptible like the tides of the sea, but of incalculable power to shape for good or ill the destinies of the African people), necessitated such an ecumenical alliance with government.

Some members knew that any alliance is risky-business. However, most believed that, in the face of limited missionary resources and the magnitude of the problem, it was a worthwhile risk. Undoubtedly, it was more than worthwhile; it was inevitable.[15]

Accordingly, Le Zoute's litmus test for unity, like previous Conferences, was not doctrinal compatibility but readiness to learn, to try new methods of missionary adventure, to recognize that unitive talk is only as "sounding brass and tinkling cymbal," if its advocates do not seek to transform into reality their ideal of cooperation.[16] As crude as it may sound, some missionary advocates believed that the alliance between colonial administrators and missionaries was in a way a demonstration of this willingness to transform this ideal of cooperation into a practical, working relationship.

At the same time, on this unity question, and looked at chronologically, Le Zoute was the climax of what the planners of the meeting had hoped to achieve in terms of missionary/government alliance. Everything was in place—the representatives of all the Colonial Powers, the delivery of various diplomatic speeches by these politicians, the presence of some native representatives, the presence of high-powered missionary representatives from all over the globe, the reception of the Reports of the Education Commissions as the basis for missionary/government alliance, the making and acceptance of common statements and resolutions on the most vexing African issues of the period. After several confidential planning sessions (and open-ended Conferences as well as months of uncertainty of what its outcome will be), many participants felt that it was good (for both the short-term and the long-term), for the IMC to pull off this very useful "summit of unity" by the North Sea.

It is, probably, difficult for us to realize what a pall Le Zoute cast upon the social scene when it assembled. Not that the need for collective action was not perceived before then. Indeed, this is what has been driving this movement from one Conference to another thus far. Previous Conferences had accustomed some to the debate about the best road to a new Africa and a new world attitude towards it. But none of those earlier meetings dared to accustom civil and business leaders to moral and social needs in Africa at a magnitude comparable to Le Zoute's experiment.

Le Zoute, therefore, rightly or wrongly, assumed the African conviction that nothing is outside the pale of Christian mission. This was evident in its view of church and missions and indigenous leaders and customs, and so on. It was doubly evident in the contribution of some delegates.

6. Some individual contributions at Le Zoute

Of the several delegates who made substantial contribution, we must mention a few. John Hope, leading a strong delegation for the American Baptist Foreign Mission Society, pleaded passionately for freedom to black American missionaries in Africa. Hope dwelt on the positive developments in America, especially the association of a new generation of black and white Americans who were willing to sit down together and talk over things. His appeal for opportunity for all was almost identical to the one he made at Hartford about a year earlier.

Z. R. Mahabane, speaking of his organization's hope for a peaceful settlement of the race question in South Africa, warned the Conference of the danger of allowing a mass exodus of African intelligentsia, few though they were, from mission-controlled church to religio-political movements. Speaking in a manner that was identical to Aggrey's presentation at Atlantic City 1922, Mahabane stressed that for the African everything was tottering. In fact, like Aggrey, Mahabane spoke of the need for missionaries to know the psychology of the African.

On Mahabane's account, there was always vacancy for missionaries who were willing to be as politically active as they were personally caring, as socially alert as they were spiritually deep, as devout in prayer as they were vigorous in doing justice. Mahabane let it be known that a reaction had taken place in the African's mind because of the advance of imperialism. Mahabane thought that what Africans needed was not imperialism but missionaries who would be on the side of the black man in all his aspirations.

Conscious that the race problem in his country was a good example of foreigners wanting to usurp all the "African gold" for themselves, Mahabane said that the idea of separating evangelism and social well-being was a thing of the past. The Church, he added, is made of people who live in a particular social situation; therefore, the Church must respond to that situation, although the social situation in "heaven" is the Christian's final destination.

Official representatives from Britain, Belgium, and Portugal delivered addresses which were, in part, frank on the necessity for cooperative action among government, nationals, and missions. On the other hand, these addresses were also punctuated with diplomatic jargons naturally designed to inflate "the good works" of colonial presence in Africa, even though these officials knew that their home countries were reaping more from, than they sowed in, the African soil, at least materially.

Jesse Jones, the man who was, above all others, a realist, spoke on why he felt that the world was looking at Africa solely as a great continent of misunderstandings, perplexities and anxieties. Gradually, he added, the world would come to see Africa as the continent of opportunities, until it is revealed to all as "the continent of responsibilities." Although this theme of a great continent of misunderstandings recalled his presentation at Atlantic City 1922, Jones was taking advantage of the presence of nonmissionary figures to drive home his call for a new attitude towards Africa.

A good ecumenical diplomat, Jones naturally lavished praise on Lord Frederick Lugard and his good friend Sir Gordon Guggisberg, Colonial Governor of the Gold Coast with whom he frequently corresponded.[17] Jones thought that Lugard had won for himself a place in the annals of African history because his achievements in Nigeria will always be regarded as standards of colonial practice.

Yet the stuff which made Jones' speech thick was not this generous remark about Lugard and Guggisberg. It was, rather, his thoroughgoing attempt to ask the right questions and to bring growing American sociological vision to bear on Le Zoute's deliberations. Jones was for frankness as the facts warranted; and, although James Aggrey was not present at Le Zoute, in Jones' remarks he was. For Jones reminded the Conference to remember Aggrey's frequent picturesque reference to the fact that even the physical form or map of the continent presents to the world one great question mark among the continents of the earth.

Jones thought that Africa's questions were of vital and international significance and that they were begging for answer. These questions included whether European

influence improved or oppressed the African people; whether African self-consciousness was real or artificial as it showed itself in the 1920s; whether colonial
governments should continue; whether the independent nations of Liberia and
Ethiopia had succeeded; whether European and American economic agencies were
necessary for the well-being of the continent; and most of all, whether missionary
work in Africa was still necessary.

To Jones, these were no idle questions of mere curiosity. Each enquiry was to
bear directly on the new forces in Africa. Le Zoute, in Jones' mind, was to "transfer the research from the realm of the descriptive and the static to the realm of the
dynamic, the vital and the real."[18] Jones was confident that, with new attitudes on
the part of colonial government, economic agencies, native people, and missions,
Africa will continue to change for the best. Jones knew that a rapidly developing
world consciousness of the African continent will continue to evolve because of dense
populations in Asia, Europe and America looking abroad for raw materials to support themselves. African cocoa, African rubber and African cotton, he added, were,
to be sure, "the forerunners" of other African resources that will lure Asia, Europe
and America into the heart of Africa.

Jones urged that the power of international altruism should be allowed to
dominate international relations with Africa. However, his idea of international
altruism came too late, for in reality powerful nations, regardless of what they said
publicly, had already staked their selfish claims of different parts of the sub-continent.

Delivered by Max Yergan, the address which some members considered "the
most impressive of all" was titled "Cooperation Between The Races: Its Difficulties
and Possibilities." Youthful but with studied restraint, Yergan seemed to have
known that the gap in material advancement or attainment was part of the problem
of race prejudice. He prayed for trust and asked that the African should be enabled
to look to the future with aspiration and hope.

Idealizing perhaps a little bit more than he would have preferred, Yergan asserted that the black man possesses "bigness of heart," "generosity of soul," "a large
fund of patience" and therefore "capable of endurance." All these, with his helplessness, Yergan thought, "should make an appeal to the white man's love of fair-
play."[19] He correctly perceived that the test that Africans bring to Christianity as
they see it is the social teaching of Jesus, and that they were more concerned with
doing rather than saying and action rather than theory. Yet Yergan knew that theory
and action are inseparable and that all true theories result in action just as all true actions generate new dimensions of thought and theorizing. However, he was par-

ticularly emphatic that action or doing is what the Christian cross, for the most part, represents.

To this Archdeacon Owen, a British missionary with the CMS in Kenya, added that, from the point of view of the Africans he knew, the problem was the European. The African, he said, was searching for an expression of Christianity not only in the missionary but also in the Christian society to which the missionary belongs.

Le Zoute was cast like a drama; and, like most dramas where motivations for publicity and substance are intertwined, and the line between reality and fiction becomes blurred, each plot was carefully designed to lead to the finale: Oldham's address on "The Relation Of Christian Missions To The New Forces That Are Reshaping African Life." Known for his frankness and reasoning power, Oldham hoped his address would convince his audience and, therefore, the Church public that there is no plateau in Christian mission or in Christian life as a whole. Putting himself in the position of his audience, and imagining what was going through their minds, Oldham began by verbalizing that which was doubtless in their minds as they followed and partook in the sequence of the Conference: What next?

Oldham's answer was that "something radically new" was needed. He did not minimize the cost that was to be paid. Instead, like St. Paul, he claimed that the cost was putting off the old nature and putting on the new one. To reach forward to new heights and new things, he continued, will demand an effort. For entrance into new life normally entails the pains of birth. Still, Oldham thought that these pains were a necessary part of the training process; and that, for all missionaries and all Christians, the rejection of old habits and the acceptance of new ones should be a continuous process.

At the same time, Oldham warned everyone against entertaining the notion that putting on the new nature and the new vision of mission will be easy. However, because the new nature was a necessary catharsis for all missionaries, the cost was to be paid by abandoning the comfort of the known to the discomfort and challenge of the unknown. In his piercing words:

> If we are really desirous to become new [people], it will mean that we shall see things differently, and think about them differently, from what we see and think at present. And this change is something that most of us do not like. Our present views are, after all, our own ideas; because they are our own ideas we are fond of them; to give them up and think differently is irksome and unpleasant. Yet such changes in our thinking must take place if something new is to happen in Africa.[20]

Oldham, like Lugard, thought that this Conference had in measure helped to make the missionary path clearer and that this Conference represented the "call to a fresh advance, a further step forward, an enlargement" of contemporary conception of the mission of the Christian Church. Whereas, in previous centuries, mission was dominated by the thought of geographical extension, and missionary policy was to a large extent determined by the idea of expansion, Oldham asserted that the new call, in light of what was becoming manifest, was that the task of Christian missions demanded not only this but also something more. The old horizon, he said, had receded. Simultaneously, new lands had come into view. The world is seen to be larger than we thought.

Oldham variously described this call as "new adventures," "lengthening our cords," "strengthening our stakes," "reaching higher," and "striking our roots deeper into the unseen world."[21] With all this emphasis on the new, it is difficult to understand why he insisted at the same time that he was not propounding a new missiology, unless he was seeking to please at once both the conservative and modernist delegates at the Conference and missionary supporters at home.[22]

Summary

A final observation about Le Zoute is that, despite unavoidable ambiguities, it addressed itself fully to proposing new means through which missionaries must understand Africa. In all, it passed eight resolutions, including one on how the resolutions were to be transmitted.[23] This was an interesting development, indicating the importance the IMC and government officials attached to this Conference.

Another interesting thing which took place was a special resolution produced by the women members of the Conference. Like the women who attended the London Meeting on African women affairs, these women believed that more women were needed in the missionary board rooms as well as the field. Their resolution set a precedent and showed the considerable interest which they also have continuously shown in African missionary concerns and the development of the IMC.

The sad part is that the Conference as a whole did not give adequate attention to issues affecting African women in general. In fact, the women delegates to the Conference, sensing the direction of the Conference made a statement which the Conference merely endorsed without debate. This statement called for more women missionaries in the context that African women would benefit more from women missionaries than their male counterparts.[24]

Judged by its purpose, Le Zoute succeeded in providing a largeness of vision to missionaries and secular authorities and so created new opportunities for the growth of the IMC. We must remember that among those who composed this august forum were some of the most gifted statesmen, missionaries, and natives, immersed in divergent political and missiological theories, and inspired by the personal visions of freedom, racial harmony, democracy, justice, and equality—perfect ingredients for an arduous debate. Some of these delegates belonged to nationalities that recently were at war. The South Africans and the Americans knew at first hand the bitterness, ignominy, and other dark aspects of racial animosity.

Needless to say, it took more than sheer luck and common sentiment of cooperation to bring about harmony of spirit. Records show that good planning—a good index of maturity and decisiveness, and self-confidence—had much to do with its success as well. Indeed, the inner-workings of the numerous preparatory meetings which were held from February 1925 to July 1926, excluding High Leigh, London, and Hartford meetings,[25] deserve a special study in themselves, especially for their help in bringing about oneness of spirit and growth in the stature of the IMC.

Le Zoute also had its problems. One of these was the fact that the negative consequences of missionary/government alliance as voiced by some native Africans were not taken seriously. Another problem, as we have already noted, was the fact that the African Church was mentioned along with devolution of power but ignored at the same time. One wishes that there was no ambiguity by the Conference on this matter of devolution.[26] But there was no dubiety as to the next course of action— publicity and implementation of the resolutions.[27]

In terms of its respect for Africa (as an important factor in modern understanding of missions), its single-minded focus on African conditions, and its good understanding of the issues that mattered, no other world conference in the period under survey can claim to be its rival. John Dube thought that the Conference had "recreated" him and that he returned to Africa with newborn hopes and new courage; and that, because of what he saw at Le Zoute, Africans will come "through their struggles, purer people."[28]

Le Zoute was, to be sure, a capital gift to the IMC which it was never to lose thereafter; and, as far as African questions were concerned, Le Zoute became at once a ready and continuing reference source for later Conferences.

NOTES

[1]Edwin W. Smith, *The Christian Mission In Africa: A Study based on the Proceedings of the International Conference at Le Zoute, Belgium, September 14th to 21st, 1926* (London: IMC, 1926), p. 28.

[2]James Aggrey was expected to be present but he was unable to attend. He was also asked to write a preparatory paper about which the editorial of the Special Africa Number of the *IRM* said: "Of the papers originally planned only two have failed to arrive in time for publication, one by Dr J. E. Kwegyir Aggrey of Achimota, the other by a Belgian colonial official." The result was that this special issue of the journal dwelt almost exclusively on South Africa rather than the whole sub-Sahara. See *IRM* (July 1926): 325–6. Aggrey later died suddenly in 1927.

[3]The deliberation was preceded by an address by Chairman Donald Fraser, a former Scottish missionary in Nyasaland (Malawi). The address charted the path along which the Conference proceeded: reliance on the past but also a look towards the future.

[4]Smith, *Christian Mission*, p. 29. Interestingly, another part of the report of this Conference states that Christianity should be presented to the African as the fulfillment and not the antagonist of his aspirations. Surprisingly, this did not settle the issue for, at Jerusalem 1928, delegates debated it as if this was a new question; see Jerusalem in the next chapter; see also appendix 1.

[5]Ibid., p. 41.

[6]This paper was prepared by Professor Westermann and was published in *IRM* (July 1926): 418–437. It should be noted that this issue of the journal, with eighteen articles and poems, was dedicated to Africa.

[7]The Conference put African customs and religious values into three categories: (1) Customs which are evil and must be rejected outright; (2) customs which are not incompatible with the Christian life and should be baptized into Christianity; (3) customs whose accidents are "evil" but whose substance is valuable. These were to be purified and Christianized. Incidentally, John Mbiti's categorization of African customs vis-a-vis Christianity follows this pattern and, therefore, not unique; see Efiong S. Utuk, "An Analysis of John Mbiti's Missiology," *Africa Theological Journal* 15, 1, (1986): 10; see also "Suggestions on Evangelism" in appendix 1, p. 275.

[8]A. Fraser, "The Evangelistic Approach to the Africans," *IRM* (July 1926): 438–449.

[9]It is important to bear in mind that, until Le Zoute, governments' policies on education for leadership was lacking and confusing, and that there was much talk

about it than action. The British Government by far the dominant political power by then was reluctant to use African resources for African education. In 1924, the Governments of Kenya, Uganda and Tanganyika were spending respectively 4, 2 and 1 percent of public fund on education; R. Oliver, *Missionary Factor in East Africa* (London: 1952), p. 270.

[10]Roland Allen, *Le Zoute: A critical Review of the Christian Mission in Africa* (London: World Dominion, 1927), pp. 19–26.

[11]See Part V, especially chapter 13.

[12]See "American Negroes and Africa" in appendix 1; cf. race relations at Oxford 1923 in chapter 5.

[13]For an elaboration of this restriction on black American missionaries, see Williams, pp. 27ff.

[14]Indeed, several studies on.labor and race relations preceded this Conference and those who took part in the discussion did so out of firsthand knowledge. The first paper was written by an anonymous writer and signed "X," indicating how dangerous the situation was for some opponents of the system even in the 1920s. The second was written by Dr. J. du Plessis and the third by D. D. Tengo Jabavu, a white and a black South African respectively; *IRM* (July 1926): 344–89; cf. in the same journal number, Callaway, "Manners and Race Relationships," 390–401; and Ellie Allegret, "Black and White In Africa," 327–43.

[15]Of the final judgement on this alliance, the jury is still out. The present generation is still too close to the colonial era to be able to make a lasting and final judgement of the morality of the alliance. This is a point often ignored by some critics of mission/colonial government alliance. For example, T. O. Beidelman, *Colonial Evangelism* (Bloomington, Indiana University Press, 1982).

[16]Le Zoute did not think of cooperation as synonymous with equality of status. Equality was found to be too loaded and many-sided a word.

[17]See, for example, chapter 4, note 17.

[18]Smith, *Christian Mission*, pp. 127–136; "New Forces in Africa: Speech by Dr. Thomas Jesse Jones."

[19]Ibid., pp. 26, 34, 38, 99–100, 178; "Cooperation Between the Races: Its Difficulties and Possibilities: delivered by Max Yergan."

[20]Ibid., p. 162; "The Relation of Christian Missions to the New Forces that are Reshaping African Life: delivered by J. H. Oldham."

[21]Ibid., p. 163.

[22]Ibid., pp. 164–170. Here, we find Roland Allen's critique of this speech to be very relevant, though we disagree with his overall condemnation of the Conference. Allen asked: "What does this mean? He [Oldham] calls to new adventures, but dis-

claims any idea of turning Missionary Societies from their distinctive function." Roland Allen, p. 26.

[23]See "Transmission of Resolutions" in appendix 1, p. 290.

[24]See "The Training Of Women Missionaries" in appendix 1, p. 290.

[25]More than eight took place in New York City, and more than the same number took place in London. Occasionally, both Preparatory Committees met together; see Le Zoute Conference, Preparatory Material, IMC/CBMS Archives, Box 217, mf. 193–94.

[26]Cf. Roland Allen and Alexander McLeish, *Devolution And Its Significance* (London, World Dominion, 1927), p. 23.

[27]As expected, the IMC carried out several post-Le Zoute activities which included Press briefings, follow-up meetings, and so on. See, for example, "Circular letter September 24, 1926 to societies asking for advance orders of Le Zoute Conference report," and "Notes of Follow-Up Meeting, Edinburgh House, December 20, 1926," IMC/CBMS Archives, Box 217, mf. 204.

[28]For more on Dube's reaction to Le Zoute, see appendix 2. Of how the Press around the world reacted see the file "Press Cuttings on Conference from Australia, S. Africa, Belgium, Congo, China, Britain, Sweden," IMC/CBMS Archives, Box 217, mf. 198–199.

PART IV

AFRICA AND ECUMENICAL ADVANCE AMID STORM, 1928–1938

10

AFRICAN WORLD AT JERUSALEM 1928

Le Zoute's implications did not quite sink home when Jerusalem 1928 assembled. Meeting from March 24 to April 8, representation from the "younger churches" was 52 out of 231 delegates, far less than the fifty percent the Rattvik's Meeting of the Committee of the Council had suggested.[1] Of this number,[2] some were African nationals, Professor Davidson Jabavu of the South African Native College, Fort Hare, and County Chief Sirwano Kulubya of Uganda. Others who represented Africa were Josiah T. C. Blackmore of the Methodist Episcopal Church in Algeria, Charles E. Pugh of the BMS in Congo, Arthur W. Wilkie of the Scottish Mission in the Gold Coast, Lars Meling of the Norwegian Missionary Society, Henri Randzavola of the LMS in Madagascar, Adolphus W. Howells of the CMS in Nigeria, W. H. Murray of the Dutch Reformed Church Mission in Nyasaland and J. J. Willis of the CMS in Uganda.

Representatives from other parts of the world included the then well-known names of world Christianity. Among these was Bishop William Temple of the Church of England. Youth organizations were invited to share in the deliberations but with no voting power. Max Yergan attended this Conference on that ticket. Oldham, having been appointed a member of the British Government Commission to East Africa to investigate labor and other questions, was absent.

Though Jerusalem is usually called a conference, it was, actually, an enlarged meeting of the Council which, according to its constitution had to bar non-delegates from full participation. Jerusalem was not a free-for-all.

Theologically, the meeting met at a time when the uniqueness of Christianity was being challenged. Politically and economically, rumors of revolution were in the air and the early and latent effects of the Great Depression loomed up before the world. Thus, when the delegates to the Jerusalem meeting gathered, it was clear, from the outset, that the changed political and economic circumstance of the world would influence its final documents and position on several mission questions. Accordingly, Jerusalem's central theme concerned the Christian Life and Message in Relation to nonChristian Systems.[3]

1. Social conditions at Jerusalem

The first African question on Jerusalem's agenda concerned the continuing and over-powering nature of African social conditions and their call for development and reconstruction. This concern took a new dimension in this meeting because, for the first time, the rural field with its peculiar problems absorbed a major part of the Council's time. Its spiritual and material poverty was recognized, particularly its peculiar inability to catch up with secular trends. Conference delegates heard that, like city folks, rural Africans are human beings, and that they required the same comprehensive attack on their problems. Like the cities, these rural areas were calling for devoted Christian workers and service.

The Council's statement on this subject began with an attempt to justify why rural mission was necessary. Addressed to both mission boards and indigenous churches, it sought to show that many rural people were "without many conditions necessary for that abundant life which our God and Father desires for all His children."[4] This was, clearly, a soteriology which understood that to be saved included having enough to sustain both the spirit and soul. It noted the disparities which existed between urban and rural centers and the attendant inequality in distribution of amenities and vital resources. Missions were to work hard towards the development of an intelligent, literate, and efficient rural population capable of sharing the economic, political and social emancipation, and well organized to participate fully in world affairs.

Moreover, the statement admitted that this branch of mission service, in all its implications for "Kingdom-building," was not sufficiently taken seriously, either as to policies and programs or as to specially trained leadership and adequate financial support. In this sense, this meeting improved upon past attempts at forging a balanced missiology for contemporary evangelists. Its beliefs that attention should be given to the social construction of rural populations, and that (if the gospel is to become the very throb of the heart of a nation), their feelings, thoughts, customs, and languages, must be known and met alike by preachers, teachers and missionaries, sounded like the resolutions reached in ecumenical conferences of the 1970s and 1980s.

In view of extensive ignorance of this field of mission, the statement stressed that, as the volume of experience increases, the National Christian Council in each country and the IMC centrally should collect and disseminate the knowledge of the problem dealt with, the solutions attempted, and the failures and successes recorded.

It was another frank admission that, on this matter, Protestant missions, as an ecumenical body, were in part entering into an unknown territory. Delegates saw this work as "so vital to the world's welfare" and recommended that as soon as practicable the IMC should appoint a competent staff member to give full-time attention to the service of "rural missions in all parts of the world." It was agreed that the IMC should create African Rural Mission Program.

Clearly, here at Jerusalem more than Le Zoute, African rural missions had a pervasive impact on emergent ecumenism. Up to this time, ecumenism was more or less seen as a "favorite pastime" for the educated and the city dweller. African rural conditions helped to make the Council rethink the locus of the peasant in world Christianity. This necessarily strengthened the idea of witness in six continents first broached at Edinburgh. Further, it was the "unveiling of the veil"—the exposure of the falsity of the notion that unity would only come from "above," that is, from the educated, the city dweller, and the rich. This led to the rediscovery of the fact that the "below"—the poor, the peasants, and the village dwellers—also have a say in "Kingdom-building."

Jerusalem knew that all cities are, in part, dependent on rural farm labor, that the disenchanted and the enchanted are not too far apart, and that the "below" and the "above" are intrinsically interdependent just as New York 1900 spoke of the East and West Siders. For, in the economy of God, the visible and the invisible are equally important. This was a further questioning of one-dimensional, perpendicular ecumenism in which everything starts from above. Ecumenism, as both a vertical and horizontal movement and as a multi-class Christian experiment, continued to press toward the surface.

Another social question Jerusalem dealt with, which also expanded ecumenical vision, was the industrialization of Africa. Like rural problems, which for years were talked about but not taken seriously, this subject was brought to Jerusalem, in the view of an editor, as "one of the facts that illustrate the development of the missionary movement during the eighteen years that had elapsed since the Edinburgh Conference of 1910."[5] At the formation of the IMC, the study of this subject was seen as one of its functions. This was reiterated at a meeting of the Committee of the Council at Rattvik, 1926.[6] Jerusalem, then, was the first opportunity in which the question was extensively studied, despite Le Zoute's references to it.

Its preliminary paper, entitled "Christianity and the Growth of Industrialism in Asia and Africa," was a product of many minds, and was prepared on the basis of material from different groups in the Continent, Britain, the United States, India, China, Japan, South Africa, and other countries. Prominent among those consulted were H. A. Grimshaw, Chief of Native Labor Section, International Labor Office,

Geneva, and R. H. Tawney of the London School of Economics, author of *The Acquisitive Society and Religion* and *The Rise of Capitalism*.

One may wonder whether the complexity of the conditions in Africa did not nullify any attempt to generalize on the situation. The fact of the matter is that, while there were differences, underneath their variety and complexity lay certain broad facts which were common to the whole situation and which justified the Council viewing it as a single problem. Although most of what was said about Africa was known to Le Zoute's representatives, Jerusalem heard that further rethinking was needed to appreciate the state of industrial affairs in that continent.

Whereas the world was accustomed to think of Africa as predominantly the continent of raw materials, the rise of primary industries, during and since the first world war, necessitated a modification of earlier assumptions. For industrialism had taken firm foothold in Africa and was gradually extending in several directions. Yet this did not mean that Africa was wholly industrialized. Jerusalem's concern was to alert the outside world that it was no longer acceptable to see Africa solely as the center for the world's raw materials. It had become necessary to think in terms of keeping its raw materials within its borders and using them in its industries and for the benefit of its teaming rural and urban population.

A catalogue of the "evils" of industrialism in Africa were made, with particular reference to its complication of the missionary task. This included the familiar questions of direct/indirect forced labor and sanitary conditions in labor camps the extent of which most people found difficult to imagine, except those who had seen these conditions face to face. Other scourges which European demand for production brought to Africa included circumscription of native trade unions and freedom of movement. Some of the questions which were asked of the conditions in Southern Africa are very identical to questions one would find in contemporary Black South African journals such as the *Journal of Theology For Southern Africa*.

These questions included, for example, whether it is justified to say that the African's wants are unimportant. Another one wondered whether the African's needs, in terms of education, sanitation, and everything necessary for industrialized life, are not enormous; and why, for the sake of justice and equity, should the wealth which might help in satisfying these needs be sent elsewhere outside Africa's borders? It was also asked whether the transition from nonindustrial to industrial, with all its accompanying negation of traditional life, was absolutely necessary in Africa; and whether this was an inevitable condition for the continent's progress. This was an indirect reference to the Marxist claim that there are inexorable social paths through which all societies must pass as they evolve from a simple to an advanced social formation or a preindustrial to an industrialized society.

On this issue, comparison, on the one hand, between West and Southern Africa and, on the other hand, West and East Africa was inevitable, in view of the fact that economic policy in West Africa had led "to infinitely better conditions," though not a rose garden. This limited "economic success" in West Africa justified asking

> whether even in more purely industrial circumstances it may not be possible to avoid the creation of a "landless proletariat," dependent entirely upon wage-earning, which must needs go through the long travail of our European working-class populations, but with infinitely worse chances of securing well-being at the end of their effort.[7]

The discussion which followed evidences a balanced attempt to at once appreciate and reject Karl Marx and Adam Smith. Because of the fear of Marxist intrusion into the ecumenical movement, a yellow light was blinking everywhere in the hall in which the meeting took place. Fortunately, the site was a perfect place to reflect on this nagging problem, for, compared to Le Zoute with its promenade and sea shore, the sanatorium in which the meeting took place was built on Mount of Olives, the site which Jesus, probably, frequented for contemplation and solitude. Although, the building was dilapidated, and hardly the same in terms of amenities to which many delegates (including William Temple, later Archbishop) were accustomed, the atmosphere of Eastertide helped to focus thought on apostolic examples.

A paper on "The Christian Approach To Industrial Problems" introduced the discussion. The meeting found that all humans are entangled together in the social and economic system, and that ecumenical action is needed to help industrialize Africa. Attempts were made to steer the discussion toward a balanced understanding of evangelism and industrial action. For this reason, it was rationalized, like Oldham did at Le Zoute, that this concern for industrialization of Africa was not a new gospel, but an extension of the power of Jesus to "a larger area of life" necessary as an adjunct of evangelism.

Moreover, it was argued that the ecumenical movement must realize the pervasive impact of existence on what many perceive to be the essential. For in all human disciplines it is impossible for a genius to suddenly appear without centuries of cultural struggle and a background of a fairly well-developed intellectual society. Similarly, it was observed that the missionary movement, through this mandate on industrial missions, was trying as God's co-worker to bring into fruition a state of society in which more individuals can "attain to saintliness" and remain the "light and salt" of the earth.

The discussion established that in dealing with industrial questions in Africa, like elsewhere, the church was confronted with the problem of getting human values out of the realm of abstraction and situating these values in the concrete. Yet it was also admitted that all that the church could do was to influence public opinion to help make changes, not to tell politicians and industrial leaders in detail how to conduct industry. However, defining human values, and creating a public atmosphere insistent on the industry heeding these values, was seen to be within the province of the church as a missionary organization.

The Council's statement on this matter, "Christ The Lord Of All Life," was very realistic. To calm the fears of doubters, this statement was prefaced with a strong assertion that the gospel message is not only for individuals but also for the world of "social organization and economic relations in which individuals live."[8] Because this Conference met during the rise of atheistic Communism, this statement said that it was very crucial for Christianity in Africa, as elsewhere, to attack something strong in the camp of the enemy, e.g. materialism.

This statement also dealt with the problem of investment of capital in nonindustrialized nations, the problem of developing African resources in a way that would be beneficial to all, the obligation of the governments of the economically more advanced nations, the vital importance of curbing friction between nations engaged in economic expansion, through the cooperation of the IMC, the International Labor Organization, and the League of Nations. Finally, it called for the establishment of the Department of Social and Economic Research and Information, an agency whose "biggest success" was the study of industrialism in Africa.[9]

This statement was the product of its times, though obviously the idea that the ecumenical movement must act as an international broker, reconciling the oppressed and the oppressors has lived on to this day. It presupposed the idea of interdependence and partnership between the have and the have-not, the industrialized and the nonindustrialized. It saw African industrialization as a continuing ecumenical predicament and reaffirmed ecumenical commitment to reconstruct society and work for social justice and peace.

On avoidance of friction between nations engaged in economic expansion, the statement acknowledged what experience had already shown, namely, that the most prolific and underlying cause of international friction was the rivalry of competing imperialisms. For the sake of the future of world civilization, the statement pleaded with all the nations engaged in this rivalry to bring it "under control" because it was ruinous alike to the metropolitan nations and to the peripheral nations and their populations. This idea that international economic rivalry should be controlled was Jerusalem's way of condemning the exploitation of the weak by the strong. It was another indication of the impact of anti-Christian forces (especially Marxism) on ecumenical thought and statements.

2. Primal religions at Jerusalem

Jerusalem delegates also learned that primal religion was still alive in Africa, that Christian converts still owed most of their values to it, and that nonChristian religions cannot be evaluated without reference to it. For example, it was made clear that women were still seen from the point of view of this primal religion (as largely inferior to men) and that no amount of Christian teaching seems to change all the old beliefs about gender roles and differences.

Discussion showed that, theoretically, the older churches were still afraid of syncretism, while, practically, many African converts were making do with what they had, without worries about the contamination of Christianity, just as many Western people had to do in the early years of their encounter with Christianity, even after the Reformation period. In order to produce a statement which represented various opinions on the subject, the Council resorted to a general statement which appreciated and condemned at the same time all human religions.[10] Although it was a statement Edinburgh could not have made, it was, clearly, in line with the missionary attitude of the 1920s, especially in its positive attitude towards all religions given their transcendental values, as opposed to rising atheistic philosophies with their so-called this-worldly values.

In other words, because Jerusalem's greatest threat (vis-a-vis the relation of Christianity to nonChristian systems) was "secularism," even African preliterate religion was seen as worthy of preservation and encouragement rather than atheistic philosophies and quasi-religions. Jerusalem clearly distanced Jesus Christ from all cultures and civilizations and all cultural expressions of Christianity. It condemned religious imperialism and affirmed that "Christianity is not a Western religion, nor is it yet effectively accepted by the Western world as a whole." "Christ," it said, "belongs to the peoples of Africa and Asia as much as to the European or American."[11] Experience continued to turn around pre-twentieth-century missiology.

3. Indigenous churches at Jerusalem

On the development of native leadership through education and responsible church positions, Jerusalem took special notice of Le Zoute's resolution on this matter. It called for the creation of the International Committee on Christian Literature for Africa (ICCLA) as one way of giving practical result to the educational hope expressed at Le Zoute.[12] This Committee was also mandated to serve as an ecumenical knot, fastening different denominations and parochial schools closely together with the aim of publishing objective textbooks for the mission schools. Yet there were still unresolved questions regarding the definition of devolution as it related to the indigenous church, and how devolution can be carried out without rupture in church life.

For Africa, this concern for a better definition of devolution was overshadowed by an immediate aspect of the question. This was the continuing lack of adequate and rapid training of indigenous leaders. It continued to be evident that the need was not just for men alone but also women. While no priority was set, delegates, including those from Uganda and Nigeria, agreed that the extension of work among the women and girls remained undone. It was said in a slightly different way from Aggrey's that a nation cannot rise above its womanhood.

A statement which was issued did not claim to have found a permanent solution to this issue, with all its theological and nontheological dimensions. Rather, it acknowledged that ecclesiastical power should be gradually shared with present and future native leaders. This meant that foreign missionaries did not consider this Assembly the appropriate place for complete hand over of authority even to Asian churches or nationals.

Bishop Howells of Nigeria, for example, downplayed the idea of devolution in Africa, given what he termed the immaturity of his flock. Arguing as if the idea of devolution was tied to one's view of the Bible, Howells claimed that Africans wanted foreign missionaries who were willing to preach, not devolution, but "the simple Gospel." He suggested that, because some Africans were not yet ripe for modernist views of the Bible, they should not be bothered with the idea of devolution. It was his view that the Africans he knew were satisfied with the Bible as it is without criticism. These Africans, he added, wanted missionaries who believed the whole Bible, not portions of it, as inerrant. To be sure, this was a conservative vote for the status quo on devolution matters.

Whether Howells' view on both the devolution question and "bible-believing" missionaries reflected a unanimous opinion by the African delegation to this meeting is hard to assess. What we can assess is the fact that some missionary bishops such as Howells continued to see African churches as immature and ineligible for immediate selfhood, a fact which had its merits and demerits, Howells' comments notwithstanding.[13]

The important point, however, is that, like Le Zoute, many missionary societies did not indicate here at Jerusalem that they were making adequate plans to wean their "African babies" or that they expected these churches to come of age very soon. On the contrary, the discussion on this issue continued to show that missionaries were in Africa for the long haul; that the ecumenical movement still was very uncertain of how best to proceed on this question; and that the refocusing of missionary aim in Africa from pioneer work to consolidation and educational work meant, to some missionaries, caution and measured action.

4. Race relations at Jerusalem

Attempts to resolve the race question also received attention at Jerusalem and brought fruitful progress to the thought of the IMC. Expert minds were asked to examine some of the real issues underlying this conflict. Like Le Zoute, Jerusalem took pain to study and prepare for the subject. This preparation did not attempt to survey the whole problem in all parts of the world. Instead, attention was focused on the problems arising from race contacts in the Southern States of America, and in South Africa, and those arising from the contacts of Oriental and Occidental peoples on the Pacific Coast of North America.

The transcript of the Council's discussion shows that Jerusalem participants, like High Leigh delegates, saw this world menace of interracial antagonism as constituting "the supreme concrete challenge to the Christian belief that all [humans] are the children of God."[14] Conducted in an atmosphere where stark facts were faced with honesty, frankness, and an attitude of Christian understanding, Jerusalem considered this subject as a human tragedy whose roots run back deeply into the past with a bundle of interlacing questions. It blamed past generations but agreed that they were ambitious and knew not what they were doing. It thanked God for the fact that the whole situation did not get out of hand because of some who were single- and clear-minded on this race question.

Yet such recognition did not mean declaring the past the sole culprit or an inhibiting sense of helplessness. Contemporary currents also had a surge of their own, thrusting themselves upon the African and the nonAfrican whether or not they liked these currents. That the conflict was ruthless was not denied. That Jerusalem had found a secret pill to cure this cancer was denied.

The summary of the discussion on this subject states that the African delegates, "whose speeches made a profound impression because of their moderation, humility, and wisdom," appealed to the Conference to issue "a definite statement of the principles that must inform any Christian attitude in race relations."[15]

The Council's statement on this issue of race relations reflected these African concerns. Like Le Zoute, all agreed that goodwill is not enough and that there comes a time when discussion proves barren unless it translates into concrete action. After the usual theological preamble, as we have seen in other Conferences and other statements or resolutions, Jerusalem hazarded what it called "A Constructive Program."

Assuming that scientific knowledge and successful experiment and perpetual adjustment to the new demands of changing situations would lead to coexistence between peoples, the Program had six parts.[16] The first part spelt out how two or more races were to live side by side in the same country. The second part dealt with subject peoples. The third part concerned migration and colonization. The fourth part dealt with other interracial problems. The fifth part emphasized further and continuing research. The sixth part made reference to Le Zoute's resolution on black Americans going to Africa for missions, and outlined what it considered "immediate action necessary." This meant that action should be directed to the ends of exchange of students and teachers of different countries and the development of the consciousness in every nation that the common courtesies of life are an elementary duty humans owe one another.

A glance at this statement on race relations would show that, as the years brought more and more experience, ecumenical gatherings were also becoming adept in resolution construction. While, like Le Zoute's, it bristled with this issue in a waiting mode, one of its great triumphs is how well it was written. Though it was the work of a committee, it does not sound as it was written by a committee. It has a flow of style, a consistency in its parts and masterful use of language in both clarity and holy ambiguity.

It may be worth noting also that the virtues of the statement, in fact, may be too disarming. One may not feel like tampering with it, for it shows that theoretical conclusions arrived at half a century ago are in many respects the same thing contemporary Black and Liberation Theologies are parading today as essentially "new." For instance, there is a condemnation of virtual hegemony of one race over another due to the establishment of financial and economic control. Where two or more races live side by side in the same country, authorities were asked to "secure that the land and other resources are not allocated between races in a manner inconsistent with justice and with the rights of the indigenous peoples."[17]

5. Cooperation and unity at Jerusalem

In regard to international missionary cooperation in Africa, Jerusalem harbored no regrets for advocating more unitive ventures among missionary societies. Its statement on this issue focused on what it described as common convictions about evangelism and its relations to local Christian communities, church renewal, church unity, and people of other religions. The statement defined the term "missionary" in a manner that officially included, for the first time, "the work of presenting the

Gospel to nonChristian peoples, whether carried on by the younger or by the older churches."[18]

A revised constitution of the Council was made, taking into account the rise of many national missionary organizations than when the Council was first formed at Lake Mohonk. Added knowledge, brought by the years, suggested that continuing development of this Council could only be ensured in part by giving more power and representation to national councils as soon as they were formed. Thus, for Africa, beside the missionary societies of South Africa, two national councils were admitted to the IMC. These included the *Societe Belge de Missions Protestants au Congo*. Each national council had one seat in the Committee of the Council and was an indication of Africa's steady ecclesiastical advance.

Here, it should be noted that these African councils represented a new phenomenon in that they were quite different from, say the FMCNA and the CBMS, which were still exclusively composed of missionary societies' representatives. Organizationally, these African Councils, like the ones in Asia, were international in character and combined, within their organization, members of mission boards from different Western countries, in addition to nationals of the country in which the national Christian council was working.

While the final statement on unity was futuristic, by looking forward to a time in which the movement will be friction-free, it also emphasized why members of each national and racial viewpoint should, with open-mindedness and generosity, welcome the maximum contribution of the other national or racial groups. Additionally, it was recognized that in the future, perhaps, more than in the past, establishing and preserving right relations between missions and African governments will, in itself, constitute a field where international cooperation will be indispensable to ensure better results.

This statement also forewarned that, while in Africa negotiations with government will, as a rule, have to be initiated and conducted by national missionary bodies, it will be most advantageous for the Christian leaders of different nations to see eye to eye in matters of policy. The world, the statement made clear, is now organized internationally; peoples and nations are tied together by one consuming quest for survival. Thus this outward unification of the world made "supremely important" the spiritual unity of the Churches.

Reechoing Le Zoute, the statement went on to say that the world situation is making increasing demands upon the Church and that there is an insistent call for "better-thought-out and better-directed policies among Christian missions."[19] On this question of unity, Jerusalem correctly predicted trends in post-Independent

Africa and even the world, especially concerning the discovery of the true international character of Christian missions based on partnership not coercion.

Yet, like many future predictions or prophecies, Jerusalem did not gamble with
fixing the precise time when these future trends will take effect. However, it knew
that new technologies and new modes of thinking were reducing the globe to a
metropolitan neighborhood and, as its statements implied, regional alliances were
giving way to alliances "organized internationally."

6. Some individual contributions at Jerusalem

At Jerusalem, the contribution of a few leaders on African questions was equally
outstanding and impressive. John Hope, whom we met at Hartford and Le Zoute,
delivered a paper on "The Negro in The United States" in which he traced the cultural and religious status of black people in America and the role of the Commission
on Interracial Cooperation in America. Hope wanted the missionary movement to
be tremendously concerned, as he was, about not only the present but also the future, particularly the effect this conflict will, inevitably, have upon all people alike,
upon the victims and upon those who do the victimizing.

Hope was not interested in blaming people for what happened in the past in
relationship to slavery. White people of today, he said, had nothing more to do with
bringing African slaves to the New World as he or any other black American had.
As a matter of fact, Hope was not interested at all in apportioning blame and dwell-
ing on past mistakes. However, he was extremely interested in what people and nations were now doing to correct past mistakes. Failure to take concrete action in the
present, he reasoned, will only prolong the problem and create new opportunities
for continuing enslavement of people.

Jerusalem continued the tradition of seeing black people as one, irrespective of
where economic forces had sent them. Thus Max Yergan's "The Race Problem in
Africa" reemphasized the social and economic changes which had brought about the
conflict, especially the rush for gold, diamonds, oil, rubber and cotton. Also, it outlined the constructive forces which were at work—a vast body of missionary workers,
qualities of improvability that the Africans themselves were demonstrating, and the
presence of some whites with progressive racial views.

Professor Jabavu also contended that one of the great difficulties repelling South
African blacks from Christianity was "the feeling that even under Christian missions,
there is no equality in Church or State."[20] Islam, Jabavu added, was gaining more
African adherents because of this racism in South African ecclesiastical and civil
life. Jabavu thought that some whites did not care about what religion native Africans
professed so long as they did not seek equality with whites. Ironically, some white

South Africans who called themselves Christians were in part responsible for driving native Africans into the waiting and open arms of Moslem preachers.

Harold Grimshaw, the labor expert, was even more down-to-earth about this race question, noting that there was much to be done to change interracial attitudes; and that input by a few black Americans and native Africans (such as Yergan and Jabavu) was necessary but insufficient. For, in Grimshaw's opinion, there was still lingering bitterness in the hearts of millions of people which was not yet removed.

It was Grimshaw's belief that the IMC should thoroughly concern itself with trying to remove every bitterness, primarily because that bitterness was potent in making foci of insurrection, rebellion, and war. Like James Aggrey who preached the same gospel of co-existence, Grimshaw strongly believed that only Christianity can temper race conflict with its doctrine of common creation, common destiny, and common destination.

Summary

For Africa, Jerusalem, like Le Zoute, ended on a positive and appreciative note. Although debates were sharp, even to the point of creating a permanent gulf between advocates of social action and soul-winning only, most delegates were exposed to why Africa insists on holistic missions. While there were ideological tension between those who advocated more liberal Christianity (e. g. W. E. Hocking of Harvard University) and those who were more conservative (e.g. Hendrik Kraemer, the Dutch missiologist), Jerusalem knew that Africa was not particularly interested in the ideological debate; for at this time Africa was more interested in practical solutions to its problems regardless of what ideology or school of thought inspired or informed such solutions.

The next pivotal opportunity for ecumenical initiation and friendship-building was Madras 1938. There, although "the centre of gravity had moved eastwards,"[21] African questions were no less significant.

NOTES

[1]*Minutes Of The Enlarged Meeting of the International Missionary Council And Of The Committee Of The Council, Jerusalem, March 24–April 8, 1928* (London: IMC, 1928), p. 6f; hereafter cited as *Jerusalem 1928 Minutes.*

[2]When scholars speak of the "huge" percentage of representative from the "younger churches" at Jerusalem, they often fail to distinguish very clearly Asia from Africa or Latin America. The fact is that Jerusalem saw more Asian representatives. Thus Hogg's statement "the presence of a large representative group of spokesmen from the younger churches provided the most readily apparent difference between Jerusalem and Edinburgh, held only eighteen years before" gives the impression that all the "younger churches" were equally represented. See Hogg, p. 245. And Bassham, following Hogg, also fails to note that the idea of a fifty-fifty basis was as yet an impracticable and unrealistic notion. However, this did not diminish the urgency and impact of African questions, but in fact made them more explosive. See Bassham, p. 21.

[3]*Jerusalem Meeting of the International Missionary Council, March 24–April 8, 1928*, 8 vols. (New York: IMC, 1928), vol. I, *The Christian Life and Message in Relation to NonChristian Systems of Thought and Life*; hereafter cited as *Jerusalem 1928.*

[4]*Jerusalem 1928*, vol. VI, *The Christian Mission in Relation to Rural Problems*, p. 232.

[5]*Jerusalem 1928*, vol. V, *The Christian Mission in Relation to Industrial Problems*, p. v; hereafter cited as *Missions and Industrialism.*

[6]*Minutes of Rattvik Meeting*, p. 24; cf. *Lake Mohonk 1921*, pp. 55–6.

[7]*Jerusalem 1928*, vol. V, *Missions and Industrialism*, p. 65. Here was another indication that the meaning of evangelism was impossible to divorce from changes in external circumstances. Again, notice that this question was asked as far back as 1928.

[8]Ibid., p. 141.

[9]For a lengthy discussion of the work of this Department, see Hudson, pp. 112–113.

[10]*Jerusalem 1928*, vol. I, *The Christian Life and Message in Relation to Non-Christian Systems of Thought and Life*, p. 402.

[11]Ibid., p. 411.

[12]*Jerusalem 1928*, vol. II, *Religious Education*, pp. 161–8.

[13]As a matter of fact there were several problems plaguing mission-related churches as well as national movements for independence in the late Twenties. One of these problems was the fact that the leaders who came to shoulder the responsibility of independence in church and state were just entering institutions of higher learning. One thinks of Kwame Nkrumah of Ghana (born in 1909), Azikiwe of Nigeria (born in 1904), and Akanu Ibiam (born in 1906). A leader such as Kenneth Kaunda of Zambia was only four years old when Jerusalem met.

[14]*Jerusalem 1928*, vol. IV, *The Christian Mission in the Light of Race Conflict*, p. 182.

[15]Ibid. Notice the progressive willingness to critique past missionary mistakes both overtly and covertly.

[16]On this statement, Bassham wrote "This was the first considered statement on race relations from an international ecumenical conference" (p. 22). Actually, as we have seen, this was not the first time. Oxford and Le Zoute, for example, did make statements on race relations. Understandably, Bassham did not study those meetings and/or did not classify those meetings as ecumenical.

[17]*Jerusalem 1928*, vol. IV, *The Christian Mission in the Light of Race Conflict*, p. 197.

[18]*Jerusalem 1928*, vol. VII, *International Missionary Cooperation*, p. 59; see also *Jerusalem 1928 Minutes*, p. 37.

[19]*Jerusalem 1928*, vol. VII, *International Missionary Cooperation*, p. 53.

[20]*Jerusalem 1928*, vol. IV, *The Christian Mission in the Light of Race Conflict*, p. 184.

[21]Margaret Nash, *Ecumenical Movement In The 1960s* (Johannesburg: Ravan, 1975), p. 231.

11

AFRICAN CHURCH AND THE WORLD: MADRAS 1938

By the time delegates arrived at Madras from various parts of the world, the intervening years between that meeting and Jerusalem had seen numerous activities in Africa which gave the Council and the movement further effectiveness, despite continuing theological crisis, particularly in Europe and America.

These activities included the declaration of Africa as a special province for the IMC,[1] the carrying out of Jerusalem's directive on the foundation of International Committee on Christian Literature for Africa,[2] the African Rural Mission Program,[3] and the Department of Social and Industrial Research.[4]

Madras was the first IMC meeting that drew several native African leaders. This reflected the fact that, during the decade 1928–1938, such leaders were beginning to emerge. Native Africans who were present included Christian G. Baeta of the Gold Coast, B. A. Ohanga of Kenya, A. B. Akinyele and M. O. Dada of Nigeria, T. S. C. Johnson of Sierra Leone, Y. K. Bina and K. L. Kisosonke of Uganda, Chief A. J. Lutuli and Miss Mina Soga of South Africa. In all, 471 persons from 69 countries or territories were present; it was, by far, the largest ecumenical gathering up to that time.

Meeting from the 12th until the 29th of December, 1938, its central theme was "The World Mission of the Church." This theme was chosen to coincide with the same stream of thought that was going on in the Faith and Order and Life and Work Movements, each of these bodies had held in 1937 a great world meeting.[5]

1. Social conditions at Madras

The concern for African social development and reconstruction changed significantly between Jerusalem and Madras. Madras began to focus more attention, not on what missionaries were doing for Africans, but on what African churches were doing with Christianity and their social situation. This was a marked improvement from

Jerusalem and happened in part because the Department of Social and Economic Research had gathered material in Central Africa for use here in this meeting.

The data which this Department gathered related to the main economic and social trends (which affected the growth of African Christianity), the relation of these trends to its development and the principles and methods by which churches in different African fields dealt with these situations. A number of African Churches were presented as examples of self-government, self-support, and self-propagation, an evangelical doctrine first promoted in the nineteenth-century but hardly taken seriously until the brink of the second world war.[6] Things were still rough but, gradually and steadily, some native churches were coming into the limelight.

One example which was cited was the Church in Angola connected with the mission of the American Board of Foreign Missionaries and the United Church of Canada. Its organization was based on the village government in vogue by the natives. Economically, this Church was struggling to grow, but it had put in place a financial system which allowed for pooling of resources among the various districts.[7] The Lutheran Church around the Kilimanjaro was the second example of what African churches were doing to support themselves and spread ecumenical vision. Economically stronger congregations affiliated with this Lutheran Church were helping the smaller and weaker congregations. Some of these congregations built their chapels, schools and churches "without mission aid."[8] In addition, it was learned that the older congregations were sustaining and sending teacher-evangelists to neighboring regions. Churches, such as these, in rural areas were seen as forming the reservoir from which the health and strength of the urban centers and nation were drawn.

Another Church was the Methodist Church of the Gold Coast. Thanks to the high demand for cocoa this Ghanaian Church was providing for 87 per cent of the budget, while only 13 per cent or about five thousand British pounds came from the Missionary Committee. This high percentage of local financial support was contrasted with what was happening in the Hyderabad Methodist Community in India where the natives and the Foreign Missionary Committee gave 7 per cent and 93 per cent respectively of the budget. These figures were not put forward as measures of faith and devotion, but as "indices of a vast difference in economic condition."[9]

From this African report and others from Asia, Madras formulated a statement which recognized the importance of self-development, the relation of Church support to Community Service, the changing economic and social order both on national and international bases. Specifically, the statement saw that the vast economic disparity between sending and receiving churches tended in the past to encourage giving subsidies to receiving churches. Unfortunately, paternalism, among other evils, was the result of this system of support. "The evils of this system,"[10] the statement added, had become evident to both younger and older churches. A conscious readjustment effort, it concluded, was being effected. That this readjustment was, however, not widespread or significant enough to generate radical changes prior to the 1960s is now widely recognized.

Some of the most significant "advanced" technology in tackling rural mission problem in South Africa were used to offer fresh insights into principles and methods of rural work around the world. Through the instrumentality of J. Merle Davis and research in African fields a renewed emphasis was made in missionary thinking, namely, the importance of the economic and social environment into which evangelistic, educational, and medical enterprises were set.

2. Primal religions at Madras

The influence of African cultural and religious values was also discernible at Madras. Although the focus was more on Oriental religions and philosophies and the threat of national religions and ideologies, the final statement recognized that African primal religion was not antagonistic to the gospel. This position must be seen as a rejection of Hendrik Kraemer's view (and, by inference, Barthianism) that there is a gulf or discontinuity between Christianity and other religions.

Of particular interest to Africa was the statement that "the Church is called to the appropriation of all that traditional cultures may contribute to the enrichment of its life and that of the Church Universal."[11] This meant traditional African spiritual heritage and permanent social values of filial piety and devotion to communal service must be taken into use. This was also a reaffirmation of the position adopted at Jerusalem.

Specifically, primal religion was to be understood as a total system of life and the assumption that Christianity and a foreign civilization may necessarily attract "nonliterate people" was found to be partly unfounded. For, as a result of incipient cultural nationalism throughout the sub-continent and back-to-tradition movements, some primal religionists, led by the educated class, were feeling the need to save those forms of life which have been their cultural home.

To address this new circumstance, Madras reemphasized what previous Conferences, after Edinburgh, had, directly or indirectly, underscored, namely, that the Church must be thoroughly familiar with the social context in which it situates in order that it may be able to "rightly distinguish good and evil elements and cleanse the communal life of its converts without becoming a party to its destruction."[12] Madras did not go into detail of how missionaries should achieve this aim of having a better sociological knowledge of the society in which they served. Since it was building on past mandates on this matter, Madras saw no reason to be more specific. It was clear, however, that the more missionaries became thoroughly enmeshed in the community in which they worked, the more it became difficult to condemn some local customs and beliefs, simply on the basis of their appearance.

3. Indigenous churches at Madras

In considering the question of African leadership Madras found, unlike Jerusalem, that there was a greater need for devolution of power to native leaders. The size of the African presence itself was quite unique and was a cause at once for applause and more work. More lay leadership needed to be developed particularly in rural Africa where the circuit system of spiritual supervision was used. Emerged was an attempt to pay respect to many unsung African disciples. Here the role played by lay workers (of whom Apolo Kivebulaya of Uganda was cited as "notable example") took precedence.[13]

A central problem concerning recruitment and retention of native workers was the fact that the ministry was found to be too narrow for educated young men. With the rise of national consciousness, a feature which was not a serious African problem at Jerusalem, there was a great demand for educated church leaders. Women leaders were also being trained but not as rapidly as the Special Group on Women's Work found. However, it is interesting to note that Miss Mona Soga was the first African woman representing Africa in a world conference.

Madras found that the education of the African "people must not be higher than that of the minister."[14] At the same time, there was no preparation made to avoid the lurking problem of elitism within the ranks of native church leaders. For, although some would disagree, the education of native pastors was already higher than the people; and, increasingly, status differentiation was unavoidable among the native clergy themselves. The task was how to overcome this potential problem which is becoming even more problematic today than it was half-a century ago, not only among the clergy of the same denomination but also across denominational lines, including the *Aladura* or Independent Churches.

Madras received a good report of the indigenous schemes for leadership by the Methodist Church of the Gold Coast. Of its thirty-two circuits, twenty nine were already in the charge of African superintendents. Similar accounts of growing African Churches were made of the Church in the Kasai district of the Congo, the Presbyterian Church of Central Africa, the Anglican Church in Uganda, and of the Lutheran Church of Madagascar. All these reports were transition stories, remarkably different from just a generation earlier, and indicative of what many anonymous Africans were doing to strengthen and plant the ecumenical church.

Moreover, these Churches showed in a practical way what indigenous leaders could achieve independent of, and with, foreign support and prayers.

In view of this African contribution and emerging leadership, the final statement, framed by a special group appointed to reflect on this subject, declared that both younger and older Churches continue to need each other. "Our task," said the statement, "is a united one. Our need is mutual."[15]

4. Race relations at Madras

Madras also went on record in its vehement opposition to racial discrimination. Although, clearly, the Jews were uppermost in the minds of the delegates in view of Hitler's "Final Solution," Africa was not forgotten. Besides, Madras was generally aware of the racial implications of Mussolini's war of aggression against Ethiopia in 1935.

Madras, therefore, made a strong declaration against racial discrimination and persecution. Calling it abhorrent, Madras called on the Church to exert its influence on the side of all movements working for "the full and equal sharing by all races in the common life of" humankind. In doing this, Madras wanted the Church "to purge its own life of any racial discrimination."[16] It recognized that race hatred stems from easy acquiescence in popular prejudices which lend unconscious support to such discrimination.

5. Cooperation and unity at Madras

The relation of Africa to the necessity for cooperation and unity in church and civil life also received attention. This was particularly an acute problem, in view of the fact that political tensions had brought unmatched world uncertainties and anxieties. To keep with past ecumenical tradition, a survey of various areas of political tension and colonial policies was made.

In Northern Nigeria, the policy of Indirect Rule was still in place, though Moslem leaders, for educational reasons, were beginning to invite missions to open work in their territory.

In the Equatorial Africa, missionary work was subjected to certain regulations with the exception of "catechumen schools" which were allowed to freely operate. These regulations mainly concerned the requirement of French as the only medium of teaching. This requirement by the French Government was seen as a retrogression from the spirit of Le Zoute, especially because the law stipulating the exclusive use of this language in schools was newly reenacted (January 1938).

Yet Madras, in view of the resurgence of nationalism, was unable to pass a resolution specifically condemning France, Belgium, or Portugal for their maltreatment of Protestant missionaries in their African territories. Since, some delegates were unwilling to approve any statement which mentioned these "Catholic nations" by name, Madras settled for a statement couched in generalities.[17] However, on balance, Madras was quite honest with itself in that this political reason was used to preface the resolution on Church and State. This action showed a growing desire to admit the impact of world politics on mission thinking and action. Moreover, it signalled the beginning of the end for the largely cozy relationship which existed between the missionary community and the Colonial Powers particularly after the Le Zoute Conference.

However, Madras predictably found that cooperative action in church and civil life was more than necessary; examples of some cooperative plans in Africa which were found to be encouraging included the Kenyan scheme that was to unite the Anglicans, Presbyterians and Methodists, the Nigerian proposal,[18] and the Congo accord which mandated all Protestant missions working in that territory to use one name: *l'Eglise du Christ Congo.*

Madras' final statement on cooperation and unity urged the older churches to take seriously into "prayer, thought and action," movements toward organic unity on the part of the "younger churches." Regrets were expressed concerning the fact that the "older churches" did not show a good example in terms of moving toward organic unity. Still, no accusing fingers were pointed to any one particular church, mission society, or nation for causing disunity, international tension or conflict. Madras reserved its harsh words for recusant European churches.[19]

6. Some individual contributions at Madras

Of many Africans who took part in the assembly, K. L. Kisosonke's contribution should first be mentioned. A layman and Schoolmaster from Budo, Uganda, Kisosonke was one of six nationals who expounded the topic the "Triumph of the Gospel." Kisosonke began by paying a high tribute to missionaries, by recalling the hazardous conditions the pioneers encountered in travelling, food, climate, loneliness and health. He was particularly grateful for the Bible but was also willing to speak of the numerous Ugandan martyrs, young and old, who died in the hands of Moslems and paid the ultimate price for the spread of the Church in Africa.

Kisosonke's greatest testimony to the triumph of the gospel was the narration of the story of the legendary Apolo Kivebulaya who in spite of serious handicap became the most famous Ugandan lay evangelist. Kisosonke spoke of how Kivebulaya escaped death on one occasion and managed to go into the land of the Pygmies to found the Church of Christ, and of how the CMS conferred on him the honor of vice-presidency in addition to the title of a Canon. Kisosonke went on to speak of spiritual awakening in the Ugandan Church and of the need for workers to ensure the final triumph of Christ over ignorance, superstitions, and "women lying wounded on the battlefield of economic warfare." Contemporary Christianity, he said, still needed more witnesses. Thus, he ended his short but informing address with a rhetorical question: "Who will go there [Uganda] to further the Kingdom of God?"[20]

Another notable contribution was made by Mina Soga who brought her black South African vision of Christ to share with the Conference. A little shy and reserved, Mina Soga spoke on why African women must be given equal opportunity in education and evangelical leadership. Realizing that Christian missionary work was dominated by men insofar as most missionaries and delegates to this Conference were men, Miss Soga wished that many women missionaries would be trained and sent to Africa. Additionally, she asked the Conference to pray and plan for the day when African women will take a prominent part in ecumenical conferences. Also, she prayed for the day when the whole African continent will raise only the banner of Christ.

Emphasizing the same theme which some delegates hammered away at London 1925, Soga wondered why African women issues were not taken very seriously, and why these issues were often discussed after many conference delegates were fatigued. Because of the vital role women play in African society, she urged the missionary community not to relent in their attempt to educate more women.

Miss Soga's account of her South African experience of racism was quite moving. She wondered what the future of Africa will be, if no radical solution was found to help all people, including children, to live together in peace. She feared most for the children who were being brought up in an atmosphere of racial intolerance. These children, she imagined, will most likely grow up to encourage this sin of racism, if nothing concrete was done to ameliorate the situation. Racial segregation was to her an antithesis of the Christian gospel.

Visionary and determined, Soga was, interestingly, articulating, though in the language of her period, some of the things contemporary feminism are emphasizing: equal opportunity to all in all areas of life, irrespective of sex, race or nationality. On this, no one could fault her. For she was on target on everything she said and for which she hoped. She was overwhelmingly positive in her reaction to the Conference and said that, on the one hand, her journey out of Africa turned her from a South African into an African. On the other hand, the journey to Madras made her "a world Christian."[21]

Of the splendid performance of the delegates on Christmas Day, 1938, it was observed that the African delegation provided a fitting climax to all that was said and done. Having chosen six of their greatest singers in the delegation, they "banked them around" Mina Soga with her powerful obbligato. Together they produced a memorable ecumenical music in an ecumenical forum and setting. It was a spectacular sight to watch, a great song for ecumenism, and a marvelous opportunity for Africans. "When they had finished," Hogg wrote, "thunderous applause broke out. The day ended on a note of perfect beauty."[22]

Summary

Frankly, it was not only the day which ended with "a perfect beauty" at Madras. The whole Conference, from a balanced perspective, equally ended on such a note. This does not mean that Madras was trouble-free.

Meeting in a world about to be shaken to its foundations, Madras did not wholly win over critics of its church-centric tendencies, did not overtly call on older churches to grant autonomy to their African churches, and did not even tacitly call on African colonial governments to hand over power to indigenous leaders. Uncertain of what the following years had in store for the world—and the ecumenical movement, for that matter, Madras largely underscored the cautionary mode which the IMC had devised for itself, although it was quite progressive on unitive matters and the sociology of ecumenism.

Although it recognized that there comes a time when the church must say to the state "thus far and no farther,"[23] Madras left national churches to discern when to say so. This meant, for mission-related churches in Africa, the continuation of the status quo, just like Jerusalem did a decade earlier, given the fact that the control of these churches was not in the hands of the native Christians. Doubtless, with hindsight, one can see that this was a retrogression on the part of the IMC, a failure it later regretted even before the second world war was over.

Still, despite Madras' equivocation on the status of indigenous churches and calling for "prayers" when forceful action was the need of the hour, Africans returned from Madras with a mood of expectancy, discovery, and anticipation. For the Conference was for them and the whole of Africa a further indication that the era of independence was a matter of time. The next two decades and a few more conferences proved that they had good reasons for their measured optimism.

NOTES

[1]This proposal started early in 1928. See Oldham to P. H. J. Lerrigo [American Baptist Foreign Mission Society], December 8, 1928 and January 1, 1929, IMC Papers, WCC Library, Geneva; part of this statement is in appendix 3.

[2]See Margaret Wrong, *Africa And The Making Of Books* (New York: ICCLA, 1934). Margaret Wrong was the first secretary of this Committee. In this book (p. 13) she mentioned the ecumenical function of this body particularly its help towards overcoming sectarianism, confusion in ecclesiastical thought, and fanaticism in missionary and native circles.

[3]Dr. Kenyon L. Butterfield was appointed the first director. This program helped to make the IMC to rethink the role of the peasant in world Christianity as those who have equal claim to God's material and spiritual resources. Lessons gained from African experiments were shared with the Asian fields; cf. Hogg, p. 273.

[4]This department, like the rural mission program, was seen as encompassing the entire scope of the missionary work. Its highly-acclaimed and shared report, *Modern Industry and the African*, published by director J. Merle Davis in 1933, made 75 recommendations which included taking action to curb the ever-widening gap between the outlooks and ways of life of the city and rural folks in Africa. Another work, production and interchange of cultural films on an international scale, was done between 1935 to 1937. See L. A. Notcutt and G. C. Latham eds., *The African And The Cinema: An Account Of The Work Of The Bantu Educational Cinema Experiment* (London: IMC, 1937).

[5]*The World Mission Of The Church: Findings and Recommendations Of The International Missionary Council, Tambaram, Madras, India, December 12th to 29th, 1938* (New York: IMC, 1939), pp. 6–7; hereafter cited as *Madras 1938, Findings*.

[6]Prior to Madras, numerous field studies were done in Africa. This included "The Church and African society." African Christian Councils took part in financing these surveys; see, "Field Studies for Madras 1938: Africa," IMC/CBMS Archives, Box 203, mf. 34.

[7]*Meeting of the International Missionary Council, Tambaram, Madras, India, December 12th to 29th, 1938*, 7 vols. (New York: IMC, 1939), vol. V: *The Economic Basis Of The Church*, p. 449; hereafter cited as *Madras 1938*.

[8]Ibid., p. 452.

[9]*Madras 1938*, vol. II, *The Growing Church*, p. 6.

[10]*Madras 1938*, Findings, p. 101. The statement was a long one but notice that the word "evil" is used to describe the system of grant-in-aid.

[11]Ibid., p. 45.

[12]Ibid.

[13]*Madras 1938*, vol. IV, *The Life Of The Church*, p. 222; see also "The Younger Church in South Africa: contribution to missionary work in S. Africa and to IMC at Madras (findings of group of African ministers at Lovedale)," IMC/CBMS Archives, Box 203, mf. 34–35. This is still an excellent study, though done several years ago.

[14]*Madras 1938*, vol. IV, *The Life Of The Church*, p. 223.

[15]*Madras 1938*, Findings, p. 142.

[16]*Madras 1938*, vol. VI, *The Church and State*, p. 249.

[17]Ibid., p. 263; see also p. 193 where it is remarked that the Roman Catholic attitude towards Protestants was still "We claim freedom for ourselves in the name of your principle, but deny it to you in the name of ours."

[18]This union scheme later debacled, see Ogbu Kalu, *The Divided People Of God: Church Union Movement in Nigeria, 1875–1966* (New York: Nok, 1978).

[19]*Madras 1938, Findings*, p. 131.

[20]*Madras 1938*, vol. VII, *Addresses and Other Records*, p. 148.

[21]Fey, *Ecumenical Advance*, p. 77; for a detailed work on Mina Soga see R. I. Seabury, *Daughter of Africa* (Boston: Pilgrim Press, 1945).

[22]Hogg, p. 292.

[23]Madras used this phrase "thus far and no farther" only when it dwelt on generalities about church/state tension. Madras continued to take the colonial order for granted. See *Madras*, 1938, vol. VI, *The Church and the State*, p. 262.

PART V

AFRICA AND ECUMENICAL MANDATES IN A NEW KEY, 1939–1958

12

AFRICAN AFFAIRS AMID WORLD WAR II

The first three years after Madras saw a succession of sociopolitical crises that led to another major war. This war damaged the relative optimism that characterized Madras' pronouncements and, with its incalculable brutalities, left a permanent mark on ecumenical thinking. But balanced against this horrifying disregard for human life and destruction was the increased awareness of the interdependence of the human family, and the continuing relevance and immediacy of African questions.

This chapter gives our ecumenical journey two important but brief stops. The first stop—Westerville—examines the issues which made African affairs attractive in a small American city, despite the war situation. The second stop—Whitby and Willingen—notes, albeit in passing, the aftermath of the war and a quest to weave post-war mandates, pulling the IMC out of its desert of indecision on some crucial issues.

I. CHURCH CONFERENCE ON AFRICAN AFFAIRS: WESTERVILLE 1942

Amid the cataclysm of the war, a revived attempt at understanding these questions helped to supply the opportunity for a much-needed, wartime, ecumenical fellowship and sustenance. The occasion was "the first general" Church Conference On African Affairs to be held in North America. The venue was Otterbein College, Westerville, Ohio. The meeting took place from June 19–25, 1942.

Organized by the FMCNA, the Conference took advantage of the upsurge of North American interest in Africa. Seeing that with the outbreak of this war, the old world had died and the peoples of Africa and the world were about to enter a new age, the Conference sought to explore ways in which, during and after the war missionary work in Africa was to be "altered, located, united, enlarged, strengthened and supported" as to give the African Church effective and efficient support in the new day which the Conference believed was a matter of time.[1]

Thus, this comprehensive warrant inspired and brought a total of 199 delegates from 52 organizations to Westerville. While Westerville regretted that, because of wartime conditions, it was impossible to have a larger representation from Africa and Europe, practically all functional interests were represented either by foreign missionaries or nationals. Hence, in addition to Jesse Jones, Edwin Smith, and A. L. Warnshuis, black Americans sent an unprecedented number of twenty-nine. Others who represented Africa were James T. Ayorinde (Nigeria), Adjei Ako (the Gold Coast), Joseph N. Togba (Liberia), and Mrs. Ntombikobani Tantsi (South Africa).

1. Social conditions at Westerville

At Westerville, the nature of the questions did not change. What changed was consciousness or imagination. This change in thinking is seen first with how Westerville deliberated on African social and rural questions. Westerville believed, for instance, that in tackling rural missions the worldwide Church would benefit from the old African idea of preserving the "holy earth." A bulletin, *The Holy Earth*, produced by the Christian Rural Fellowship gave a classic expression to this commitment.

Discussion led to the discovery that labor questions, especially the exploitation of women, are tied to the whole problem of "unmoral partition" of the earth among the millions who live on it. Christians were to recall that the processes of agriculture which Africans take for granted, are divinely appointed and that, if Christianity is to function in the daily living of Africans or in any other people, then predominantly it must function in whatever they do for a living.

Westerville's recommendations on socioeconomic questions moved beyond Madras in specifying that voluntary corporate and governmental actions should be put in place in order to prevent as far as possible the exploitation of Africans in industry, to help them receive a larger economic reward, and provide them better housing and recreational facilities. This recommendation was also an affirmation of the fact that any isolational or sectional attempt to deal with this enormous task would be stupid and futile.

2. Primal religions at Westerville

On indigenous cultural and religious values, no one has to read far or search deeply to discover that Westerville did not seek to erode ecumenical convictions of the preceding two decades. Instead, it strengthened and refined them. Influenced by American anthropological and sociological studies, Westerville evidences a desire—even an obsession—to give African values the benefit of the doubt. For example, Westerville acknowledged that Africa's gift of radiance of religious life and spirit, social solidarity, simplicity of life, religious value of the soil, and closeness to nature must be embedded deep in ecumenical mission thinking.[2]

Westerville also knew that the modern African community is no longer solely bounded by the horizons of a past generation, and that modern African children are born into a heritage compounded of elements old and new. How to maintain the traditional emotional understanding of God and the view that religion interpenetrates every activity of daily life was not sufficiently fleshed out.

Likewise, although Westerville spoke of Africanization or *Africate*[3] of Christianity and expected the missionary to initiate the process, it failed to understand sufficiently that by the time the missionary learned African ways and thought patterns, Africans have become inoculated with foreign ideas and have adopted foreign customs. Consequently, when missionaries have awakened to the inherent good in traditional African societies and attempt to preserve these values, they find that often the natives question their motives and argue that missionaries are trying to keep them on an inferior level.

Nevertheless, in spite of Westerville's laudable appreciation of strains of cultural change and innovative understanding of Africa, it failed to recognize that in the clash of two cultures, industrial and nonindustrial, the former, because of its flexibility and output, is bound to subject the latter to its own systemic laws and inner-logic.

This notwithstanding, Westerville attempted to apply latest social techniques to understanding indigenization questions. It was said, for example, that Christians should, for a moment try to look at the missionary enterprise as a historian and a sociologist might look at it. For, while Christians would tend to see the dominance of Christianity over nonChristian systems, the historian and the sociologist would see Christianity in terms of its long contact and collision with nonChristian cultures and the emergence of new civilizations, struggling at once to attract and repel nonChristian elements.

Additionally, Westerville mandated that missionaries must see Christianity as a creative and stimulating idea which began in the mind of Christ naked and unorganized. In its Palestinian environment, and the life and work of the early Christians in particular, it made itself a body. The implication was clear: no religion exists in the ideal state. On the contrary, all religions only begin to make sense to mortals after they take on the language of mortality and sin, change their state from static to dynamic, and bring to humans a sense of affirmation and being amid the constant threat of nonbeing, contradictions, and ambiguities of human life as we know it.

This manner of speaking owed a lot to American pragmatic tradition and innovation. It showed that, like Hartford, Conferences held in American cities tended to be ahead of their times and were more willing to borrow theoretical ideas from diverse intellectual disciplines and sources to support the making of ecumenical mandates. Further, whereas Conferences held in European cities felt that they owed much to traditional missionary thought, Conferences held in America lacked such abiding subservience to tradition, though not on all missiological issues. For, after all, America as a nation, with its religions—civil and noncivil, was born because of peculiar immigration circumstance and willingness to call tradition into question and explore new directions, no matter the uncertainty of the future and the difficulty of a complete break from the past.

3. Indigenous churches at Westerville

On the rise of indigenous churches and how this affected church-mission relations, Westerville, in view of the wartime conditions, was more forthcoming than Madras in seeing that foreign missionaries after all are only a temporary evanescent feature in the African scene.

Discussion on the particulars of devolution from mission to church was still marred by a failure to recognize that the logic of cross-cultural missions in itself superimposes a limit on how far a foreign worker can actually train "indigenous leaders." The recognition that the war had shattered many things did not spur most delegates to recommend immediate transfer of responsibility to nationals. Indeed, the whole treatment of the question assumed that the war was bringing into existence political and social realignment only among Colonial Powers. Westerville failed to perceive that, while the colonial order was disintegrating, at least politically, tortured Africa was also seeking to realign itself.

The decisive aspect of this question of devolution was the sad fact that, after more than thirty years of talk about indigenous leaders, missionaries were not training adequate "leaders" but were in fact training only "followers," or "Western indigenous leadership," not "African indigenous leadership." To be sure, the Conference was dismayed to find out that, although African mission councils had on their staff indigenous workers the master/servant, superior/inferior mentality still conditioned actual relations between church and mission. Little wonder that the political calculation of the committee which dealt with African leadership and the political situation was clearly futuristic, anticipating several decades of Indirect Rule but not outright independence.[4]

This notwithstanding, Westerville received remarkable reports that, despite the war, some indigenous leaders were doing comparatively very well, for example, in Tanganyika. Doubtless, for those African leaders who managed to keep the nascent church alive and growing during these years of unplanned weaning, this war was a blessing in disguise, because it helped them to gain some confidence in their own leadership and managerial abilities.

Some delegates, for example Warnshuis, feared that when the war is over and missionaries returned to their African posts they would fail to realize and understand the changes which have taken place and will try to take back again the positions that they ought never to have had in the first place. This fear was not unfounded because, willy-nilly, someone's livelihood was tied to those positions. For, contrary to popular thought, the enterprise was not only beneficial to Africans. It was also extremely beneficial to metropolitan countries and individual missionaries in more ways than the purely religious. Thus, if one truly wants to know why there was too much foot dragging on the devolution question, this factor of vested interest must be taken into consideration.

Westerville's frank admission of this problem of vested interest (happening as it did at a time when native underground political movements for independence had become foreground movements, and some rules of colonial politics were about to be changed), served as the point of departure for the framing of special recommendations. A wartime product, these recommendations reflected the political and economic situations of several African territories. Also, unlike Madras and, perhaps, because of America's distance from Europe and the war situation, the recommendations mentioned territories and countries by name and represented over a third of the 169 recommendations approved by the Conference and had specific messages or petitions for both church and state. However, they stopped short of urging either ecclesiastical self-government for the African Church or suggesting political independence in African colonies.[5]

4. Race relations at Westerville

Westerville also subjected the race question to an intensive scrutiny. This scrutiny exhibited not only a vivid contrast with past conferences, including Jerusalem and Madras. It also served as the first time this growing body came to the understanding that the racial problem is not a black problem, but "truly seems in many respects to be a white problem." Also, the Conference found that the involvement of black people in the second world war more than in the first had brought a new reality:

color does blind and bind. The war had helped to challenge old assumptions, call familiar ideas to question, and enable people to see things differently. A statement gave a vivid expression to this discovery and fact and emphasized the importance of recognizing social problems even in American society:

> [Color] binds us so that sometimes white Christians in America who have strong prejudice concerning Negroes here can nevertheless contribute generously for Christian evangelism and education and medicine in Africa. It would almost seem as if in the past some gave to the cause of African missions with escapist motives. It was easy to give to foreign missions without disturbing the economic or social or cultural or religious structure here at home. But that is no longer possible. American Christian failure in America in the matter of race is now well known over the world and generous foreign missionary giving cannot hide the stark facts. Nor can the success of Christian missionary work abroad fail in turn to help alter and correct our weaknesses here. Countries are no longer compartments in which actions affect only those within.[6]

Consequently, Westerville's mandate on this question stressed humility in view of the defects in American society. It saw racial discrimination as ecumenical abomination and suggested that instead of looking upon human species in "superior" and "inferior" categories, they should be considered as "advanced" or "retarded."[7] Clearly here Westerville's imagination was not particularly "advanced," for, by speaking of retardation, it failed to recognize that it was replacing one stereotype with another.

Westerville reaffirmed that this problem of race both in America and Africa cannot be separated and that steady improvement in America will lead to steady improvement in all parts of Africa. Tribute was paid to black American missionaries in Africa who in spite of restrictions had managed to make significant achievements. For the first time, the ecumenical community minced no words that the decisive reason why black Americans were prevented from going to Africa in great numbers was because they might "raise forthright questions—even more quickly than most white American missionaries."[8]

This statement marked another milestone in ecumenical thought and was an improvement on Le Zoute's and Jerusalem's. However, it was also indicative of the power of the vote even in ecumenical gatherings. For this was the first ecumenical conference on Africa with so many representatives from the black American missionary and church community; and they demonstrated by their presence and vote that, on this matter, they were not interested in any ambiguous resolution. The time had come, they believed, to be more straightforward in ecumenical dealings.

5. Cooperation and unity at Westerville

On the issue of cooperation in church and civil life, Westerville also sought to break new grounds. As a wartime gathering, Westerville wished that there should be more mission/church cooperation as well as mission/government cooperation.

Also, it suggested that there should be more cooperation between missionary societies controlled by whites and the ones controlled by blacks. Recalling Hartford's suggestion that white Christians must not think that they can support missionary work in Africa but ignore social conditions in their own backyard, the meeting suggested that everyone, including black churches, should work together. Cooperation abroad would be meaningless, Westerville stressed, without cooperation here at home.

Given that some black churches in America were still leery of cooperative ventures with white churches (because of the fear of losing the relative autonomy and power they had acquired for themselves over the years), Westerville assured all churches that the ecumenical movement was in the business of spiritual unity rather than organic unity. To what extent this assurance assuaged those churches, particularly the minority ones, to abandon their apprehensions is not clear.

One thing that is clear from our sources is the fact that, in light of rising tensions in all parts of Africa, Westerville resolved that colonial regimes must no longer see themselves in terms of "trusteeship" but in terms of "guardianship." Short of a forceful action, this resolution amounted only to a word game, despite Westerville's good intention to remind those colonial governments of the ephemeral character of their African exploits.[9]

6. Some individual contributions at Westerville

Westerville also featured outstanding individual contributors. Mrs. Tantsi spoke on behalf of African women. She stood for a comprehensive ecumenical view of education and demonstrated this by talking about John Dube's project of educational advance in Natal. Mrs. Tantsi could not resist the temptation to compare conditions in America with South Africa.

She saw the powerlessness of black people written all over every discussion touching social, economic, and missiological matters. Seeing that America, despite laws to the contrary, was developing into two societies—black and white—largely separate and unequal in everything, including burial grounds, Mrs. Tantsi feared that a similar situation was gradually being codified into law in South Africa. This, she said, not knowing that apartheid would receive the imprimatur of the legal statutes about five years later.

The Nigerian delegate, James Ayorinde, was concerned with the building of the indigenous church. Ayorinde believed that missions in Africa would be better off with the missionary at the background, while Africans build the church and have the upper hand in deciding its destiny.

Showing his knowledge of the rapid growth of the *Aladura* Churches, particularly, the Cherubim and Seraphim Church which had spread in Nigeria within a few years despite internal divisions, Ayorinde wondered whether the mission-related churches would ever be allowed to experience the same sense of freedom enjoyed by the Independent Churches. It was his belief that the Spirit of God should be allowed to control these indigenous churches rather than missionary boards acting as absentee landlords.

Joseph Togba dealt with the ecumenical problem of making both the missionary and the missionized to see themselves as *en route* and co-workers, both in translation work and pastoral care. For Togba, much remained to be done in terms of building ecumenical trust and mutual confidence between the foreigner and the indigene.

As one who was familiar with indigenous attempts to create ecclesiastical structures suitable to underpin a lasting bridge between the aboriginal people and the emigrant population in Liberia, Togba stressed the need for unity in every action of the contemporary church. Togba's was an indication that there was friction among nonwhite peoples and that the ecumenical movement should not only be concerned with relations between whites and blacks.

Some black people in Liberia, he said, were waging an undeclared war against their fellow countrymen and distant kindred. This war, he added, should be brought to a stop as soon as possible, otherwise Liberia will disintegrate given the fact that the various groups were imperfectly weaved together. The church, he declared, must find elastic ways to link black Americans churches with Liberian churches in a formal ecumenical venture.

Summary

Finally, Westerville strove to take Africa seriously. Although it continued the unfinished task of previous Conferences, it was also a product of the war years. More important, it was also indicative that the center of gravity which had moved to Asia was moving across the Pacific to the United States. Politically, Westerville was very sensitive to Africa's role in world politics. It wanted the United States to fill the power vacuum that the war had made possible in Africa. Thus Resolutions 85 and 86 were directed to the United States relations with Africa.

In particular, they called for the United States active participation in international conferences on Africa, and to consider creating, in the State Department, a separate Division for African-American Affairs, since the old system in which Africa was considered part of the Near East or Western Europe seemed inadequate "for the present and future."[10] The American Committee on Africa, the War, and Peace Aims, formed in 1941, studied and presented at this Conference a preliminary report that focused attention on Africa as an important variable in enduring world peace.[11]

Westerville adopted a series of resolutions which, taken together with the Le Zoute resolutions of 1926, and the Madras resolutions of 1938, looked toward more comprehensive and effective understanding of the idea of partnership. One of these, Resolution 143 (B), condemned the Belgian government policy in Congo which was "developing in Congo a privileged class of Roman Catholics and a seriously under-privileged class of Protestant Africans."[12]

As in earlier occasions, there were loud expressions of disgust with oppressive conditions in Africa but no radical action as such was taken. In this, Westerville merely reaffirmed the ecumenical significance of African affairs and, despite its highly unusual political awareness and statements, failed to see that the era of decolonization was about to begin. In the next and first post-war conference, Whitby 1947, such a miscalculation became impossible.

II. TOMORROW IS HERE: WHITBY 1947, WILLINGEN 1952

The period after the war evidenced a growing realization that the second chapter of African-European interaction, like the first, was brought to an abrupt end by a war. While what was to follow in the next chapter was not yet exactly clear, at Whitby it was clear enough to dismiss as an idle dream the expectation that Africa, after a short interval of unrest, will plunge into its ancient way of life again, and let the West do its will.

Accordingly, the Whitby Conference[13] gathered on the assumption that the old as such will not return, and that, for the second time, the burden was on Christian missions to readjust themselves to a changed world order, with all the honesty of vision, and all the wisdom they could call to their aid. Yet, because this was 1947 and not 1921, when this Council was born, Whitby also rightly assumed that most of the tactical findings of the previous Conferences were still sound and relevant and that its main task was "to seek fresh insight on the broad strategy of the missionary task in our sadly shattered world."[14]

1. Social conditions at Whitby

As a transition Conference which formally made manifest what earlier Conferences had merely assumed—partnership, Whitby treated Africa with more respect and admiration than any other previous Conference. Whitby's review of African social questions and their impact on ecumenical necessity brought humility. For it was discovered that, for the most part, rhetoric, not reality, followed the reports of the previous Conferences.

In particular, Whitby saw no reason to boast in view of the fact that the church was contributing to the depopulation of African villages and the decline of agriculture, by continuing to offer a form of education that was largely unrelated to the environment[15] and the needs of the urbanized African; in Nigeria, Gold Coast, South Africa, and Kenya, cities were beginning to show signs of unplanned growth as more and more people sought "white collar" jobs in the cities, creating new foundation for future social instability in these countries.

Similarly, Whitby in part blamed the missions for exacerbating the fissiparous tendency of modern African life, given the continuing differing tempers and approaches to social questions by missionaries in different African areas. Whitby confessed that the "needs of the industrial areas and the injustices and disintegration of capitalist economy have received only a faint challenge."[16] Ecumenical workers were urged to take note of this oversight and inaction, given that past Conferences, beginning at Jerusalem, had pointed out similar lapses.

Another statement, "Christian Witness in a Revolutionary World" minced no words regarding the IMC continuing commitment to both social action and spiritual rebirth. It declared:

> As Christians, we are pledged to the service of all those who are hungry or destitute or in need; we are pledged to the support of every movement for the removal of injustice and oppression. But we do not conceive these things, good in themselves, to be the whole evangelism, since we are convinced that the source of the world's sorrow is spiritual, and that its healing must be spiritual, through the entry of the risen Christ into every part of the life of the world.[17]

2. Primal religions at Whitby

On other matters, however, such as the use of African religious and cultural values in church life and worship, Whitby's attitude was, predictably, less orthodox and more understanding. Given the drastic effect of the war and the realization that, once again, the so-called developed world (and, by implication, Christianity itself) was largely responsible for the war, it was found no more necessary to consider Christianity, as it has manifested in the West, as largely above culture. If, after the first world war there was something left to be said to exonerate Christianity from any blame, after this second war, no delegate in Whitby could pretend that it was easy to defend Christianity amid the shattering effect of the war.

Therefore, Whitby's view of the relationship of Christianity to other religions was necessarily far more positive than we have seen thus far. Whitby allowed no more deification of any nation. It unapologetically reaffirmed, the supranationality of the church and missions and, by implication, approved the relativity of all cultural forms. An abiding implication of this understanding of culture was the abandonment of the old notion that aboriginal African customs must be destroyed and the acceptance of the current notion that African customs and primal religions are not all bad after all.

Whereas, at Madras, national loyalties prevented any specific criticism of the nation state and undue homage to Western nations was still discernible there, here at Whitby, it was another opportunity for a litany of self-criticism, confession, and inaction: "Looking back[, a statement began,] upon the years of war and the events which led up to them, we are conscious of many failures at this most critical point."[18]

3. Indigenous churches at Whitby

But Whitby did not only regret the way the ecumenical movement had in the past dealt with other religions. It also regretted the slow pace the movement was dealing with the issue of church and mission, during the past four decades. This is why, on the question of African leadership and devolution of responsibility from mission to church, Whitby moved quickly, in light of the changed climate in world politics, and uncertainty which characterized the future of missions, to underline the Madras principle of growing integration of mission and church.

Yet no specific timetable was put in place to encourage giving over the definition and direction of missionary effort into the hands of African church leaders.

Similarly, although the discussion assumed the position that the colonial era in missions, as in world politics, was ending, Whitby, like Westerville, did not call at all for decolonization of Africa. However, an interesting theoretical point which Whitby raised related to doing away with the terms "younger" and "older" churches. Whitby suggested this change in terminology because it felt that "the distinction is largely obsolete, and that for the most part the tasks which face the churches in all parts of the world are the same."[19]

Additionally, another section of the statement called for full partnership in which Asian and African churches would put away once for all every thwarting sense of dependence on the older churches and stand in the ecumenical movement as "absolute spiritual equality." This was a marvelous statement but it bordered more on wishful thinking than reality, given the continuing problem of inadequate preparation for self-reliance on the part of Asian and African churches and missionary societies themselves.

4. Race relations at Whitby

In the same fashion, the issue of race discrimination at Whitby brought penitence. A statement captured this feeling when it regretted that it was too easy for Christians to unquestionably accept whatever they were told about their national interest and racial inheritance when, as Christ's disciples, they should have been critical of it. In light of the war and how Christian churches participated in it, the statement stressed that the IMC was deeply conscious of the danger of identifying Christianity too closely to national ideals and interests. It pledged the IMC to work for greater alertness to this peril. It promised that the IMC "will make it unmistakably clear to the world that Christian missions transcend all national and racial differences."[20]

However, what brought more humility, self-criticism, and further calls for ethnic-free Christianity here at Whitby was the *prima facie* evidence of the massive aid that the orphaned German missions in Africa and elsewhere, once again, required. Though, financially, the need was for thousands of American dollars, the worse part was the fact that the wound of the first world war was not yet perfectly healed before the second one began to bleed profusely. It was another mourning time for foreign missionary workers, and another serious blow to missionary work and confidence.

Luckily, this Council was on a better, though not perfect, foundation than when it had to face similar circumstances in the 1920s. For the growing African churches, like other churches, were up and ready to make their contribution[21] to this unitive body as it sought to recover from this terrible blow, finding new ways to restore its confidence and recover its largely tarnished public image.

5. Cooperation and unity at Whitby

Whitby summoned the churches in Africa and elsewhere to continue to see mission unity as a primary need. The necessity of cooperation in Africa was found to be still acute and was very likely to become "more pressing in the near future." Needless to say that the war experience had some impact on how the Conference perceived unity. Consequently, one was more likely to hear presentations in defense of mission unity rather than against it. Indeed, the word unity or something akin to it runs through the reports of the Conference like a colored thread. For example, the preamble to the major report stated that, despite the separation brought about by the war, Christians have known through faith and experience that the Church is universal; and that no worldly principality or power can change that universal conviction. The war experience was seen as a crucible and a new opportunity which had made Christians to become more aware of, as never before, the need for unity.

Doubtless, humans, after passing through the crucible of war or any major disaster, tend to reflect more on their mortality and appreciate more the necessity for interdependence. Whitby's delegates were no exception. This is, perhaps, one reason why they readily underlined Christianity as a universal religion and missions as supranational. Moreover, they hoped that, increasingly, the Church may be seen as a great global and ecumenical fellowship within which great differences are brought "together—racial, national, cultural, and economic—but which by its very existence is token of a Kingdom in which these differences have been overcome."[22]

Whitby's action also led to one of the first fruits of cooperation between the IMC and the WCC: the formation of the Commission of the Churches on International Affairs. This Commission was one aspect of the IMC/WCC cooperative activity which later led to the integration of the two bodies.[23]

6. Some individual contributions at Whitby

Whitby witnessed significant contributions from African delegates. The report by the Literature Secretary, Miss Margaret Wrong, on the state of Christian literature in Africa reiterated the importance of unity. She regretted the fact that the war had hampered some efforts but she remained optimistic that the churches would redouble their effort in the production of new texts for use in church and schools.

Miss Wrong was careful to remind all cooperating mission societies that the post-war period was not the time to fall behind in whatever they were doing in their different school systems. Christian literature, she asserted, has contributed immensely to the intellectual growth of the natives; and that there was more demand for literature authored by the indigenes themselves.

Miss Wrong wanted the Literature Committee to remember the spectacular growth of its history from the dark days of uncertainty when Jerusalem mandated its establishment. After two decades, Miss Wrong felt that there was something tangible which the IMC could show for its efforts. She urged the Council not to forget Africa as it sought to mobilize the missionary forces for post-war evangelism.

Christian Baeta of the Gold Coast spoke vehemently against the mistakes of the past, particularly the problem of orphaned-missions in Africa. The fact that there was such a thing as orphaned-missions, he suggested, was due to the persistence of nationalism even in the missionary community. This is why Baeta was against missionary societies which continued to tie the success of their work to the colonial aspiration of their home countries.

Knowing that it is the ground which suffers whenever two elephants fight, Baeta urged that Christian missions be denationalized because on two occasions missions stood to suffer simply because two major powers or power blocks decided to settle their differences by taking up arms rather than negotiations. Baeta saw no reason why more mission societies should not be organized internationally as some societies such as the SUM attempted to do. Thus he wondered why French mission societies limited themselves to French territories in Africa and why, after a century of Protestantism in Africa, British societies were still largely concentrated in British Africa and not very much in French or Portuguese Africa.

Baeta was delighted that, after the war, the IMC was beginning to take the idea of partnership seriously. Yet he wondered what kind of partnership the IMC had in mind, given the fact that ideas were not widely sought from both the sending and receiving churches on how this concept of partnership should be understood, let alone given a structural framework in light of the dawning of a new day for missions in Africa.

With his penetrating insight, Baeta argued that partnership must not mean a reshufflement of the old structure of ecumenical mission relations. To reshuffle things and call them new, he suggested, was not good enough. Africa, he claimed, needed a whole new structure of international relationship.

Seth M. Mokitimi of South Africa spoke of the wartime conditions in his country, and how these required concerted missionary action to remedy the situation. Mokitimi did not see any immediate change in race relations in Southern Africa. Indeed, it was his belief that the war had, in fact, made the work of the church more difficult. How would you, he asked, tell people to live together when Hitler sought in his war efforts to exterminate the Jews in the name of the Christian God and his country? Mokitimi found solace in the fact that some Christians such as Dietrich Bonhoeffer (1906–1945) were willing to stand up to Hitler. He prayed that the South

African situation should not come to such a showdown, a prayer many still are praying for that beautiful and wealthy land with unparalleled ecumenical potential.

Mokitimi also chaired one of the three sections of the meeting, The Equipment of the Church, from which the statement on the spiritual and social life of the church emerged. It was Mokitimi's view that the equipment of the Church requires more than "earthenwares" or worldly armor. True equipment, he said, must be spiritual rebirth followed by sanctification. Yet he did not turn his back against "earthenwares." The Church, he stressed, unlike the world, must rely on earthenwares ecumenically manufactured. Strengthening native economies, erecting new church buildings, and creating a better climate for the Church to grow uninhibited were among his suggestions.

Whitby closed with the awareness that missionary tutelage was ending, but it left implicit its desire that the younger churches of Africa, like that of Asia, should be given more weight in the formulation of missionary policy than ever before.

Willingen 1952. This concern for a *fresh reformulation* of the missionary mandates was taken up by Willingen 1952, a gathering which largely repeated many things which Whitby[24] had mentioned and therefore deserves only a brief mention here.

Of the important mandates which relate to our general theme, we must note Willingen's increased preoccupation with the shape of the world. According to Norman Goodall, Willingen was planned to be a time of reflection and stock-taking, not the end of process, but a beginning. More important, every effort was made from the outset to avoid creating the impression to the outside world that the IMC had an inner cabinet secluded to a hidden resort and charged with the responsibility of producing a theology of missions "in even temporary forgetfulness of" events in South Africa, Korea, or China.[25]

Willingen, like Whitby, found that the distinctions suggested by the terms *younger* and *older* churches, and *national* and *missionaries* "were more than ever subordinate to our common calling in the Church and our common missionary obligation."[26] Similarly, the temper in which the whole subject of unity was discussed was revealed in the suggestion that it was no longer sufficient to speak of Africa, Asia, Europe, mission *and* unity and so on; "the call now is to 'Mission *in* Unity.'"[27]

After decades of resistance, another important outcome of the Willingen meeting in particular was the fact that members, apologetically, recognized that Johannes C. Hoekendijk's God-world-church formula of missions was, in fact, not "heretical" as it first appeared. As a member of the Dutch delegation to this meeting and an influential missiological figure in both Protestant and nonProtestant circles, he, beginning in 1950, rightly saw the church as the illegitimate center for missions. For the world, including Africa, was in his thought the proper center for missions.[28] Also, Willingen, despite its lack of significant theoretical originality, must be credited with reviving a very ancient missiological term which grew out of the Trinitarian discussions: *missio Dei*.

Summary

At both Whitby and Willingen, the final statements on the indigenous church, the role of the missionary society, and reshaping the pattern of missionary activity took for granted the principle of partnership. At Willingen, for example, these statements were made in a way which underscored past resolutions on the necessity of unity and partnership among churches; and in a way which made it abundantly clear that the IMC alone was incapable of framing ecumenical mandates that can be accepted by all missionaries and all churches at the same time. The IMC was to do its part in consultation and dialogue with other ecclesiastical bodies and power-centers.

Clearly, this was an assumption few missionaries at the turn of the century could have made; but, it was another indirect concession that the world will continue to have something to say to mission thinking and doing.

The African delegates who joined in issuing "A Statement By Younger Church Delegates" were probably left speechless, regarding how African conditions were helping to make mission agencies to be very anxious to devolve or even "abdicate" direct responsibility to even ill-equipped indigenous leaders. On this James Scherer observed: "So swift and complete was the devolution of responsibility that the wisdom of this policy had to be called into question in later years."[29]

Both Whitby and Willingen were, undoubtedly, further indications that events in the African world cannot be ignored and that redefining mission policy and attitudes is a task for each generation and era.

NOTES

[1]*Christian Action in Africa: Report of the Church Conference On African Affairs held at Otterbein College, Westerville, Ohio, June 19–25, 1942* (New York: FMCNA, 1942), p. 1; hereafter cited as *Christian Action in Africa, 1942*. The Conference was also called on behalf of the IMC. See the report of the IMC for 1940-41 to the Foreign Missions Conference of North America in *Report of the Forty-eighth Annual Meeting of the Conference Of Foreign Mission Boards In Canada and In the United States, Hotel Hildebrecht, Trenton, New Jersey, January 12–15, 1942* (New York: FMCNA, 1942), pp. 80–81. The report began by noting that, because of wartime conditions, it was necessary to remind the North American Boards that whatever was being done by the FMCNA should be recognized as being done in the name of the IMC and vice versa.

[2]Notice that the Vancouver WCC Assembly declared that the ecumenical movement should be concerned with justice, peace, and integrity of creation. Marlin Van-Elderen, "Justice, Peace and the Integrity of Creation," *One World* 111 (June 1986): 12–13.

[3]This was compared with *Brittate* or *Americate* of Christianity. The idea emerged as part of the historical and sociological analysis of African spiritual heritage and was used to convey that Christianity must necessarily take various forms in history. *Christian Action in Africa, 1942*, p. 68.

[4]Ibid., p. 158. Lester A. Walton, the American Envoy in Liberia and a member of the Conference did not even think that a few African leaders may rise up when they did to reject even shared political leadership.

[5]*Christian Action in Africa, 1942*, pp. 175–9.

[6]Ibid., pp. 143–144.

[7]Ibid., p. 170; Resolution 63.

[8]Ibid., pp. 140–1. Again, colonial governments' ignorance of real life in America also stood in the way, despite resolution after resolution at Conferences. Most of these governments in Africa thought that all black Americans were followers of the two most-dreaded black movements at the time, Garveyism and Pan-Africanism. In an attempt to overcome this misunderstanding, "isolation and ignorance," the Phelps-Stokes Fund, the Carnegie Corporation, and others sought to educate European administrators of African areas by bringing some of them to America to see things for themselves.

[9]Ibid., p. 171; Resolution 79.

[10]Ibid.

[11]Ibid., pp. 155-159; see especially the section of the report entitled "Africa and Enduring Peace."

[12]Ibid., p. 177.

[13]The first part of this section is devoted to Whitby, while a brief mention is made of Willingen at the end of the section.

[14]C. W. Ranson, ed., *Renewal and Advance, Report of the Whitby Meeting* (London: Edinburgh House, 1947), pp. 6-7; hereafter cited as *Renewal and Advance*.

[15]Ibid., p. 46.

[16]Ibid.

[17]Ibid., p. 215.

[18]*The Witness of a Revolutionary Church: Statements Issued by the Committee of the International Missionary Council, Whitby, Ontario, Canada, July 5-24, 1947* (London: IMC, 1947), p. 36; hereafter cited as *The Witness of a Revolutionary Church*.

[19]Ibid., p. 174.

[20]Ibid., pp. 173, 175-184.

[21]Indeed, some younger churches had during the war sent gifts to the church in Germany "in token of Christian love and a partnership shared together." K. S. Latourette and W. R. Hogg, *Tomorrow Is Here: The Mission And Work Of The Church As Seen From The Meeting Of The IMC At Whitby, 1947* (New York: IMC, 1948), p. 113.

[22]*Renewal and Advance*, p. 220.

[23]Ibid., pp. 45-50. In 1948, the WCC was formally inaugurated after ten years of unofficial existence. See *The First Assembly Of The World Council Of Churches Held At Amsterdam, August 22nd to September 4th, 1948* (London: SCM, 1949); and, Visser 't Hooft, *Genesis*, pp. 56-57. For more on the integration, see our study of Accra 1958 in chapter 13.

[24]Because of the IMC's closer relationship with the WCC, there were other Conferences which dealt with mission mandates prior to Willingen. These were, in particular, Amsterdam 1948 and Rolle 1951.

[25]Norman Goodall, ed., *Missions Under the Cross. Addresses delivered at the Enlarged Meeting of the Committee of the International Missionary Council at Willingen, in Germany, 1952; with Statements issued by the Meeting* (London: Edinburgh House, 1953), p. 13.

[26]*The Missionary Obligation of the Church: Willingen, Germany, July 5-17, 1952* (London: Edinburgh House, 1952), p. iii; hereafter cited as *Missionary Obligation*. Notice that the WCC at its inaugural assembly also indicated its desire to seek a "fresh" theology of mission. Its thematic study "Man's Disorder and God's

Design" pointed in this direction. See *Man's Disorder and God's Design: The Amsterdam Assembly Series* (New York: Harper and Brothers, 1949).

[27]*Missionary Obligation*, p. iv.

[28]For some of his early defense of this formula, see his "The Call to Evangelism" *IRM* (1950): 162–175; "The Church in Missionary Thinking," *IRM* (1952): 324–336; contrast this with how I noted this development elsewhere, namely that at New Delhi, 1961, this formula was "baptized with no apology into conciliar rubric." Efiong S. Utuk, "From Wheaton to Lausanne: The Road to Modification of Contemporary Evangelical Mission Theology," *Missiology* XIV (April 1986): 207.

[29]James Scherer, "Ecumenical Mandates for Mission," in *Protestant Crosscurrents in Mission*, ed. Norman A. Horner (Nashville: Abingdon, 1968), p. 39. For the statement by the delegates from the younger churches, see *Missionary Obligation*, pp. 39–41; cf. Norman Goodall, pp. 233–235.

13

AFRICA AND THE WEAVING OF POST-WAR MANDATES

The years following Willingen made many concerned observers to wonder whether mission mandates actually reflected the reality of post-World War II. The old world as many, including the IMC, knew it had already collapsed in many respects beyond recognition. Anybody who thought that the pre-war years could be recaptured was simply hallucinating.

Nevertheless, there was nothing substantial in the ecumenical movement resembling an adequate reaction to this new situation. The WCC, through its World Conference on Faith and Order (Lund, Sweden) held immediately after Willingen and its Second Assembly (Evanston, Illinois) held in 1954, had sought to bring the churches out of their closets and to respond missiologically to this collapse. Even so, none of these Conferences had sufficiently come to terms with the idea that tomorrow, as Whitby endeavored to show, had already dawned. The missionary enterprise was confronted with harsh realities and hard decisions; yet it appeared that the ecumenical movement was not ready to risk its capital by confronting these harsh realities with the courage and radicalism which the new dispensation required.

Many concerned missionaries found this to be shameful and inexcusable. Seeing that African and other events were moving faster than expectations and that past mandates were being invalidated by the rapid turn of events, this concern conceived the idea of "The Christian Mission at This Hour" and the Accra Assembly which met to consider it.

This chapter brings our ecumenical tour to its destination with an examination of the two Conferences which, in their own ways, helped to usher in this new ecumenical dispensation: Accra and Ibadan Conferences.

I. AFRICA AND THE CHRISTIAN MISSION AT THIS HOUR: ACCRA 1958

By all measures the last but one Assembly of the IMC which took place at Accra made one of the clearest statements ever of its debt to, and concern for, Africa.

A product of the profound impact and understanding of changing African and other conditions (particularly the attainment of independence by Ghana in March 1957), to which adjustment had to be made, the Assembly was planned to coincide with the first All-Africa Church Conference at Ibadan.[1]

1. Social conditions at Accra

With a theme which aroused considerable attention and suggested urgency in all its deliberations, Accra brought to a focus of thought a considerable body of experience that, in many ways, reflected the ongoing uneasiness and uncertainty in the ecumenical circles. The Christian mission at this hour meant vis-a-vis social conditions in Africa a thoroughgoing commitment to expanding social services to needy communities and supporting indigenous attempts to steer the new Africa to a more industrialized and fair social formation.

Accra assumed that past decisions regarding social conditions in Africa had begun to bear tangible and visible fruits. Yet, as its chief political host (Kwame Nkrumah) emphasized, Accra knew that much remained to be done in terms of modern education, hospitals, agriculture and transportation. For this reason, Accra urged all missionary societies to see "this hour" not as a time for reveling in past achievements but as a time for a renewed sense of human and evangelistic sacrifice. Christian missionaries, it declared, still have a vital contribution to make to post-colonial Africa.

An alarming fact which was brought to the fore concerned the enormous amount of money which the powerful nations were wasting on weapons of destruction (instead of "weapons of construction") when many dependent peoples throughout the world can barely feed themselves. This revelation brought Accra's theme nearer to the plight of Africa's masses, and confronted the Assembly with a problem which required a radical decision. Nkrumah also ensured that Accra's discussion of social matters were based not on hear-say but on some face to face encounter with the masses. For, in addition to an official cocktail party which he organized to honor the delegates, some delegates were given a tour of some places of interest within the city of Accra.

Thus, with respect to economic and political questions, Accra did not condemn the world for being the world and moving along sometimes in spite of the church.[2] Instead, it felt that these and other questions concerning rapid urban growth in many parts of Africa, compelled a new study of the subject. With its deliberation on the impact of social change on missions, Accra provided a starting point for this new study. This was later completed and published by Paul Abrecht, one of Africa's outstanding servants, as *The Churches and Rapid Social Change* (1961). With its desire to make its social policy to reflect the actual conditions in which the poor live and work, Accra provided a foundation, often ignored, for the people's theology of mission—something contemporary theologies of "liberation" should examine.

2. Primal religions at Accra

Accra's view of African customs and religious values rejected the notion that African Christianity must be composed of Christians caught perpetually with the dilemma of "a dualism of loyalties." Hoping to alleviate the dangers associated with this dualism, Accra felt that African Christianity must be expressed in indigenous cultural patterns, and in the very "structure of society itself." This focus on the world meant precisely that Christianity must not remain "an alien institution and even an alien faith by failing to be radically incarnate in the daily life and thought of community."[3]

Accra reaffirmed that idiosyncrasies also had much to do with how quickly dual personality can be overcome in African society. However, like previous Conferences, it made no attempt to point out that, perhaps, the ambiguity is insoluble as long as there is a qualitative difference between the missionary's standard of living and that of the missionized. Nor did it recognize that it may well be that the split personality that goes with conversion is inherent in the Christian life itself—something any convert who is born in a predominantly "Christian culture" may or may not experience as acutely as those born and bred in a predominantly "nonChristian culture."

Clearly recognized, however, was the fact that some native leaders were themselves a source of trouble in relation to the use of indigenous religious customs. For some of them opposed, just as some continue to do today, the adoption of some indigenous customs, for example, dowry, largely because of how they were trained in their youth.

A deeper look at Accra's theme in relation to primal religions indicated to the delegates that it was no longer useful to waste time debating the minor points of inter-religious encounter, knowing that there is no one answer that can satisfy everybody in an organization so wide and diverse as the Christian church. Past Conferences, it was believed, had laid down the broad path along which dialogue can proceed, for it was time for the missionary community to move on and look ahead to other more important challenges such as civil religions.

Another important development on this matter was the fact that some delegates, seeing what the war had done to Jewish people in part because of anti-Jewish teachings on the part of Christians, were particularly reluctant to condemn primal religion and its value system. The old chapter of widespread fear of syncretism came to an end, leaving behind those who refused to change. The new hour and dispensation required more tolerance far more than what Whitby explicitly required. It emphasized chewing bones, not drinking milk, ecumenical hope, not ecumenical despair. This brought a remarkable relief to the missionary movement, though the charge of its misrepresentation of primal religions, in the early days of the encounter with Africa, appears destined to remain for many years to come.

3. Indigenous churches at Accra

Accra, more than any other Conference, witnessed increased African pressure to reconsider past views on indigenous leadership and actual practice of the idea of mission as partnership. In this connection, and in view of the Ghanaian independence, Accra discussed the issue of power as it relates to foreign missionaries vis-a-vis indigenous colleagues.

Accra found that missiology must continue to grapple with this problem, in view of the fact that "today power is not in the missionary's hands,"[4] and that lack of power in some cases was leading to frustration or "lost directness" (Freytag) and uncertainty of the future due to political causes. Ironically, discussion established that this sense of missionary powerlessness has arisen in part out of a situation for which previous generations of missionaries and conferences had prayed.

Accra reaffirmed Willingen's insight concerning new forms of mission, particularly the exchange of personnel and the recruitment of lay persons—men and women—as propagators of the gospel. However, delegates also regretted that, "despite Willingen's clear statement of its new insights and concerns, few new forms of mission have as yet arisen from that stimulus."[5] Still, in spite of this past inaction, new recommendations were made.

Of these new recommendations, the establishment of the Theological Education Fund was the most interesting and novel suggestion. Designed for a more adequately trained and effective ministry in Asia, Africa, Latin America, Oceania, and other areas, the Fund was made possible by John D. Rockefeller and nine mission boards in America.[6] Unfortunately, although this Fund was a post-war development, Accra's understanding of how the Fund should be administered was based on a narrow definition of the ministry which gave too much importance to "theological scholarship." In so doing, it inadvertently helped to foster in African churches (particularly the so-called mission-related ones), an understanding of the ministry which, despite avowals to the contrary, tends to encourage clericalism, perpetuates colonial mentality, belittles nontheological studies, and looks at mundane activities as a preserve for the "devil."

4. Race relations at Accra

As in previous meetings, the same temper of reaffirmation was applied to race relations. Yet the Assembly was aware of the political significance of this gathering for the first time in African soil. Thus, before reaffirming the Evanston[7] statement on this matter, it was explicitly stated that a declaration must be made, because the IMC was meeting as an ecumenical body for the first time on African soil and in the country of Ghana. This declaration expressed happiness for past achievements and for Africa's emergence as a partner in ecumenical struggle against all forms of prejudice and injustice.

Clearly, this was a preemptive action to allay the apprehensions of critics, and it shows how ecumenical missions kept responding to African political realities such as this Ghanaian attainment of independence. Even so, it was a wise and timely move on the part of the Assembly. For, it showed the IMC's willingness to be flexible and adaptable on some issues including race relations, particularly "at this hour" of a new understanding of missions.

Accra looked forward to a time when the WCC/IMC Joint Committee will appoint a consultant to "help the churches to help one another more effectively in the field of racial and ethnic tensions."[8] This was an important decision because it represented a radical departure from the past and a willingness to commit the ecumenical movement financially, a commitment which later culminated in the formation of the WCC's Program to Combat Racism.

5. Cooperation and unity at Accra

The concern for unity for the sake of mission ran through much of the discussion at Accra. In view of the Assembly's theme and the reality of the world situation, there was no more reason to spend more time justifying the need for international missionary unity. All delegates had arrived, from different parts of the world, deeply conscious that past divisions must give way to a deeper and wider ecumenism in virtually all aspects of missionary work "at this hour" of a new dispensation.

Therefore, because of its mature approach to this question of unity, and the time it devoted to prayers, thanks to its ecclesiastical hosts (Ghanaian Christian Council), Accra can be described as a Conference of Prayer. For more time was spent on prayers for divine guidance in post-war missionary cooperation. This was a subtle but important change and development in ecumenical conferences, something which needed to be done more often throughout the years under survey. With this emphasis on prayer as an important basis of unity, it appeared that the Spirit had finally spoken in a modern ecumenical gathering just like the day of Pentecost in a strange and unexpected hour and place—Africa. It was a fitting occasion to watch. For at last, a continent, once thought to be wholly dark, became the *mountain top* where the transfiguration of ecumenism partly took place.

At the same time, Accra did not allow the emotion of meeting on the African soil for the first time to overshadow unitive questions; careful use of the fund of reason and thought was still considered inevitable. While references were made to comity issues in Africa and other regional areas, the focus of the discussion on unity was the "Draft Plan for Integration" of this Council and the WCC.[9] At Accra, no other issue was more hotly debated than this integration issue.[10] Opposition and support came from various regions. Latin American members feared that integration will result in the collapse of national Christian Councils, especially because such Christian Councils "have long included in their membership societies which have shown themselves unwilling to be associated with the WCC."[11]

Missionary workers in the Congo opposed it, because they wanted to preserve the little working unity that mission societies in that region were enjoying. Z. R. Mahabane, speaking for the black churches in South Africa, was "heart and soul in favour" of this integration idea. But that is not how Dr. Akanu Ibiam and the Christian Council of Nigeria saw the proposal. Ibiam was hesitant to vote yes, because the Nigerian Christian Council was "faced with great difficulties," particularly the fact that not all the missionary bodies in Nigeria were members of the Council. However, in the end the Assembly voted to accept in principle the integration idea.

A significant outcome of this integration debate was the acceptance of the fact that the regionalization and broadening of ecumenical structure is an ecumenical asset not a liability. Thus, Accra affirmed implicitly what, Aggrey and others at Atlantic City 1922, and Max Warren, CMS Secretary and a leading participant in this debate, had already said explicitly.[12]

One point is in order here. This embracement of nationalism as an ecumenical asset reflected in part the reality that the new and soon-to-be nations in Africa cannot be denied their quest for full independence even if it is only on paper. At the same time, it showed that even Africans were more willing to embrace nationalism more than Ethiopianism with all its transnational possibilities for an All-Africa ecumenical body. Indeed, progressively, as some of these natives became more conscious of themselves and were willing to pursue differing interests outside the control of the churches, very little was said about the Ethiopian Movement in this or any other Conference after Edinburgh. As to why this was the case, one can only speculate.[13]

6. Some individual contributions at Accra

At Accra, various African members made substantial thematic contributions. Among these, we must mention Prime Minister Nkrumah, Christian Baeta, now Chairman of the Ghanaian Christian Council[14] and Peter Dagadu, its Secretary. Others were, inter alia, Mrs. Annie Baeta-Jiagge of the Ghanaian Y.W.C.A., Z. R. Mahabane and Seth M. Mokitimi of South Africa, Daniel Lungwa of Tanganyika, and Akanu Ibiam of Nigeria.

Of these contributors two are noteworthy. Nkrumah's, "coming from one who spoke not as a member of the Assembly, but as the political leader of his country, [was] an unusually interesting comment on and illustration" of Accra's central subject, the Christian mission at this hour.[15] Offering something one would expect from a politician—the gospel of the soap box—and, in accordance with his political philosophy that the political kingdom must precede other things, Nkrumah asserted that the task for "young emergent Africa" was nation building. This task was to him equally missionary in character and obligation.

Nkrumah granted that the whole world must be the base for contemporary mission. Taking advantage of the presence of some international opinion makers and shakers of events, Nkrumah thought that Africa's need for missionaries was not over. Missionaries, he emphasized, were still needed in all phases of nation building. Although he knew that missionaries were limited in what they could deliver in this new era, Nkrumah wanted them to return home with an accurate, not distorted, picture of the new Africa.

All of you, Nkrumah continued, missionaries and nonmissionaries, have seen Africa in its bareness. You have seen its ambitions and hopes as written in the faces of its citizens who, so far, have received only the "crumbs of civilization falling from the rich tables" of the world. Post-colonial Africans, he added, are only at the beginning of their quest for statehood. For this reason, he brought out a shopping list which included mostly items which were in short supply throughout Africa: education, economic advancement, and financial capital for a head start, among others.

Looking back at his list, Nkrumah regretted that, unfortunately, the Great Powers, who could have helped to sufficiently prepare Africans for the new era, were busy pouring out their treasure, which included Africa's wealth, "on sterile arms." Thus the precious capital that could have helped to raise up Africa and Asia was being abused and misdirected. "What," he asked, "has this [militarism] to do with the Christian charity proclaimed by the west? Or the human brotherhood we hear so much about from the east?"[16] In light of Africa's needs and aspirations, Nkrumah saw this abuse of resources and the rivalry between capitalism and socialism as senseless.

Thus, for Nkrumah, "the Christian mission at this hour" called for a critique and transcendence of ideological divides, challenge to the military industrial complex, and a field in which "priest, pastor, educator and social worker must cooperate."[17] This brought relief to some in the meeting who, because of Nkrumah's previous political statements, had feared that he would seek to "embarrass" this Assembly by speaking of socialism as *the only* Christian mode of production, as if the Bible cannot be used to justify practically any preconceived economic system. Actually, his balanced view of both socialism and capitalism is now becoming widely acknowledged as more and more socialist states adopt some capitalist ideas, just as some capitalist states began, as far back as the 1930s, to adopt some socialist ideas.

The second noteworthy contribution was made by Akanu Ibiam under the title "The Witness of the Christian Layman in Nigeria." Ibiam was uniquely qualified to speak on lay leadership in church and state. Through his medical work in Uburu beginning in 1936 and principalship of a Presbyterian high school (Hope Waddell Training Institute) in Calabar, he became thoroughly involved in the Nigerian Christian Council activities and spread of Presbyterianism along and beyond the banks of the Cross River.[18] His complete immersion in the missionary movement, through the Calabar Mission Council, gave him special insight in interpreting developments within mission theology.

With the unchurched outnumbering the churched in Nigeria, in spite of the presence of all kinds of denominations, Ibiam believed that contemporary missiology must develop a theology of lay leadership in which all adults and children are taught their Christian responsibility "including evangelistic work." Yet this was nothing new but in fact a reemphasis of the oft-forgotten Protestant principle of the priesthood of all believers.

The missionary movement, Ibiam suggested, tended to forget that Christianity did not become the dominant religion in the Roman Empire simply because of the Augustines, the Tertullians, and the Cyprians. Commoners and lay people, he added, also acted as facilitators and carriers of the good news. Similarly, in Africa, Ibiam continued, the missionary movement must never forget how it managed to survive through the lean and dry years when the future of Christianity was on the line: heavy reliance on the laity.

Conscious of the slow process of recruiting and training new ministers, Ibiam believed that for many decades to come, the ecumenical movement in general and the African Church in particular will not be able to do without the contributions of the laity. In this sense, the "Christian mission at this hour" meant, as far as Ibiam was concerned, finding new ways to tap the varied and useful skills of lay Christians for the organization of missionary work.

Mission at this hour: action not rhetoric. Because of the dawning of the new era, Accra prepared its delegates, particularly nonAfricans, for what they were about to see and hear at the Ibadan Conference. Foremost in this preparation was the issuing of a statement. Interpretative and lamentative, this statement was also commended to the IMC constituency because it expressed "certain convictions which came home to those who shared in [the Accra Assembly] with great insistence or in a new form."[19] In it, the Christian mission at this hour was thought to include the discernment of God's action in history or "What is God's will in this situation?" not "How will this affect us?"[20]

The statement went on to admit that, although the new patterns of relationship demanded by the post-colonial age was not yet seen "with full clearness," two things were, doubtless, plain. One was the fact that the ecumenical movement knew exactly the immediate demands of the present age to which it was called. The other was the fact that the problem was no longer a theoretical one, but in fact a practical one. Or, as the statement concluded:

> In regard to the[se tasks], it is not knowledge that we lack; it is the will to do them. That, we believe, is why we still grope for fuller understanding of the nature and form of Christian mission in our day.[21]

Summary

Thus, Accra closed with the recognition that "the condition for receiving further [ecumenical] insight is to act upon what we have" and that "ideas are no substitute for decisions; the exchange of thought is no substitute for action in common obedience."[22] Accra felt that the credibility of the church was about to be fully restored, because the missionary movement has separated itself from any alliance with imperialism. Thus it was no longer necessary to see the Church as a Western phenomenon and missions as heralds of imperialism. The Church, Accra believed, was now physically and truly God's own family with its roots firmly planted in all corners of the inhabited globe far more than New York had hoped or could have imagined.

Accra was, then, the first IMC gathering to reflect more on what is shaping up as a significant finding of this study: the continuing gap between theory and action. There, again, no pre-1958 IMC gathering was as privileged as Accra to meet on African soil, propose concrete plans for the development of regionalism within the ecumenical movement, and most important, feel

happy to think that immediately after this Assembly there will be
held in Ibadan, Nigeria, an All Africa Christian Conference, at
which representatives of Christian Councils and churches from
every part of Africa will meet to consider their calling and their
task as followers of Jesus Christ.[23]

II. THE CHURCH IN CHANGING AFRICA: IBADAN 1958

When, then, on January 10, 1958, in a native African city, Ibadan, the long-awaited
first All-Africa Church Conference opened, two things were certain. First, the Conference was not a coincidence. It was a deliberate ecumenical design in which the
Christian Council of Nigeria took the initiative. Of this initiative, a participant
wrote:

> Some Christian Councils might have felt unable to accept an in-
> vitation from the IMC itself, but this difficulty was overcome by
> the magnanimity of the Christian Council of Nigeria, which
> thereby, in the words of a conference resolution, 'earned for it-
> self a proud place in the annals of the emergent Church in
> Africa.'[24]

Second, it was clear that, at last, Africa and the ecumenical movement stood at
the threshold of a new age. For one thing, following Accra, the Opening Address
and two of the Addresses of Welcome were made by indigenous leaders.[25] For
another thing, although physical circumstances had made it necessary to limit the
number of delegates to 200, a statistical breakdown of the meeting indicates that, by
all indices, Ibadan was a much more widely representative gathering of African
Christian leaders than had ever before come together for any purpose in Black
Africa.[26] Indeed, in view of the role that the Church has played in Africa, it was fitting that African ecclesiastical leaders should precede African political leaders in
holding, for the first time, a continent-wide, modern assembly on African soil.

Hence, of the actual attendance of 195, 96 African churches were represented;
74 were African men, 16 African women, and 6 Europeans represented the white
churches in South Africa. Of the missionaries from countries outside Africa 46 were
white, 1 black-American and 1 Asian. Racially, 96 were blacks, 92 whites, and 7
Asians.[27] Among well-known Christian leaders in attendance were W. A. Visser 't

Hooft of the WCC, John A. Mackay, President of Princeton Seminary and Chairman of the IMC, and Bishop Stephen Neill, Church of England. Among the African leaders, we must mention here some daughters of the soil. For, after many decades, the hope of many people, including James Aggrey and Mina Soga, was partially realized with this unusual number of African women in an ecumenical forum. These included Mrs. Yudith Chidosa (Tanzania), Mrs. A. S. Banjo (Nigeria), Mrs. Rebecca Mulira (Uganda), Dr. Irene Ighodaro (Nigeria), Mrs. Phyllis Mzaidume (South Africa), Mrs. Elsabet Karorssa (Ethiopia), Mrs. Esther L. Coker (Sierra Leone), and Miss Edith T. Hlatshwayo (South Africa).

The agenda at Ibadan was not substantially different from other Conferences. However, in view of the fact that more than two dozen African nations were on the verge of independence, discussions were characterized by an atmosphere hitherto lacking in conferences on Africa: deepest frankness and commitment to relating Christianity to the actualities of African life without fear of reprimand.[28]

1. Social conditions at Ibadan

On socio-economic questions, Ibadan advised churches to be aware of the systemic changes which were going on in different parts of Africa, particularly the steady movement from a wholly agricultural economy to a partially industrializing one. Instead of the churches heaping blame on people, as they seek to withstand and adjust to these changes, Ibadan said that the church must be the *avantgarde* of change, helping people to adjust in customs, consumption habits, manners and patterns of behavior.

Ibadan also took for granted that the issue of polygamy will not be immediately resolved. Thus, while Ibadan reaffirmed the monogamy ideal, it did not view any form of marriage as sin-free. Ibadan agreed that the Church should discourage clitoridectomy given its "unjust discrimination against the woman." This position was consistent with the idea that the status of African women "in the ministry of the church required urgent examination."[29] For past Conferences did not sufficiently settle the question; nor did they prescribe or define in exhaustive and specific terms what role women should play in the new Africa. Full emancipation of women, and, therefore, full emancipation of men, remained an ongoing task. This fact was brought to the Conference through a Consultation on "Men and Women in Africa Today" which preceded the Conference. This Consultation did not make any attempt to soft-pedal the shortcomings of the marriage institution in Africa. Indeed, the Conference, through this Consultation, decreed that the term *bride price* as often used in relation to marriage was unacceptable and should be replaced with the idea of *dowry* or "exhange of family gifts."

Ibadan devoted much attention to the theme of the Church and Citizenship,[30] showing the major concern of the delegates regarding how African Christians should conduct political affairs, in view of the fact that, in Kenya, for example, the Mau Mau Revolt was coming to an end. After hearing reports from churches in many different parts of Africa, it was affirmed that African Christians must take active part in national independent movements, and like past meetings, many saw nationalism as double-sided, positive and negative. African Christians were to seek the positive side, seeking self-respect and group integrity only in the context of internationalism as Aggrey understood it with authoritative comprehensiveness.

Unlike previous meetings, such as Westerville, which failed to mention the need for political freedom for dependent territories in Africa, Ibadan unequivocally called for "self-determination and self-government" for all African territories. This was an important decision because it helped to prepare the ground for the meeting of the Conference of Independent African States, a precursor of the Organization of African Unity. Moreover, it was an important contribution which Ibadan brought to the making of ecumenical mandates. For it showed that there are times when the Church, notwithstanding the cost, must abandon the safety of the politics of neutrality and throw itself wholeheartedly on the side of the oppressed, the voiceless, and the poor.

A statement pledged the churches to work for social justice and to relate prophetically, educationally, and pastorally to society. In view of the special circumstances that surrounded the emergence of new political institutions in Africa, Ibadan believed that Christian ministers may be thus called but they were to resign from their pastorates during the period of their political service.

2. Primal religions at Ibadan

The question of the contribution of African traditional culture and religion to Christianity came to Ibadan via the report of the groups which dealt with "The Church and Culture" and "The Church, Youth and the Family." Ibadan did not discover any exciting way to deal with this question; indeed, like other meetings, opinion was sharply divided, ranging from those who espoused a permissive approach to everything aboriginal to those who opposed anything traditional that tended to "pollute" Christianity.

Understandably, therefore, the final statement merely repeated the familiar call for a sympathetic spirit and evolutionary attitude toward many African religious customs. Yet one can discern that many native delegates were proud of the contribution which primal religions have made to them as African Christians. Thus, they were not willing to throw the baby away with the bathing water. Since this was the first conference opportunity many natives had to brainstorm on the issue, they were more willing to maintain the status quo than to implement a new policy which was not carefully devised. It was also indicative of the kind of caution and conservatism on this issue to which some African leaders have subscribed, following the expectation of their Western mentors and the social realities of post-war African life. Ironically, the same people who were largely liberal and unrestrained in political statements were not as liberal and open-minded on some native customs and religious values.

3. Indigenous churches at Ibadan

On the question of indigenous leadership, Ibadan focused on the appalling conditions African youths had found themselves. These young people were poised between "two civilizations [and] between two worlds, unable to see their place early and lacking any definite standards of life and thought."[31] The worse finding was that past evangelistic services to them had failed to be the antidote to their puberty crises and restlessness.

The missionary promise, made explicitly or implicitly over several decades, to turn African villages into miniature Paris or London, had not materialized; and for that generation of Africans who were brought up to await its realization (and groomed to be unrealistic in their expectations), maturity revealed that such a "paradise" was still too far away, if realizable at all. The "Kingdom" was at hand and yet still too far away and beyond reach. "Violently drawn into the political preoccupation of their age and country," these youths found no time for life in the Church; it was, to be sure, a bad omen for the future. Delegates viewed this exodus from the church as the result of youth inability "to discern how God speaks through Him who is the Way, the Truth and the Life to the political conflicts of Africa today."[32] However, they did nothing to substantially reduce the youths' high expectation of an imminent solution to Africa's social problems. All African Christian Councils were urged to set up a strong department for youth leadership and work.

Ibadan witnessed preliminary discussions on the consequences of unplanned devolution of ecclesiastical power from mission to church. Because some missions were still dragging their feet on this issue, while others were abandoning shift without adequate warning (in view of many missed opportunity in the past), Ibadan helped to prepare the ground for the moratorium debate in the 1970s, amid charges of continuing paternalism on the part of Western churches and mission agencies.

4. Race relations at Ibadan

A similar trend of thought dominated the discussion on race relations. In addition to reaffirming past statements on this question, Ibadan also resolved that "the land question in various countries of Africa is one of the greatest barriers to the achievement of racial peace."[33] Its anthropology rejected any social system which makes "color and ethnic origin" the sole determinant of life chances. It rejected all theories irrespective of their origins, including the Bible, that taught racial segregation and discrimination against nonwhite peoples.

However, because this meeting took place in West Africa, less time was spent on this issue than if the Conference had taken place in East or Southern Africa. Apparently, delegates felt that mere affirmation of past statements on the issue was all that the Conference could handle at the time, knowing that the emergent African Church will have its hands full as it grapples with the problem in subsequent years.

Provisional Committee for the AACC. Ibadan also based its view of race relations on the understanding that the Conference was only the beginning of the new platform for Africans to voice their rejection of all forms of social and racial injustice. For a resolution which laid the foundation for the formation of the AACC, through the appointment of a Provisional Committee, was unanimously passed.[34] Adopted on January 18, 1958, this resolution also expected the Committee "to give consideration to the implementation" of the Conference's report. Chosen to represent all the delegates, this ten-person Committee was a crucial achievement as well as an appropriate culmination of one phase or chapter of *missio Dei* in Africa.

By this act, Ibadan marked the critical turning-point which put the mission-related churches in Africa on the road to growing autonomy, several decades after the Independent African churches had made self-determination for the African Church a matter of time. Appropriately, the air was full of optimism and bouyant confidence, not unlike New York 1900, though for an entirely different reason: the perceived coming of age of the entire African Church.

5. Cooperation and unity at Ibadan

Within the general theme of "The Growing Church," Ibadan also tackled the issue of unity, the ordained and unordained ministry in church and society. Reports from churches in many African and nonAfrican lands brought a fascinating opportunity to learn about other parts of the continent and the world, thus laying the foundation for the emergence of the AACC. Many were thrilled to hear that the gospel had spread so widely in Africa and were equally challenged by the knowledge that many remained unevangelized and unchurched.

All recognized and accepted the new relationship of church and mission. However, discordant notes were heard regarding premature weaning of the churches which could not stand on their own. Arrangements were made to improve relations with, and witness to, Moslems in various parts of the sub-Sahara through a movable study center on Islam. This recommendation later materialized in a project called "Islam in Africa Project." A remarkable project, it brought to partial fruition Kumm's evangelistic concerns expressed at Edinburgh.

6. Some individual contributions at Ibadan

Ibadan featured many native African contributors who were mainly new faces on the ecumenical scene. Many of the old faces made presentations during the evening sessions designed for information and reports about ecumenical agencies and undertakings of current importance to African churches. Christian Baeta, now an official of the IMC, spoke on behalf of the Council regarding the IMC/WCC integration plan. He felt that African churches should continue to work, study, and pray for the plan so that whatever came out of the newly integrated body would not become "too rigid or . . . alienate some of the Protestant bodies at work in Africa."[35]

Peter Dagadu, the Ghanaian member of the WCC's Central Committee, defended the ideals of that organization and believed that it promised to be of ecumenical benefit to all churches. Dagadu suggested that the formation of the WCC will help to curtail parochialism and enable congregations to see the needs of their local church and country from a world perspective. Moreover, Dagadu thought that the WCC will enable people to see that the continuing task of the Church is determined by the "historic moment" in which the Church finds itself.

With presentations like these by native African leaders in support of the IMC and the WCC, the official duties assigned to George Carpenter (Secretary of the IMC) and W. A. Visser 't Hooft (General Secretary of the WCC) were made lighter as they, in their presentations, concentrated on other functions of their respective organizations. Each necessarily spoke on the realization of the missionary dream of seeing Africans take their rightful place in ecumenical organizations. Each was jubilant because of the great promise which the African Church represented as indicated by the willingness of the Christian Council in Nigeria to host the Conference.

Of the new faces, we must first mention the contributions of two women, South African Edith Thoko Hlatshwayo and Liberian Georgia S. Jones. Both developed the theme "Laywomen in Church and Society." While Miss Jones' was more descriptive, outlining the contribution of the Liberian Episcopal Women to the growth of the African Church, Miss Hlatshwayo's was largely interpretative.

A Welfare Officer in Johannesburg, Miss Hlatshwayo sought to contribute to the WCC statement on Cooperation of Men and Women in Church and Society. Reviewing the failure of the church to fully emancipate women, she posited that the ecumenical movement should "look anew at the Bible," understand why Jesus attached so much importance to women, and follow suit. She wondered whether the Church can be considered as alive when all the members are not given equal opportunity to contribute to the building of the "fullest kind of partnership." She added that each group in the Church (young and old, men and women, rich and poor, literate and illiterate) should have its "rightful place."

However, Miss Hlatshwayo did not indicate what she meant by "rightful place," given that such a phrase has been used several times in the history of the church to defend the status quo as a divine right of which women themselves have borne the brunt of the conservatism and abuse. In conclusion, she advised the movement to learn from Augustine, Bishop of Hippo in ancient North Africa who said: "'If at all I am thy child, O God, it is because of the mother you gave me.'"[36]

Dr. Irene Ighodaro's contribution was particularly interesting because she dealt with the problem of polygamy. As a modern medical practitioner she naturally rejected traditional arguments for plural marriages. It was her belief that the Church should concentrate more on educating men and women rather than issuing prohibitions which only encouraged people to become polygamous, since they believed that the more they sinned the more God's grace was available for them.

Dr. Ighodaro also argued that some women were slow to want education and that those who were educated were so far not accepting their full responsibilities either as wives and mothers or as professionals or business women in the new Africa. Yet she knew that many women had innate spiritual and intellectual abilities second to none, and that they have a far more active role to play in order that polygamy as a form of marriage can be abandoned. She realized that the wounds of the African family are deep and that the ones caused by plural marriages will remain unhealed for many years to come.

Many African men—and equally "new faces" in the ecumenical scene—delivered excellent papers some of which are still very relevant today. For example, Henry Makulu, Assistant Editor, Africa Sunday School Curriculum, delivered the paper on "Industrialization and the Church." Philippe Seppo of the Camerouns spoke on "The Church and Citizenship." The Archdeacon and Treasurer, Anglican Church in Uganda, the Rev. Disani K. Mukasa, spoke on "The Growing Church: Give an

Account of Thy Stewardship." J. H. Nketia, a Ghanaian sociologist, spoke on "The Contribution of African Culture To Christian Worship."[37]

Summary

Ibadan was a special and climactic gathering; and its members were conscious of this fact. For this reason, they issued a Message which stressed the special significance of the meeting for Africa and world Christianity, and asked that it be read as widely as possible throughout African churches. This reading was to take place on Easter Sunday, 1958, symbolizing that Christ's resurrection was not only a past event, but also a continuing one of which the rise of African ecumenical initiative was an example *par excellence*.[38]

An adopted-African, while conceding that it will be years before one can know, even partially, the full meaning of this Conference to Africans and nonAfricans alike, dared "to believe that it will be in the category of 'Edinburgh 1910.'"[39] Whether one should go that far to put both Edinburgh and Ibadan in the same category is a different question.

Nevertheless, it is also self-evident that, at Ibadan, thanks to both externally and internally generated forces, indigenous Africans presented their ecumenical credentials, and had a chance to demonstrate their capability in a new political atmosphere more than they did in any previous Conference.

These African leaders also announced that they were no longer *objects* of, but interested *participants* in, missions. In so doing, they helped to put ecumenical development and partnership in a fundamentally new key. In this, one can see the contrast between the turn of the century and the middle of the century, New York 1900, and Ibadan 1958.

George W. Carpenter who, as the IMC Secretary, was in a better position to see what Ibadan had achieved believed that the remarkable feature of the Conference was the fact that, for the first time, in the history of modern ecumenism, "the African Church found its voice." While in the past Africa's spokespersons were largely foreign missionaries, here at Ibadan foreign missionaries were politely urged to keep quiet and to watch how the new fact of our time was unfolding before their very eyes. In Carpenter's penetrative and graphic words:

> It was most heartening to see the African churchmen and churchwomen themselves come forward one after the other, speaking capably, confidently and effectively; and to watch the growing sense of personal responsibility, initiative and commitment with which they dealt with the issues before them.[40]

Suitably, the last word was spoken by indigenous Africans themselves who testified that Ibadan was a fitting climax to colonial ecumenism[41] and "the greatest chapter in the history of Africa, to be added to the Acts of the Apostles."[42] Whether they were right or wrong remains to be seen. For the AACC, the most visible symbol of Ibadan's achievements, is still in many ways experiencing puberty crisis. But that Ibadan symbolized the end to colonial ecumenism, as far as contemporary Black Africa is concerned, cannot be denied. Similarly, there is no gainsaying that it was an important step toward full African participation in the ecumenical movement.

To criticize its lack of significant theoretical breakthroughs on all issues would be to miss the point about Ibadan. Ibadan was not called to radically change nearly six decades of ecumenical mission mandates; instead, it was called to announce the beginning of a new ecumenical era in Africa—and the world.

Understandably, therefore, the more Ibadan recedes in time the more it grows in stature. It remains for us to reflect on this Africa's ecumenical journey and transition by way of concluding observations.

NOTES

[1] Of the close connection between Accra and Ibadan, the IMC secretary for the New York Office wrote that, in evaluating Accra, one must take Ibadan into consideration because fully one-third of the delegates to each conference took part in both. *The Church in Changing Africa: Report of the All-Africa Church Conference* (New York: IMC, [1958]), p. 5; hereafter cited as *The Church in Changing Africa*. For more on Ibadan 1958, see the last section in this chapter.

[2] *Minutes of the Assembly of the International Missionary Council, Ghana, December 28th, 1957 to January 8th, 1958* (New York: IMC, 1958), p. 5; hereafter cited as *Minutes of Ghana Meeting*.

[3] Ibid., pp. 22, 95.

[4] Ibid., p. 96.

[5] Ronald K. Orchard, ed., *The Ghana Assembly of the International Missionary Council 28th December, 1957 to 8th January, 1958: Selected Papers, with an Essay on the Role of the I.M.C.* (London: IMC, 1958), p. 154; hereafter cited as *Ghana Assembly Papers*.

[6] Note that appeals were made to the Fund's benefactors after a survey of Africa was made. See Stephen Neill, *Survey of the Training of the Ministry in Africa* (London: IMC, 1950).

[7] Evanston's statement on race relations said, inter alia, that "all churches and Christians are involved, whether they recognize it or not, in the racial and ethnic tensions of the world." This underscored past resolutions on the subject. Peter Dagadu, General Secretary of the Christian Council of the Gold Coast, gave a speech that in many ways indicated a change in African concerns. About this speech it was remarked that "no one who heard him could feel immune from the dynamic indignation and sense of the sacred he brought to the Assembly from his native continent" (David Gaines). For this speech, see *The Evanston Report: The Second Assembly of the World Council of Churches, 1954* (New York: Harper, 1955), p. 37–38. For the statement on race relations, see the same Report, pp. 151–160. For another angle on Dagadu's address, see David P. Gaines, *The World Council of Churches: A Study of Its Background and History* (Peterborough, NH: Richard R. Smith, 1966), pp. 740–743.

[8] *Minutes of Ghana Meeting*, pp. 39–40.

[9] See Ernest A. Payne and David G. Moses, *Why Integration? An explanation of the proposal before the WCC and the IMC* (London: Edinburgh House Press for the Joint Committee of the WCC and the IMC, 1957), p. 31.

[10]Another point of debate was the structure and function of the newly created Theological Education Fund. But it is evident that no other point required more sessions than integration. *Minutes of Ghana Meeting*, pp. 6, 20-21, 29-30, 35, 39, 85-88. Appended to the minutes is a separate report of the integration discussion, pp. 123-157.

[11]Payne and Moses, *Why Integration?*, p. 26.

[12]Max Warren, "Nationalism as an International Asset," *IRM* (1955): 385-93.

[13]One should not be surprised with this development because, once the Independent Church Movement was pushed out of the control of the missionary community, Ethiopianism went with it, though, there also, it began to wane somewhat as these churches became institutionalized and division became partly a way of life. Pan-Africanism or the idea of the United States of Africa was still alive, though it too began to wane after Ghana's independence.

[14]Baeta was chosen as one of the vice-chairpersons and other Africans were appointed members of various Committees of the Council. *Minutes of Ghana Meeting*, pp. 13, 105-109.

[15]*Ghana Assembly Papers*, p. 13.

[16]Ibid., p. 150; "A Speech by Dr. Kwame Nkrumah, Prime Minister of Ghana: delivered at a Garden Party to Members of the Assembly of the IMC and Others."

[17]Ibid., p. 149.

[18]Ibiam was at Accra as a non-member Council observer. He was later the Governor of Eastern Nigeria, the Provisional and first President of the AACC, and the first African appointed a President of the WCC. See also note 25 below.

[19]*Minutes of Ghana Meeting*, p. 89.

[20]Ibid., p. 90.

[21]Ibid.

[22]In contrast with the past, especially the Conferences of the 1920s, one can say, following W. Freytag of Germany: "Then missions had problems, but they were not a problem themselves." At Accra, the question was action in a radically new situation. Ibid., p. 138.

[23]*Minutes of Ghana Meeting*, p. 113.

[24]L. B. Greaves, "The All Africa Church Conference: Ibadan, Nigeria: 10th to 20th January, 1958," *IRM* (July 1958): 257.

[25]The opening address was made by Akanu Ibiam, while the Addresses of Welcome were presented by a representative of the old order in Nigeria, Oba Akinyele, the *Oluadan* of Ibadan, and two representatives of the new order, Chief Obafemi Awolowo and Sir John Rankine, Prime Minister and Governor of Western Nigeria respectively. *The Church in Changing Africa*, pp. 9-14.

[26]It should be noted that in 1955 there was an All-Africa Lutheran Conference on the slopes of Mount Kilimanjaro. See Paul D. Fueter, "The All-Africa Lutheran Conference Marangu 1955," *IRM* (July 1956): 289-96. It can also be said, because of this initiative, that the Lutheran Church occupies a special place in the annals of ecumenism in Africa.

[27]The IMC staff were very pleased with this statistical distribution of representatives. Secretary George Carpenter wrote "thus the attendance conformed very closely to the original intention that it should be one-half African church representatives, one-fourth missionaries, and one-fourth others." *The Church in Changing Africa,* p. 6. For a similar enthusiastic African appreciation of this development, see Donald G. S. M'Timkulu, "All Africa Church Conference," *IRM* (1962): 63–66.

[28]The IMC survey of the years 1947–1958 reflects numerous political activities which served as the backdrop to Ibadan. See, for example, Margaret Sinclair, "Survey of the Year 1956," *IRM* (January 1956): 3-85.

[29]*The Church in Changing Africa*, p. 30; see also, Betty Hares, "Men and Women in Africa Today: A Consultation (Ibadan, Nigeria, January 1958)," *IRM* (1958): 306–311.

[30]*The Church in Changing Africa*, p. 89; "Reports From Churches In Many Lands." The idea of Church and Citizenship was a cautious and perhaps more accurate phrasing of the original "The Church and Politics." See also the section "Africa" in Margaret Sinclair, "A Survey Of The Year 1957," *IRM* (January 1958): 3–83.

[31]*The Church in Changing Africa*, p. 58.

[32]Ibid.

[33]Ibid., p. 46.

[34]See Donald G. S. M'Timkulu, p. 63f. M'Timkulu was later named the first AACC secretary; cf. D. T. Niles, "The All Africa Conference of Churches," *IRM* (1963): 409–413.

[35]*The Church in Changing Africa*, p. 97.

[36]Ibid.

[37]Notice also that there were many other "new faces" than we have mentioned here. Nketia's paper was later published in *IRM* (July 1958): 265–78.

[38]See appendix 4 for the whole Message. Notice in the Message, the phrase regarding the Christ who arose and "lives today in Ibadan." Notice also that, while the Message, in this final form, concludes "We declare ourselves to be in Christ," in an earlier draft the "we" was prefaced with an explanatory phrase: "whether black or white, whether educated or illiterate, whether so-called civilized, whether in-

digenous African or adopted African." For an extensive comment on the making of this message, See Greaves, pp. 260–262.

[39]*The Church in Changing Africa*, p. 7.

[40]Ibid.

[41]A South African participant, the Rev. Canon A. H. Zulu, St. Faith's Mission, Durban, thought that, because of several reasons, it was good for such a Conference to take place in West Africa and not in South Africa. One reason was the fact that Ibadan allowed the issues to be met with realism. Another reason was the fact that West African peoples had privileges and responsibilities in their countries. The third reason was the fact that it brought shame to the apartheid system, given that Ibadan featured "Africans doing jobs which carry responsibilities to which [indigenous Africans] may not aspire in South Africa." A. H. Zulu, "The South African Church in the Light of 'Ibadan, 1958,'" *IRM* (1958): 377–378.

[42]Greaves, p. 264. See also Ibiam's statement concerning the Conference to a meeting of the East Asia Christian Conference (EACC), now Christian Conference of Asia, at Kuala Lumpur in 1959 in U. Kyaw Than, ed., *Witnesses Together: Being the official report of the Inaugural Assembly of the EACC, held at Kuala Lumpur, Malaya, May 14–24, 1959* (Rangoon: EACC, 1959), p. 145.

SOME CONCLUDING OBSERVATIONS

Evidently, the construction of ecumenical mission mandates did not evolve without African building blocks. The evidence for this, as the text has shown, is secure and needs no further elaborate exegesis to establish it. Indeed, what we have presented here is only a tip of the iceberg. Several documents exist to indicate that in many aspects of the making of these mandates, African questions had much more to do with them than has been covered in the present study.

As we journeyed through the various Conferences, certain points emerged, however, regarding our principal themes, which must be stressed and brought together to give the entire analysis some theoretical and constructive coherence. This is done without pretending to be exhaustive or giving equal weight—and space—to all the recurring themes. Also, it must be remembered that each theme met and reinforced each other; and that the issues, events, and actors (both African and non-African, named and unnamed) which we have described were in a dynamic state, constantly shifting and changing like any active volcano.

1. Social conditions

On the impact of African social conditions on mission thinking and doing, we have seen how Christian missions moved from an easy-going attitude to a preoccupation with them. When Protestant missions began in Africa, the establishment of schools and hospitals, etc., was seen as philanthropic and a means to an end: soul-winning.

This was to be expected, given the fact that, at home, churches had not yet come to grips with the ethical problems brought about by the Industrial Revolution. This is not to deny that there were isolated reforms, and that there were foundations of many charitable organizations prior to missionary encounter with Africa. But on this socio-economic front, collective Christian witness in Europe or in America was not impressive. Indeed, in England, for example, Benthamism and labor militancy impacted social conditions more than the influence of the Churches; and in America the mainline Churches seemed, for the most part, to have lost their collective prophetic role as they continued to see their nation as the New Israel but failed to denounce the exploitation of women and black people as vigorously as was necessary, until those groups initiated the struggle for their liberation.

Encounter with African conditions helped to reorient the Protestant social conscience and, with this reorientation, came the need for liberalism and united action in the social sphere. To say that here missions were reactors rather than actors is not an exaggeration. For, as the text shows, the missionary community, being by nature conservative, embraced social Christianity reluctantly, and only after, among other things, African laborers began to organize and protest through their labor movement.

It is not surprising that when, at Jerusalem, the Department of Social and Industrial Research was established, "the biggest success" of this Department was the study on Africa and industrialism. However, this success was tempered by the fact that it was used to placate the foes of the department who, unable to prevent its founding, succeeded through the budgeting process and other delaying tactics to limit its effectiveness.

Without ignoring the exceptional social work which some individual missionaries performed, the text shows that the IMC, as a corporate body and, unlike the Life and Work Movement, initially lacked full commitment to social Christianity. Thus, it is significant that the IMC began in part to gradually embrace some social Christianity only as it became clear that African conditions, among other things, would have it no other way.

The shift in perspective which began in New York and culminated in Edinburgh paved the way for such gradual but steady embracement of this holistic approach to missions. But one must not underestimate the impact of the African insistence on the sociological manifestation of Christianity. Being largely a practical people and motivated by conflicting and mixed impulses (admittedly, some self-serving and others altruistic), many native people wanted to hear and see more of the social teaching of Jesus. For, like in other cultures, they knew in their lives that it is more important to give priority to practical social matters than to waste precious time on esoteric issues such as the hereafter.

This is why ecumenical emphasis on social Christianity became a fait accompli by the time the Education Commissions made their Reports public. From Atlantic City through High Leigh and Hartford, the dominating idea vis-a-vis social conditions was that the time had come for "the gospel of education" and, therefore, more, not less, social Christianity.

The willingness to *redefine* Christian understanding of education and industry, the rise of the educated class, the struggle to explicate the role of the indigenous church in social matters, the understanding that Christianity cannot be planted in Africa without modern roads and hospitals, trade and modern agriculture, combined to make it extremely impossible to completely return to nineteenth-century missionary practice vis-a-vis social conditions.

Each Conference shows in its own way the drastic changes which was going on in the economic sphere, especially the emergence of new forms of industries, varied employment opportunities, new paths for social mobility, and, of course, new and more pronounced forms of social inequality. Each also reflects the cumulative effect of the emergence of a new social structure with its effect on living conditions, new relationship between myth and reality, community and individuals, men and women, parents and children.

Whether the IMC was right or wrong to buy this predominantly social attitude to Christianity on the part of Africans is questionable. The point is that African social conditions helped to bring about a discernible change in missionary understanding of mission. If, after the Le Zoute Conference, there remained any lingering doubts as to the importance of this approach, the Jerusalem and Madras Conferences made it abundantly clear that the genie of social and economic revolution was already out of the bottle, and, therefore, uncontrollable; and that Christianity must come to terms with this reality, and the fact that human beings, including Africans, were consistently marching towards a new world order.

2. Primal religions

The presence and persistence of primal religions have certainly helped to change old missionary attitudes toward nonChristian religions. Prior to these ecumenical Conferences, one heard little about the forces and relationships in African society which Christianity had to master and make to serve its own ends. Conversely, one heard practically nothing about the relatively successful attempt primal religionists made to master Christianity and make it to serve their own ends.

While, throughout our survey, we have seen arguments for and against an all-out effort to baptize all aboriginal values into Christianity, it is indisputable that, progressively through these conferences, the *tabula rasa* image of Africa was modified, if not completely abandoned. Thus, at Le Zoute more than Edinburgh, Jerusalem more than Madras, Ibadan more than Whitby, churchmen and churchwomen came to consciousness of what had remained unconscious for too long, namely, that in modern Africa, just as in ancient Britain, Germany, and other European nations including Russia, Christianity and primal religion borrowed heavily from each other especially in the early years.

Consider, for example, the impact of Druidism and German and Scandinavian primal religions on Christianity, before and during, the so-called Dark Ages (A.D. 500-1000), and even contemporary Western myths and legends, e.g. the origin of Christmas. Not to mention the prehistoric monoliths (Stonehenge) on Salisbury Plain, England, now a good tourist attraction and focus of anthropological and religious speculation. Time and again, the Conferences show that primal religious values acted as uncompensated allies to Christian values just as it happened in the Roman Empire and in Europe, even when the English evangelized the Germans, and Celtic Christians took some of the fire and brimstone of their *peregrini* tradition to degenerate French Christianity in the seventh and eight centuries.

To be sure, for Christianity, as the novel religion in Black Africa, learning and borrowing from many quarters was the rule rather than the exception. To be candid, it would be impossible to imagine Christianity existing amid all the wealth and vigor of primal religion, had Christianity not drawn pith and flavor even from its host (primal religion). This native religion, as the Conferences brought to light, is by no means less superstitious in character than bygone European and Mediterranean religions, but it fertilized the African soil for Christianity, and the new grain and seed which fell upon it benefited from that manure, sent down its roots, and grew to be a mighty tree. And, like all mighty trees, it did not constitute a forest by itself. Certainly, statistically, it is outgrowing the other trees in some areas, but it is also dependent on them for its own organic growth.

In this regard, encountering this religion with its tolerance and unitive capacity has been both a boon and a bane to Christianity. On the one hand, it has helped to remind Christian people that Christianity's tension between the so-called scandal of particularity and universality is a life-long tension and, therefore, unlikely simply to go away. On the other hand, it has helped to show that the success of the Church in Africa hinges, not on denying the challenge of other religions, but in its bipolar, dialectical approach to them—repudiating as well as simultaneously courting and embracing them. Religion, unlike humans, Christian or nonChristian, cannot pretend to exist in a sterilized form.

One must not minimize the fact that the World Wars and the rise of totalitarian regimes and secular ideologies, from within Christianity's heartland itself, made significant contribution to the emergence of this positive attitude towards indigenous African culture and religion. But it is also salient that, before the first of these Wars, Edinburgh inaugurated a new mentality and temper which made possible the affirmation, in later Conferences, of Christianity's benefit from the hallmarks of the primordial—communal solidarity, collective consciousness, unitive and open-ended propensity. What Edinburgh started vis-a-vis primal religion was completed at Oxford—and more so in later Conferences—when it became clear that Protestantism must protect indigenous religion in part as a camouflage for its own freedom of expression and growth in Black Africa.

Seen from the perspective that African missions began with some arrogance concerning the "reasonableness" of Christianity and, therefore, the supposed "unreasonableness" of what was mistakenly called "animistic" religions, this affirmation of the primordial stands out as a veritable African gift to ecumenical imagination. More than this, the study has shown that Christian people are not different after all from primal religionists, as far as humanity and the quest for symbols of social integration are concerned.

One then should not be surprised that, after passing through the crucible of learning, Christian mission mandates today reflect more of the mentality, not of swallowing up every and any irritant, but of recognizing and appreciating them. Therefore, except for psychological reasons—the restoration of some sense of personhood and self-esteem to the African—there seems, therefore, no reason to claim, as some have done, that this African gift to Christianity must precede in importance the missionary factor. Obviously, no people, nation, or church, for that matter, can afford to live with a low, let alone negative, self-image.

However, while it is understandable and instinctually natural that African scholarship would like to pay back, with the same coin, the debt it owes Western scholarship, there is no need for reverse arrogance. Actually, the "African factor" and the "missionary factor" (or, as Sanneh calls them, "software" and "hardware," respectively) belong and have always belonged together. Against this attempt to overemphasize one at the expense of the other, we insist that, although "hardware" and "software" are distinguishable, they are inseparable. Without one the other is rendered practically useless and vice versa, and neither must be allowed to become an end in itself. Religions are perhaps far more identical and interdependent in basic tenets and aspirations than some humans are willingly to concede.

In all this, what strikes one as incredible is the fact that missionaries, from the beginning, largely ignored the history of missions in Western nations. Except for sheer humanity and socialization, how do we explain why those who were supposedly "enlightened" and "civilized" could not tolerate anything that did not conform to their mind-set?

There is no question that the charge of highhandedness on the part of some missionaries (especially in the early days of the encounter) could have been prevented if they had been more tolerant of African culture from the outset of the enterprise; though, admittedly, they brought to Africa the same evangelistic method which was used during the Christianization of Europe and even America: a combination of violence, coercion, education, threat, outright warfare, and occasional tolerance.

This raises an interesting theoretical problem, namely, whether or not cross-cultural evangelism of a new and any territory is possible without using this familiar carrot-and-stick approach. In Africa, it does not appear that Christianity would have succeeded without this approach or the familiar *Bible and the Plow* method reflected throughout the conference discussions. Certainly, many African primal religionists lacked modern education and were, therefore, easily attracted to Christianity because of its appurtenances and particularly the power and prestige associated with reading and writing.

In this, too, African reaction was not unique, because throughout Christianity's long history various other preindustrialized peoples have reacted almost in identical manner. The major difference in Africa was the color factor which succeeded to cast a strong spell over the future of the enterprise in Africa. To say that Africans reacted purely out of religious reasons would be an oversimplication of a complicated situation; and would reinforce the current myth surrounding African religiosity as if it is unique instead of a common attribute of preindustrial or industrializing societies.

Clearly, for ecumenism to rise, having a literate culture and all the other tangibles was not enough. Men and women had to encounter other cultures, other peoples, other religions, and, indeed, what Lesslie Newbigin has called other "fiduciary frameworks." In this sense, it is understandable why these Conferences were ecumenical training grounds for the missionary, the nonmissionary, and the African; and it is prudent to conclude that the rise of modern sociology and anthropology helped the missionary movement to see the enduring values in primal religion and to become, beginning at Lake Mohonk and more so at Oxford, its partial promoter rather than its destroyer.

3. Indigenous churches

The same understanding is applicable to church-mission relations. The rise of these indigenous churches, whether independent of, or affiliated with, Western missions, helped to make Christian men and women reflect more seriously on power questions and to realize that even Christians must not take them for granted.

In the nineteenth century, it was largely assumed that in order for the African "younger churches" to be authentic members of "Christendom" they would have to "dress," "think," and "behave" like their Western parents. As these indigenous churches emerged and sought the *rites de passage* from puberty to adolescence, they also helped to make the distinction between older and younger churches theoretically superfluous and anachronistic, a fact acknowledged at both Whitby and Willingen.

Their search for new patterns of mature relations and partnership challenged and rejected established ideas and made for ecumenical consciousness. Their swift, shocking, and persistent demand for recognition helped to initiate a gradual process through which the idea of pluralism in the ecumenical movement became accepted.

Accordingly, the largely "asset" view of the alliance between missions and colonial governments came to be seen as equally a liability and debilitation.

The numerous Conferences held between 1921 and 1925 evidenced unprecedented missionary moves to enlist the help of as many "moderate" native leaders as possible. Interestingly, these Conferences took place against the backdrop of increased pressure from the Pan-African movement and the rise and spread of Independent Churches such as the Kimbanguist Church in Zaire, and the Prophet Harris Movement as well as the Garrick Movement in West Africa.

The role played by the Education Commissions is also noteworthy. Their Reports must be seen as the dividing line between the period of opening up new frontiers and mission stations (with its emphasis on quantity of converts) and the period of consolidation (with its emphasis on quality of converts). They helped the IMC and its constituency to see mission as a two-way street, to appreciate the fact that industrial culture can learn from preindustrial or industrializing culture, and to continue to move away from ignorance and parochialism to cautious respect and understanding of Africa.

The rise of these indigenous churches fostered ecumenism and brought African writers and interpreters of the continent to the fore. These Africans, gradually, became vocal and strident. They made clear their desire to be part of a *new order*, not just to make small gains in the *old order*. Their quest for *self-identity*, not merely for *recognition*, helped to arouse the movement to look more favorably at pluralism within the ecumenical body. Their steady growth in spirituality and the important doctrines associated with Christianity helped the ecumenical movement to find a hospitable home in Black Africa.

The picture which emerges of the masses is as significant as the role played by educated African and foreign missionary agents. Insurmountable in courage, and indomitable in spirit, they showed acts of kindness to many missionaries, provided local idioms to Bible translators, and served as hewers of wood and drawers of water to many missionaries and administrators, services which compel us to see them as they were: true *douloi*, slaves or servants, of God. Certainly these were indispensable services some of which were done despite economic deprivation, inadequate social and economic rewards, and little or no appreciation of their importance. Yet, together, they helped to bring Christianity down to the level of the peasants and commoners, a fact acknowledged at several Conferences especially after Jerusalem. With these services (often taken for granted like the services of many housewives and powerless people throughout the world), these unsung Africans helped to remind the movement that in God's economy every contribution is significant and appreciated. To be sure, they were and are, indeed, the backbone of ecumenism and the threads of church planting in Africa and elsewhere.

In the beginning Protestantism treated the masses as if they were stupid, lazy, and dependent. After more experience and particularly the publication of the Reports of the Education Commissions, it became evident that what was actually wrong was not the people themselves, but *how* the message was presented to them. By tapping their local experience and building on their preindustrial skills, Protestantism was helped to blossom, though not like the Roman Church which had won the masses over to its side at a quicker pace. To be sure, although many of them remain nameless in historical records, they are not nameless in local history and knowledge; their names may elude contemporary historians, but they will never elude the final roll call of *missio Dei*. If contemporary ecumenical movement cannot erect tall monuments to keep alive the masses' contribution to the planting of the church in Black Africa, contemporary missiology must pay this debt at least by constantly acknowledging what it has learned over the years from this unlikely source: the underside of history—the university of the African masses.

If today it is difficult for this generation to think of ecumenical gathering without representation from diverse groups and "clans," it must be remembered that it was not always that way. Concrete plans, as we have seen, provided native Africans the educational, social, and theological skills (needed to participate in ecumenical forums), brought several African and nonAfrican church leaders together, canonized friendship and prepared the way for contemporary, post-colonial evangelism.

In short, the idea of freedom and self-identity in a pluralistic ecumenical movement, which is gaining ascendancy today, did not begin *ex nihilo*. African and non-African problems, individuals and churches, struggled together in these Conferences to bring this idea about.

4. Race relations

On the race question, clearly, a drastic change is discernible. But evidence does not support attributing this change simply and solely to missionary goodwill and foresight. Evidence is overwhelming that, at the beginning, missionaries were no more insightful than the average of European scholars who misappropriated Enlightenment principles and misused Darwin's *Origin of the Species* to popularize one race theory after another, thus setting the stage for decades of negative image of Africa that is still with us, though in varying forms and degrees.

It is evident that, if some missionaries are to be faulted, it must be because, at the beginning, they painted an unrealistic picture of Christianity, claiming that it was predominantly above culture. The fact is that Western Christianity had no separate linguistic and cultural system programmed to prevent racial prejudice. Nor did any other forms of Christianity.

Humanly speaking, one can understand why, when some Western people looked around and saw that their nations were the ones leading in modern economic and scientific achievements, even though they borrowed a lot from the Islamic civilization of antiquity, organized systematic discrimination and prejudice set in. Contrast that Western mood with the modern one brought about by the rise of the Japanese economic empire, the rise of new forms of civil religion among Islamic peoples, or the self-assertion of political power by African nations whether real or perceived.

Although this discussion focused on Africa, it is important to bear in mind that the subject of racial relations was not limited to whites and blacks, though, certainly, this was and still is a major concern. The fact is that the English, for example, were not too fond of the Germans. Nor did the Germans fail to see the French as a fair game. Not to mention the whole rivalry between the so-called Catholic and Protestant nations or the maltreatment of Jews throughout the history of the church.

It is true that, by becoming overly concerned about black and white relations, the tendency in the literature is to give European peoples a superficial unity even when we know that the World Wars were not fought because of black and white problem and, certainly, the superpower struggle today has little or nothing to do with skin color, in spite of South Africa.

The evidence is also against giving Conference resolutions on this matter, and studies done either before or after 1900 more credit than they deserve, for bringing about the change in racial attitudes and prejudices. Instead, great importance is to be attached to educative opportunities (such as the Conferences we have examined), in which Africans and nonAfricans came into face to face, interpersonal contact on a continuing basis. The presence at these meetings of James Aggrey, Mina Soga, John Hope, Max Yergan, Z. R. Mahabane, John Dube, Robert Baeta and numerous others, certainly spoke louder than words. In this sense, their tangible contributions were as important as the intangible ones.

Credit must also be given to the Education Commissions which were very useful in tearing down prejudices. They diagnosed that, far and above, the external manifestations or symptoms of racial conflict (in East and South Africa in particular) was the great question of how people of industrialized culture, with inherited tendencies and aspirations of their civilization, imbued with modern ideas of economic progress, could have opportunity for full development and find satisfaction in their lives alongside another people, far outnumbering them and just emerging from the pastoral stage, and who, for the most part, could not even understand the ideals and aims of the other.

It is ironic, but not surprising, in view of modern educational opportunities, that black Americans took the lead before native Africans. Appearing sometimes in the deliberate guise of the Old Testament prophets, their contributions were not academic; they brought the experience of the "oppressed" into ecumenical forum. With this, it is clear that predominantly black American churches have been interested in unitive Protestantism as far back as the origin of the movement itself. This testifies to their sincerity and devotion to the missionary enterprise.

Black Americans, joined in time by educated Africans, showed in person that individuals largely embody the mental and moral culture of the social formation in which they are raised, and that this social fact and divine grace must be taken into consideration in any evaluation and comparison of individuals and civilizations. For, as some Conferences such as Jerusalem recognized, a mathematical genius or "ecumenical genius," for that matter, cannot appear without a background of a fairly well-developed intellectual society and ecumenical world.

While it is difficult, for the purposes of historical analysis, to assess the precise effect an open-policy toward black American missionaries in Africa would have had, it is regrettable that white missionary societies were slow to catch up with black American ecumenical aspirations throughout these years. Certainly, while changes had occurred over time in how resolutions on the matter were crafted, the real political reason which was to keep black Americans, as much as possible, away from Africa, only began to change during the second world war.

This is one aspect of its history the ecumenical movement cannot be proud about. For, in spite of at least two resolutions, mission policies were dictated more by government attitudes than by the attitude of Christ in terms of self-emptying or sacrificing oneself for the other.

For this reason, black American mission societies deserve special commendation. This is not because all black American Churches enthusiastically supported African missions as they should have done, but because the AME, for example, helped to produce the first set of African ecumenical leaders, such as James Aggrey, by providing him with a rare opportunity for advancing his education, at a time, when most missions did not think that Africans were fit for higher education.

It is also clear that, without these early pioneers and the IMC's involvement, the story of racial conflict in East and South Africa would have been far more tragic than it is today. Indeed, there exists a relationship between increased black higher education, consciousness-raising, and determination to forge better social relations in that part of the continent, just as it was and is in America.

By standing firm and protesting against layers and layers of social, economic, and religious dividing walls, these Africans, and their Western supporters, helped to reveal to Western peoples the higher side of the African heritage of tolerance. In so doing, they helped to give the ecumenical movement a more representative and catholic cast and the understanding that African culture has sufficient religious resources to give the life of the Christian churches in Africa forms of expression proper to them; racism is and will always be an aberration of Christian teaching.

5. Cooperation and unity

There can be no question that African problems helped to create a need for unitive Protestantism. This necessity for knitting-together Protestant missionary forces took most mission societies off-guard. When these societies initially embarked on African missions, they did not plan for, or anticipate, serious challenge to emanate from aboriginal conditions. It is not that they left without baggage. It is that they had a bag, but full of wrong implements.

In the search for appropriate ones they had to unpack the old, thus bringing to being a frantic search for workable and relevant implements. While this was a set-back, it must not be likened to a congenital defect. Instead, it must be likened to a congenital disruption which is almost always correctable by surgery.

Comity, then, came to represent this unavoidable reconstructive surgery. At the start, it was thought that only the field required this surgery. Exposed to this field in all its bareness, it became a standard requirement for both the missioner and the missionized. It is striking that, with time, even the so-called "faith missions" looked upon comity as a modus vivendi which was, of course, what it came to represent for many mission societies. Comity was and is always a half-way covenant.

New York 1900 began to see, far more than the nineteenth-century Comity Conferences, that Christianizing even preliterate societies, without the cooperation of local and colonial authorities, was no easy task and, with its comprehensive, rationalist program, initiated a new Protestant missionary atmosphere. Prior to its face to face encounter with the real world of the nonChristian, Protestantism presumed in part that all it takes to Christianize simple societies is a band of pious and zealous missionary enthusiasts; and that the same free-enterprise, laissez faire, privatization scheme which had brought unquestionable social advance to "Protestant nations" could logically be extended to church planting, uncurbed and untamed. After firsthand encounter, it gradually became evident that such notions, while not incompatible with the evangelical process in an alien territory, could not be left to their own whims and processes.

This is what these ecumenical Conferences were about. Through them, Protestantism began to capture, in a painful but unavoidable manner, the real meaning of the saying that unity is strength. It was, therefore, not frivolous when these divines believed that a conference based on taking account of the real world of the African may tend to lessen the estimate of all that separated Protestantism. Or, that by making delegates feel as missionaries do when in nonChristian lands, many stay-at-home Christians would come to grasp something of the irrelevance of naked denominationalism.

The rapid spread of Western commercial, political, and immigration interests into Africa, along with the rise of indigenous anti-missionary groups, also meant danger for "divide and rule" evangelism. The move to influence colonial governments, encourage favorable foreign and native public opinion, and cooperate with these diverse interest groups was in part occasioned by these anti-missionary forces. The embracing, at Le Zoute and other Conferences thereafter, of the African holistic conception of religion as a many-faceted system of being, stood for this desire to give life a constructive unity.

Cooperation with native leaders and other non-governmental organizations was a source of strength and effectiveness for the missionary community. This was so, particularly because colonial governments, despite claims to the contrary, continued right up to, and during World War II, to interpret their mandate to rule Africa as a carte blanche for voracious exploitation of native resources at the expense of the natives.

For this reason, and in view of its inability to stop this social rape, ecumenical movement's overall political performance during the colonial period in Africa deserves a poor grade; and in matters of decolonization, war and peace, it, like the League of Nations, woefully failed.

6. Individual contributions

Of the numerous men and women who gained ecumenical prominence through their relationship to Africa during these years, and grew in understanding as they came to terms with African questions, much remains to be said. The analysis has shown only a tiny proportion of these disciples, and only as they struggled to find answers to the main themes in this study.

Explicit in the analysis, however, is the progressive change of the intellectual and political atmosphere as Africans from all backgrounds, and few though they were, rose to take their place in these Conferences and helped to explain Africa to outsiders. In this, one can see why New York was different from Hartford and why Ibadan was different from any of the other preceding Conferences. One wonders how Africans would have related to Westerners, both missiologically and nonmissiologically, if Ibadan 1958 took place in 1900.

Certainly, the text suggests that African missions would have taken a different, more respectful direction from the beginning. But it would have been more difficult to sell the Christian message just as it has remained difficult in Asia. For it is a known historical fact that Christianity tends to do better where it encounters less resistance (and primal religions in particular) than where it encounters the other "book" religions. In this sense, African technological lag and the absence, for the most part, of a strong religious resistance, particularly in the early days of the Christianization effort, must be seen as a boon and a major plus to ecumenism making.

On the other hand, the evidence is overwhelming that the problem, from the beginning of Western encounter with Africa, was not because Christianity as a religion was "superior" as such to African primal religions. It was rather the fact that missionaries felt in part a sense of superiority as the Industrial Revolution gave the West a unique economic and political advantage over all other civilizations.

This Revolution is in part what gave Christianity the apparent air of invincibility and superiority. Stripped of this economic advantage, make-up, or trappings, Christianity's true color as a human symbol system emerges. To appreciate this fact, one must contrast Christianity's status in the so-called Dark Ages with its status after the renewed confidence brought to the West by the rediscovery of Aristotle, the revolution in ship-building and seamanship, and the eventual discovery of the trade-route to the East behind the backs of the Moslem middlemen.

No indigenous African was more aware of this technological disparity than James Aggrey. His contributions at the various Conferences assumed this qualitative difference between Western nations and Africa. His statement that missionaries were shunning Africa, because it did not confer on them the same prestige that Asia conferred, indicated this awareness and pointed to the humanity of the missionary who, like other humans, not infrequently, sought power, prestige, recognition, attention, and reputation.

Aggrey believed that Africans and all colonized peoples may turn out to be more ecumenical than their colonial masters, particularly because of their exposure to diverse cultures and numerous nonAfrican languages. For, whereas metropolitan culture, for the most part, and at least initially, shunned African languages and folkways, Africans, in order to survive in the market and other public places, could not, for a long time, afford to ignore the invading culture.

As great ones always do, Aggrey was deeply concerned with how the affairs of this world impacted and controlled the pace of ecumenical missions, and whether missions will stand aloof from, or boldly relate their Christian witness to, the major forces which were helping to shape the African of the future. It is sad that he died when the ecumenical movement needed more Africans of his caliber. One can only imagine what he would have done, if he had lived to see the Ibadan Conference, not to mention post-Independent Africa.

Clearly, throughout this period British hegemony, naturally, meant that British missionaries had to take the lead in virtually all phases of missions. And it is with this context that we must, indeed, understand what indigenous Africans and non-Africans did to enhance mission unity in this period.

Seen from this context, the question becomes not whether Africans had made any contribution to the ecumenical movement, but whether British missionaries did their best according to the biblical ideal that to whom much is given much is expected. Seen in this light, the burden, which is often incorrectly and primarily put on the African's shoulder, shifts to the British and other nonAfrican peoples who were privileged to carry the gospel message to Africa and given the material means to actuate it. It is instructive that mission is always initiated by those who feel that they have something to sell to others and have the power, will, and means to do so. Cross-cultural evangelism is rarely, if ever, carried across the border by a poor to a rich people; maybe we need the poor, and Africans in particular, to create a precedent by taking more initiative in this regard.

Whatever else other British subjects and other nonAfricans did, it is clear that one individual who was seriously influenced by African questions was J. H. Oldham. If one measure of a public man is his ability to understand his times, respond, and lead in a resonant way, then Oldham was more than a prophet; he was an ecumenical giant. If one measure of a good person is the extent to which one seeks for all people the necessities of life that add up to a decent standard of living, then Oldham was surely among the best of humans. Oldham knew how influence on the makers and shakers of political events was crucial for getting things done. In the 1920s, Africa and the IMC needed protesters and builders, and Oldham was both. At the beginning, it was a hands-on role. He worked to build an institution and he travelled Europe and America, and later, East and Southern Africa as drum major for the cause of Africa and missions.

By the 1930s, when he moved on to Life and Work duties, Oldham had not only promoted Africa and world mission in several capacities, he had also left a vacuum which the next generation found hard to fill. With this change, Africa lost one of its most compelling symbols—a symbol which shows that people can inform themselves, overcome blatant cultural prejudices, protest, dream, reach, build, and succeed in making other peoples' shoes their own shoes.

Oldham was not without his weakness, especially his occasional retreat into the safety of ambiguity and obscurantism. Yet, because Oldham was a Christian not a Christ, we may say without hesitation that he was an Africanist, through and through, who rekindled the fire of anger at the misuse world powers made of Africa, the downtrodden.

To say this, is not to deprecate those who were slow to change or were not so endowed with Aggrey's or Oldham's gift of far-sightedness. Nor does it imply that other leaders, African and nonAfrican (such as Jesse Jones with his prophetic *elan*) did not leave behind their architectural skill and imagination. It is to indicate that ecumenical missions as embodied by the IMC cannot be fully assessed, without reference to how African questions influenced and shaped many ecumenical leaders, and how they, in turn, sought to influence these questions. In this interplay, it becomes even more clearer why these questions, not personalities, are enduring; and have helped to institutionalize and continue to shape worldwide unity among Christians, irrespective of their creed, color, or nationality, while personalities come and go.

BALANCING THEORY AND ACTION

Viewed from this perspective, the most important general conclusion which has emerged from this study and which missiological thinkers must confront is not the secondary issue of ecumenical representation and personalities, or whether, as claimed by some, political, economic and social factors should determine and shape our understanding of missions; missions have always been determined in part by political and social circumstances. It is, rather, the apparent gap between theory and action, consciousness and fact. There are several facets to this tragic split, but within existing constraints, I want to highlight a few dominating points.

The first and most obvious one is the problem of unnecessary repetition of issues and, therefore, inadequate follow-up to, and implementation of, Conference resolutions. Consider, for example, the relation of African religious values and customs to Christianity. The debates at these various meetings were often conducted as if nothing ever had been said about it in previous meetings. The result was several resolutions and statements which, strictly speaking, were only impression makers.

Then, there is the whole question of why a resolution should be made, if there is no way that it can be implemented and prosecuted to the letter. A conference such as Le Zoute made an insightful resolution on economic questions: land and labor relations. Yet Jerusalem repeated the same ideas. The Department of Social and Industrial Research study reports were largely left unimplemented. Still, at Westerville, one hundred and sixty-nine resolutions were passed, with several on social and industrial matters, even when members knew that some were repetitious and feared that they may end up being "a loud noise."

One wonders how labor relations in Black Africa would have been today, if the recommendation that churches must pay more attention to industrial missions had been prosecuted with vigor and to the letter. Accra, for example, saw this apparent ecumenical weakness when it declared that, in essence, the IMC's problem was that tasks were lying around even when "many of them have been familiar for many years." Even before Accra, Hartford and other Conferences underscored the need for prompt implementation of Conference resolutions. Yet, nothing directly was done about them.

A glance at an issue such as race relations would show that several lofty proposals were made, including seeking for all the fullest opportunity for growth and progress, and the Westerville meeting even recommended that black people be appointed to mission boards in order to empower and offer a larger place and opportunity for them. But the reality is that such hopes and plans were not fully realized.

Unquestionably, it is in failures such as this that those who oppose the church and its claims find abundant evidence to develop their anti-Christian theses. Quite frankly, it is visible that an enormous ecumenical and interracial point would have been scored, if the proposal to send out joint evangelical teams had taken off, after several years on the drawing board.

The whole problem of inaction is a serious one. It is a matter which requires urgent attention, especially in view of the fact that the situation has not radically changed in the post-colonial era. Whether they are worldwide or regional meetings, good evidence exists to indicate that the ecumenical movement is still plagued with making new resolutions when the old ones have not been implemented.

Another facet of the problem is how modern missions can in practice be on the offensive rather than defensive. Obviously, the problem is more compounded today than half-a century ago. However, among the things that are striking, as one goes through these Conferences, is the fact that these meetings in themselves embodied, in a pointed way, both the problem of inaction and the defensive posture of the church.

Conferences were held after the fact, called after troubles had already started, and, therefore, chiefly served, for the most part, as damage control sessions. This is not to deny that it is possible to argue that in some respects some of these Conferences were a mixture of offensive and defensive weapons. One may even say that the Education Commissions were also good examples of offensive posturing. However, such a case would only be credible, if it could be established that Protestant missions began in Africa in the 1920s and not more than a century before.

Moreover, such an argument would make much sense, if it can be shown that adequate planning went into each Conference; and that their organizers were fully certain of how to followup Conference decisions.

The point is that, by the time ecumenism got underway, and missionaries began to debate how to "soften" the blows of full-scale Western incursion into Africa, the damage had already been done. For several nations had already staked their claims of various parts of Africa and were not out to listen to rearguard action by the missions.

If there is a lesson to be learned it is that ecumenical missions must find ways to take preemptive action, to do more and talk less. For, unquestionably, the text shows that it is relatively easy to plan for conferences, but extremely difficult to carry out conference decisions. To put it mildly, there has been far too much talk and very little action, far too many resolutions but very few follow-ups.

Some Implications for the AACC

Before pursuing further what the entire ecumenical movement must do to face this problem of inaction, there are some implications of this study for the AACC which I must briefly outline. Apparently, Africa has a very rich and surprising ecumenical past of which the AACC and the whole African Church should be proud. It is a past which shows a remarkable side of African tenacity and capability to withstand the most adverse condition and, in a puzzling manner, still wants to be Christian and ecumenical.

The process of transition from an object of, to a participant in, mission was unquestionably rapid, considering the odds which were stacked against such rapid transition. Similarly, the process of adaptation or self-rediscovery was astonishingly rapid, considering the means available, the total lack of information as to how to proceed, and the recurrent dangers of abuse, loss of self-respect, and status inconsistency.

Nevertheless, while the past may furnish the AACC and the whole African Church moments for elation, the underside calls for more action, not regret or despair. First and foremost, the delicate task today is not to exaggerate or ignore ecumenical achievements and failures during the colonial period. Nor is it to pretend that Africa has arrived and can go it all alone. It is, rather, to critique and learn from past mistakes and successes, knowing that the ambiguity of transcendence and finitude is not limited to any one period, people, movement, religion, or system.

For this reason, the AACC has the added responsibility of taking seriously this colonial period, which is its past. The irony is that this past was formed, largely, at a time when African cultural nationalism was based more on the sentiment of

Ethiopianism than on the nation state as we know it today. Whether the AACC should regard the nation state as a boon rather than a bane is hard to fully assess at this point in time. But there can be no question that the "partition" of Africa on national lines has complicated the ecumenical picture in Africa. Thus, it is clear that the AACC not only has to worry about externally imposed conditions that create instability in church and national life. It has also to worry about African separatist and nationalist claims which will threaten its very basis.

As new generations grow up with a dimmer knowledge of Africa's colonial past, and as being a Zambian, a Nigerian, a Kenyan (or a Commonwealth member, not part of the Francophone) becomes more important than being an African or a Christian, it will not be enough, in order to strengthen the AACC, to appeal to consanguinity, religious affiliation, primordial bonds, or common colonial experience. Increasingly, the task will be for the AACC to find new ways to strengthen and recreate opportunities for *koinoia* (fellowship). Indeed, it is already clear that the days in which external factors provided a common target for unity is over. Its *Nunc Dimitis* was sung long ago, despite claims to the contrary. Who would have thought that the impact of Ethiopianism would wane as nationalist sentiment and separatist churches gush forth in burst of quick succession!

Accordingly, certain things will have to be done differently by the AACC, knowing that it has no precedent as such. By that I mean that the African situation is very different from what most other peoples have experienced. In dealing with it, it should not be considered a sin to deviate from or modify popular developmental and ecclesiastical patterns or understanding of the kerymatic Christ. As the past does not have the sole key to solving Africa's continuing problems, the AACC and African churches must be pragmatic and open to new ideas, however shocking and eclectic.

They must begin to think through the faith they hold and not swallow any and every mission attitude that may or may not be relevant for contemporary African and world life. For instance, there is no reason to continue to treat African Independent Churches with disdain, simply because they are supposedly "theologically unsophisticated" and are not historic or mission-related. In the past, no adequate steps were taken to direct the exuberance of these indigenous churches to produce lasting ecumenical results. This is one unwritten task the AACC must undertake.

Because the next "battle for Africa" would concern ecumenism, the forces of ecumenism now in Africa must be pitted against the forces of denominationalism, division, and sectionalism. For at stake is this question: Who will control Africa's ecclesiastical future, ecumenical or nonecumenical forces? Also, more affirmative action should be taken to overcome the Protestant/nonProtestant split in Africa. That it has outlived the colonial period is regrettable. The AACC must take more *pro-*

active steps to overcome this transplanted schism which should have no place in Black Africa or any other part of the world. The time has come for a real thaw and even a real rapprochement.

Existing programs of economic empowerment must be strengthened and given serious and single-minded prosecution. Although these programs will take time to materialize, the important thing is to make a start and plan for the future, particularly the reversal of aid-dependency and its demeaning psychology to one's sense of personhood. The truth is that indigenous initiative holds the key to African missionary and economic expansion, not foreign aid, however generous. Some resolutions on industrial conditions (such as an active involvement by the church in industrial missions) which have been left largely untouched need to be reexamined. Indeed, the industrial recommendations, except certain outdated points, made by the Department of Social and Industrial Research, in the 1930s, read as if they were recently written, given that the issues they raised are still very much relevant.

The AACC must learn from the Conferences we have examined to try to ask what's important, what's worth pursuing, and what's not worth pursuing, and not to confuse the game with the quest. Right answers can only be preceded, not by asking just any question, but by asking the right question. And not infrequently, as the text shows, right questions come only after one has been shocked to discover that one has been operating under false consciousness and false premises, and only as one faces the fact that old formularies can undergo dynamic change and take on creative power and form. The AACC need not postpone until tomorrow what it can do today. For, in Whitby's phrase, "tomorrow is here."

This means that, while there is a place for continuing reflection on theoretical matters, a larger place must be given to concrete actions. At present the lurking epistemological temptation is for the AACC to waste its energies in attacking "enemies" no rhetoric will ever be able to subdue. This study offers some of the most striking illustrations of the powerlessness of some resolutions and rhetoric. If these alone were to be enough, there is no doubt that past ones would have appreciably changed African-European relations.

This is another way of saying that Africa must adjust to the brute reality that there are constants it must always have to deal with and that, if moral suasion and protests alone were enough to rid African societies of injustice, it would have been accomplished long before the emergence of Independent African nations, and even the AACC.

In this regard, it is clear that, as long as African churches and nations, for the foreseeable future, have to play catch-up with their Western "parents," there is no reason to think that these "parents" will suddenly come to a standstill and let their children catch-up with them. Admittedly, it is sad to say this. However, it is a fact of life even for ecclesiastical communities, and the earlier African churches come to this realization, the better it will be for us all; to be forewarned is to be forearmed. The truth is that, during and throughout the years we have examined, the gap between these churches was widening, not narrowing. Likewise, extensive documentation is not necessary to show that, from Africa's vantage, since 1958 ecumenical expectation has not caught up with ecumenical reality.

We know, for example, that in Christian understanding partnership is supposed to be the basis of missionary life, and, indeed, much was said about it even before the Whitby Conference made it its sole theme. However, the fact that the churches and the missions waited until the World Wars to take the idea of partnership seriously has thrown the weakness of our inchoate body of churches into vivid light. The AACC, therefore, needs to realize that, in a community of churches just as among nations where very powerful and very weak churches are bound together, there is no immediate antidote to exploitation and easy way to achievement of impartiality.

The AACC must act forcefully in order to put its house in a better economic and spiritual order. The task of evangelism is not over. Its better and global understanding is just beginning. At stake is the question whether the ecumenical world is ready to give up what it is used to, and comfortable with, for a new wave of unconventional evangelism.

Further general implications

Accordingly, the whole ecumenical movement itself must not continue to do business as usual, making resolutions and promises it cannot keep. In view of our common creatureliness and the biblical charge that gifts, talents, and privileges should not be misused or wasted, East/West, North/South polarization must not be the basis of post-colonial evangelism. Nor should the Western churches buy the siege mentality that the nonWestern churches are taking over the control of the ecumenical movement and that a neat separation of the realms must be rigidly maintained.

Western Christians have a greater and continuing role to play, if equality is to be realized in all spheres of ecumenical relations, and if the present divides in our world are to be overcome, at least in part (Matthew 25: 14-46). They, like others, still have more account to render regarding their stewardship and faithfulness to the Christian world mission.

Africa has had enough of ecumenical promises and resolutions. The point is to act. The mission boards and agencies are between two worlds, old and new, colonial and post-colonial. Many are still tempted to act as though the former would return, and the temper suited to it will be enough. It is hard to understand how changed the situation has become for Africa and for the world missionary community. It is hardest of all to stand away from the dear, familiar colonial world as the West—and even nonWesterners—knew it.

Yet this is what the Western churches are called to do: seeing what their African brothers and sisters are seeing, and hearing and understanding what they are saying, even when it appears unreasonable, overly ambitious and infuriating.

The whole ecumenical movement is called to act and to go beyond politeness and tokenism. Acting means a willingness to receive as well as give. It means devising ways resolutions are to be carried out before they are made, for it is very tempting to make resolutions and quite different and difficult to implement them. It means evaluating ecumenical hopes and aspirations, means and methods, group and individual ethics, organizing to influence and organizing to act, and building fellowship and friendship which rises above nationality and economic class. It means thinking and acting out problems, not from a nationalistic, economic, or ideological viewpoint, but to do so in the light of Christian teaching. This is where the Bible has several warrants concerning how to act, and none is perhaps more appropriate than the Lukan account of how the early church shared resources quite literally (Acts 2: 43-47; 4: 32-37).

The path this action must follow is equally clear. It must not travel the thoroughfare in which one sees one's own civilization with the eyes of love; singling out the best in it as normal and glossing over the worst; but when one looks at another civilization one has another standard: comparing the best in one's civilization with the worst in other civilizations. It must follow a narrow and rugged path which enables a person to see life and Christian mission from the angle of others, not of one's race or tradition.

Ecumenism was born out of Christian rediscovery of Jesus' prayer that the Church should be catholic (John 17:20-21) as well as the realization of human weakness and interdependence. This theme must be developed and made the basis of cross-cultural action. It was born because people saw how limited is the power of one people to see all things as they appear to another, trained in other habits and traditions and bred to perceive reality, including the numinous, from a certain vantage and not others. It developed through the experience of shared activities.

Africa helped to provide that opportunity with its challenges and problems. Also, it helped those who were engaged in its service, both at home and abroad, to increase daily in Christlikeness, in largeness of vision, in breadth of sympathy, in power of understanding, in sound judgement, and in adventurous faith. It arose as a bridge to cross over to the other side and read the colonial scene from the angle of vision which Africans had on that other side.

The two have met, but never completely; and they will only completely meet where places are fully traded, "hearts" and "pockets" are fully converted, waste of scarce resources is overcome, goods and services are sent where they are needed most (not to the highest bidders), and nonAfricans are helped to understand how dependent they are on Africans, just as Africans are dependent on them. Ecumenism means that things cannot continue to stay the same. It must not mean too much talk about mission crisis. Rather, it must mean more appropriation of the opportunities that crisis has offered.

Ecumenical commitment to action and following the narrow path is not the only condition; but nothing can take its place. Action must also be generated by more not less history and criticism of religion and culture. We know from this study that no dent would have been made by the missionary movement, for example, on prejudice and parochialism, but for the gradual adoption of the rationalist temper and historical criticism.

Here we see the interlocking nature of history and theology of missions, religions, and ecumenics. Biblical theology provided the impetus for missionary adventure and zeal, history tempered that zeal with some realism, and encounter with religions and cultures helped to generate pluralism and ecumenism.

Despite the negative effects of this rationalist temper, especially its crippling debilitation and obsession with theorizing, there is no question that its positive and constructive proddings are among the things that have brought ecumenical mission thinking thus far. We must insist on more not less dispassionate cultural study. This will continue to help overcome the disposition to be parochial in mission vision and hagiographical in writing about its past.

Hopefully, such continuing thinking-action would lead to a clearer understanding of the ecumenical movement (as a symbol with divine and human aspects), whose goal of creating a worldwide fellowship in which all people come to know Christ as equal participants (in his justice and saving promise for the world), is a continuing task.

Africans and nonAfricans who went before us charted the path and have shown us the way through their sacrifices and willingness to admit their faults as they became conscious of them. In Christ Africans and nonAfricans need each other more than ever to translate these largely ignored mandates from empirical knowledge into concrete action. This need for action, I suggest, is the agenda put on the shoulder of contemporary Christianity and all those concerned with the future of our world by the nature and impact of African questions.

APPENDIX 1

RECOMMENDATIONS AND RESOLUTIONS AT LE ZOUTE 1926*

A. SUGGESTIONS ON EVANGELISM

The spirit of evangelism should permeate all the services of the missionary and the Church. The primary purpose of all missionary activity is to relate every aspect of African life to the Lord Jesus Christ. No moral standard for the African Christian which is content with anything lower than likeness to Christ is adequate. The forces which make for the regeneration of Africa are spiritual.

The Conference would emphasize the need of the fullest possible knowledge of the vernacular of the people for a true approach to the African mind in presenting the Christian Gospel and in building up a Christian habit of life.

The Conference re-affirms the conviction that Africa will best be evangelized by her own children, and therefore to search out and train those whom God has called to this work is of the utmost importance. The careful supervision and guidance of these evangelists is essential.

1. The life of the African is essentially social and based on tribal conditions and customs. Therefore everything that is good in the African's heritage should be conserved, enriched and ennobled by contact with the spirit of Christ. While the Church cannot sanction any custom which is evil, it should not condemn customs which are not incompatible with the Christian life. Customs whose accidents are evil but whose substance is valuable may be purified and used. Where in the light of more comprehensive knowledge a change of practice is suggested it should be made only with due care not to wound the feelings of the African Christian. In all questions regarding indigenous custom the counsel of mature well-instructed African Christians will build up a body of Christian custom, true to their genius, and covering the whole of their life.

2. This Conference is convinced that Christian society must be built on Christian family life, and that the ideal of the Christian family life can only be realized in monogamy.

---

*Source: Edwin Smith, *Christian Mission*, pp. 108-126

3. The greatest care should be used in the exercise of discipline to maintain a high standard of conduct within the Church. But such discipline should make for edification and not for destruction. It is the duty of the Church to shepherd those who have been disciplined so that they be not lost to the Christian faith. Care should be taken for the better co-operation in Church discipline between neigbouring missions. When members or teachers apply to be received into another communion information should always be sought from the communion from which they have come, with a view to the maintenance of discipline.

4. The Conference recommends that missionary societies provide full opportunity and time to African missionary, by means of recognized courses at home and on the field, to study Native languages, customs and religion, that they may make an effective approach to African mind.

5. In each where there is a considerable Muhammadan population provision should be made for special training in Islamics and in Arabic.

B. EDUCATION

I. The Christian Ideal of Education

Many definitions of the aim of education are being offered today which the Conference could accept as true and valuable in themselves, as consistent with the religion it professes, and as peculiarly relevant to this age and the conditions existing in Africa; but all together these would form only a partial statement and come far short of the height and breadth of the Christian ideal of education. The members of the Conference see in Jesus Christ all the elements of human greatness meeting in the perfection of grace and truth. To have the mind of Christ is, in their estimation, the mark of maturity for any man. This Conference, therefore, regards Christlikeness as the supreme moral achievement, and to them that definition of the aim of education which, traced out in all its implications, is felt by the consent of our whole nature to be at once the highest and the most comprehensive.

The following outline of recommendations and proposals is inspired and governed throughout by this faith and conviction.

II. Policy

Inasmuch as Native education in Africa is a co-operative undertaking in which Governments, missions, Natives and the non-official European community are all concerned, the Conference, while recognizing that conditions differ in various parts of the continent, offers the following general recommendations regarding the distribution of educational effort at the present time.

1. The formulation and general direction of educational policy, the general administration of the educational system and the supervision of all educational institutions are among the proper functions of Government. To advise and assist the Government in the functions mentioned above, and to secure co-operation among all the bodies concerned with Native education, there should be established in each territory, as has already been done in many cases, an Advisory Board of Education on which Government, missionaries, Africans and the European non-official community are represented. Provision should be made for regular and special meetings of the Advisory Board.

2. While the right of Government to inspect schools is acknowledged, inspectors of Native schools should be competent educators, in sympathy with missionary effort, and able to speak one or more of the Native languages current in their circuits.

3. To improve the work of existing schools and especially village schools, to relate the work of the schools closely with the needs of the community, and to promote health and general well-being of the people, visiting teachers of the Jeanes[1] type, both men and women, should be appointed. These teachers should ordinarily be trained at a central institution controlled by a governing body on which missionaries are adequately represented. These visiting teachers should work under the direction of the missions, or (in exceptional circumstances) under the Government.

4. Under the particular conditions obtaining in Africa the special responsibility of missions and of the Native Church seems to lie in the field of village, central village, intermediate and secondary schools, and in particular in the training of teachers, and it is desirable that these branches of education should be entrusted to them so far as it is possible for them to undertake the work. In places where for any reason the missions are unable to provide adequate education of this nature, or to maintain such education at a sufficiently high standard, it will be necessary for the Government to provide this type of education also.

5. Higher and technical education instruction such as that given in colleges and advanced industrial, agricultural and medical institutions should, under present conditions, ordinarily be conducted by the Government through the agency of government bodies on which missionaries are represented. This, however, should not prevent missions or united groups of missions from conducting such colleges and in-

---

[1]See *Education in East Africa: Report of the Second African Education Commission*, pp. 54-56.

stitutions, provided they conform to conditions laid down by the Government.

6. The extent to which missions can share in the task of education will depend upon the financial assistance provided by the Government. Such provision should be made on bases to be determined in consultation with the Advisory Boards.

7. In cases where the Government undertakes such school work as is ordinarily undertaken by missions, the expenditure on the government schools and the grants paid to aided schools should be so adjusted as to secure for the latter equal opportunity of attaining the same standard of efficiency as is aimed at in schools under the direct control of Government working under similar circumstances.

8. Inasmuch as the funds for Native Education, apart from the missionary and church contributions, will as a rule be derived from either the general revenue of the country (including the Native tax), or from special cesses or levies imposed upon particular districts or tribes, the Conference is of opinion that the best policy is to regard the general revenue of the country as the main source for educational grants and expenditure, and that the money derived from this source should in time be sufficient to put an elementary education within the reach of all Native children. In order to provide additional educational facilities, Native chiefs or councils and other local governing bodies should be encouraged to supplement the amount of money derived from the Native tax or general revenue. Such local contributions should ordinarily be expended in the districts in which they are raised.

III. Curriculum

The curriculum of all types of schools should be drawn up with complete awareness of the life of the community. Character development based on religion should be the colouring of every educational activity. Hygiene and health should be emphasized, not only in the practice of the school and home but in the reading, writing and arithmetic of the school. Agriculture and industry should be taught in the classroom as well as practised in the field and workshop. The building up of a sound home life should receive consideration in the school as well as be exemplified in the home, and the value of recreation should be taught by both practice and precept. In higher institutions, which should aim at the training of men and women as leaders of their people, the curricula should be based on the same principles, together with an historic and comparative treatment of civics or citizenship, economics and the development of civilization.

If it be true that 'great importance must be attached to religious teaching and moral instruction' and that 'both in schools and in training colleges they should be accorded an equal standing with secular subjects,'[2] it is essential that adequate provision should be made in governmental codes and curricula for sufficient time for religious instruction during school hours, and particularly for the training of the teacher to give such instruction.

IV. Education of Women and Girls

In all these resolutions dealing with education we have had in view the absolute necessity of the education of women and girls being developed simultaneously and in full co-ordination with that of boys. This will involve among other things:

(a) The gradual creation of an adequate staff of women inspectors of schools.

(b) Mutual consultation in regard to programme and curricula of boys' and girls' schools.

(c) In some places a completely new emphasis upon the education of women and girls.

We therefore suggest that the International Missionary Council be asked to set up a commission or committee to help and advise those engaged in the education of women and girls.

V. The Medium of Instruction

For educational and other reasons education should be conducted through the medium of the vernacular at least during the early stages of the school life of the child. In Africa, as well as in other parts of the world where there are very small language groups, it may not be possible to give full effect to this accepted principle, and in such cases the language of a neighbouring large group might with advantage be made the medium of instruction for the smaller, provided that it is acceptable to them. No attempt should, however, be made to impose upon larger units any African so-called lingua franca.

Instruction through the medium of the Native language should be the rule for all subjects in the primary stages of instruction (extending ordinarily through the first three or four years of school life) and for some subjects throughout the whole school life of the child, attention being directed in the higher classes to the grammatical structure and the literature of the language.

---

[2]*Education Policy in British Tropical Africa: Memorandum submitted to the Secretary of State for the Colonies by the Advisory Committee on Native Education,* p. 4.

In classes beyond the primary stages the teaching of a European language should be begun in order to enable the pupils to meet the situation arising from the rapidly increasing contacts with European civilizations, to profit by them, and on their part to make a full African contribution to the shaping of a developing society.

VI. Religious Education

The need for giving to Africa an education which is based upon religion, and which in all its parts is infused with religion, is vital to the missionary cause. It is also one of the chief reasons why both Governments and missions are convinced that missionary co-operation is essential in the education of Africa. This being so, it is obvious that the missionary body must see to it that the religious instruction and practice of its schools is raised to the highest possible level of efficiency.

To this end we propose that the International Missionary Council shall set up an *ad hoc* commission whose task it shall be, in consultation with existing agencies, to survey the whole field of religious education in Africa, and to advise the various societies thereon.

In order that this body may at once turn its attention to those questions which are most exercising the minds of the missionary body in the matter of religious education we submit the following suggestions as a starting-point for their deliberations:

1. We desire that a clear statement should be made concerning the aim of religious education, and that the missionary body should be assisted to discover wherein their present theory and practice of religious education succeeds or fails in the attainment of this aim.

2. If, as we expect, in the persuance of this aim the content of our own religious education will be found to include (a) the transmission and development of religious knowledge, (b) the translation of such religious knowledge into ethical practice, and (c) its relation to worship, we ask that this commission shall include in its report reference to the following points:

(a) The general technique of religious instruction. (b) Special problems related to the teaching of the Holy Scriptures, naturally including among these the question of graded syllabuses and appropriate literature. (c) The methods through which theoretical instruction can be immediately and inevitably related to appropriate expression in the life of the individual and community. (d) The place of worship in the life of the school and the possibilities that exist for training in worship.

In all these matters we ask that the subjects may be reviewed not only from the standpoint of psychology and pedagogy, but also from that of sociology.

3. And believing as we do that although special classroom periods are essential in religious instruction, yet such periods of instruction will be of little value unless religion colours the whole curriculum, and not only the whole curriculum but the whole of life and activity of the school. We ask for special study of the religious implications of the school as a community centre and the kind of practice which is essential if these religious implications are to be made actual in the life and work of the school.

4. In all these suggestions we ask that the commission shall have very clearly in mind the problems of the little non-residential village schools as well as those of central schools, boarding schools and training institutions, and that the educational influences of the home may not be neglected.

5. We suggest further that help is needed not only in respect of the actual content of religious education under varying conditions, but also concerning the methods by which such training of missionaries and teachers can be devised and put into execution, so as to secure that this content is preserved and such supervision on the field exercised as shall make improvement in the religious education on the lines suggested progressive and assured.

6. It is urged further that this commission shall conceive it to be part of its duty to set in motion forces which shall lead to the production of such literature, or the utilization of appropriate literature, if such exists, as shall be deemed by them to be necessary in the pursuance of the policy of religious education which they devise.

7. In the pursuance of the work of such a commission we deem it probable that any effective survey of religious education in Africa, still more any large change of policy in religious education in Africa, will involve the setting apart by the missionary body in each of the several principal areas in Africa some group to undertake the specific task of studying the local problems of religious education and encouraging experiments in this field.

VII. Conclusion

The Conference would conclude this statement as it began. All those measures which are here proposed—the willing and loyal co-operation with Governments and all the agencies of a properly constituted society, the setting up of boards and councils, the drafting of codes and curricula, the establishment of schools and colleges, the appointment of supervisors and other educational officers, the relation of a village to activities of the rural community and the emphasis on instruction not in word only but in deed and truth, the training of teachers and the preparation of suitable textbooks—are nothing more, and nothing less, than means to one end, uniting Africa to the whole world of men. 'Until we all come unto the unity of the faith and of the knowledge of the Son of God, unto a full-grown man, unto the measure of the stature of the fulness of Christ, that we may be no longer children.'

C. LANGUAGE AND LITERATURE

We record with thankfulness that, as a result of missionary devotion and labour, there are now at least some portions of the Christian Scriptures in 243 African languages, and that in 190 of these there are also other books.

2. We are, however, profoundly impressed with the inadequacy of existing vernacular literature for the needs of the African people. From the results of the recent survey it appears that in only 17 of these 190 languages are there more than 25 books, and more than half of these languages have less than 5 books each as their entire library.

3. The survey reveals the lack of any definite plan of production, and suggests the necessity for a selection of the more important languages in which literature should be developed.

4. For the most part the existing books are the work of foreigners and have the foreign outlook. African authorship has to be discovered and encouraged, and a greater master of African speech and thought attained by the foreign missionaries.

5. We are convinced that for the purposes of education and for the full development of the life of the Christian Church in Africa the use of the vernacular is essential, and therefore that the time has come for the missions to set themselves to secure an immediate and rapid increase in the production of the literature urgently needed in African languages.

6. We thankfully welcome the establishment of the International Institute of African Languages and Cultures, and we earnestly commend to all the missions working in Africa, and to the home boards, the importance of co-operating heartily with it. We believe that the Institute will be of far-reaching service to missionaries in helping (a) to solve linguistic problems, (b) to remedy and to prevent expensive mistakes in the choice of orthography, (c) to prepare school text-books adapted to the needs and conditions of African life, (d) to promote a better understanding of the distinctive character and contribution of African peoples, (e) to bring about an increasingly sympathetic attitude on the part of Governments towards African vernaculars, and towards the valuable elements in the African heritage.

7. We urge the missions to consider without delay what is the minimum programme of publication needed in their own language areas. We recommend the co-operative preparation and publication of literature wherever possible, and suggest that the fol-

lowing items are so sure to find their place in the minimum programme that the preparation of manuscripts along these lines should be at once undertaken. To secure the widest possible usefulness of such works we recommend that copies of the manuscripts in English or French should be circulated in the different language areas and so made available as basic texts for translation, adaptation or suggestion.

A. Graded Readers, including African fables and folk-lore.
Graded Nature Talks.
Graded text-books in Geography.
Graded text-books in Bibliography and History.
Graded text-books in Arithmetic.
Handbooks on Hygiene, First-Aid and Nursing.
Handbook on Agriculture.
Handbook on Child-Welfare and Mother-Craft.

B. Graded Bible Lessons and Stories.
Books on Christian Conduct and Fellowship.
The Christian Ideal of Marriage and the Home.
Why I am a Christian.
The Bible and how it has come to us.
Bible Dictionary and Helps to Bible Study.
Single-volume Commentaries.

C. Books for Advanced Readers.

In addition, we urge the educational and evangelistic importance of pictures, and recommend the preparation and co-operative publication of pictures suitable for African school, family, community and church life.

8. We strongly advise the establishment and strengthening of periodicals in African languages, and that these should include a section specially devoted to the interests of African women.

9. We specially recommend the preparation of a suitable book with reference to the life of the African women, bearing upon all the different needs of the home, and we request the Committee for Christian Literature of the Conference of Missionary Societies in Great Britain to consider this matter with view to the problem of such a manuscript, which might be made available for translation into the various African languages.

10. The permeation by Islam of many parts of the continent of Africa calls for a simple literature to give to the African Church information upon Islam, and inspiration and guidance for her task of evangelizing Moslems. We appeal to the Central

Committee for Christian Literature for Moslems to enquire into the type of literature that may best serve the African Church in this respect, to request some one acquainted with the impact of Islam on animistic people to prepare a handbook for the instruction of Christian leaders on the origin and character of Islam and how it differs from Christian teaching, and to submit suggestions and other basic texts to the Christian Literature Committees working for the areas concerned.

11. It is confidently hoped that in the production of the books in Section A of resolution 7, the co-operation of Governments, and of the International Institute of African Languages and Cultures will be available. We however remind the missions and Churches of Africa that this will not release them from their obligation to provide the Christian literature which Africa needs.

12. We urge the International Missionary Council to bring before the boards and their missions the necessity of strengthening and perfecting the co-operative organizations both in Africa and at the home base for promoting Christian literature. No one mission nor Church, nor any one provincial group can be expected to produce at an early date all that is required for the schools and Christian communities within its area. The task can only be accomplished by wide co-operative effort, sustained with enthusiasm. No missionary expenditure will in most areas be more remunerative than that which is devoted to a wisely directed scheme of co-operative publishing of African Christian literature within the next decade.

13. We urge the mission boards that African Christian literature demands a regular assignment in the budget of any mission that seeks to fulfil its task completely, and the seeking out and setting apart for the task of authorship of workers, foreign and African, with literary aptitudes.

14. We recommend the Literature Committees in North America and Europe to consider the joint appointment and support of a full-time officer or organizer of African Christian literature.

15. We call the attention of the mission boards to the necessity of new missionaries having an introduction to phonetics and the principles of African language study before going to their mission field.

D. HEALTH AND NATIVE WELFARE

It is the conviction of this Conference that the problems of health and population are basic in any plan for the sound development of Africans and Africa. In view of this conviction the Conference deems it of the utmost importance that mission societies and missionaries shall have a clear understanding of their responsibility in health ministry to the Africans.

1. Recognizing that the health of any people is ultimately dependent on education along sound lines, we would draw attention to the fact that the necessary machinery already exists whereby the teaching and practice of the laws of hygiene and personal cleanliness can be carried out, we would stress the importance of utilizing such machinery. We refer especially to village schools, which exist in most areas, and where health education on the simplest lines can be imparted as an integral part of the daily curriculum.

Among the subjects which we deem to be of primary importance we include education in housing, food, personal and moral hygiene, general sanitary habits and simple measures against existing diseases.

All teaching should be of a simple practical nature, and wherever possible, illustrated by object lessons intimately connected to village life.

It is obvious that education along these lines can be carried to a further stage at the centres of higher education; but we would stress the point that all teaching should be essentially the elements of mother-craft, first aid, and responsibility towards the sick.

(a) From the above suggestions it follows that Native teachers for village schools will themselves have to be trained in the above subjects, and such training must be an integral part of the education they receive at the normal schools.

(b) If health education is to be carried out along these lines it will be necessary to survey existing local conditions, and among other measures to provide simple primers in the vernacular dealing with the subject taught. A start has already been made in its direction, and it has been found to be of great assistance in several countries to publish simple health tracts in the vernacular for free distribution.

(c) We would draw the attention of mission boards to the vital necessity of establishing maternity and infant welfare centres along with other general health measures. This ought to be possible in any district where there is a hospital in existence, or where a maternity training school can be established.

2. We recommend that the International Missionary Council be requested to consult with the missionary boards regarding the desirability of establishing an international advisory board, whose task it shall be to survey the whole field of medical missions with Governments, with various philanthropic and scientific agencies, and with the League of Nations, in the campaign against disease. We would suggest sleeping sickness, tuberculosis, venereal disease and helminthiasis as especially requiring attention. Another point would be the training of an African medical staff.

(a) In the survey of the field of medical mission work in Africa such an advisory board would correspond with representatives of the various mission areas with a view to collecting information as complete as possible concerning all factors bearing upon the health of the Native population.

(b) We believe that the need for medical and welfare workers in Africa must be met from among the African peoples. In most large areas of the continent definite efforts have been made to train such workers, frequently with a large measure of success both by Governments and missions. Building upon these foundations already made in established institutions, efforts should now be put forth to increase as rapidly as possible the number of trained African workers of all types, looking to the provision in the near future of institutions capable of giving a complete medical training. In the establishment of such medical schools Government and inter-mission co-operation should be sought.

3. In regard to the entire programme of the promotion of health this Conference wishes to assure the various Governments that they can count upon the missionary societies rendering all possible assistance to Governments in the forwarding of any particular measures of Public Health which it is desirable should be carried out.

E. ECONOMIC QUESTIONS

I. LAND

Missionary experience is unanimous in emphasizing that the question of land holds a central place in the consciousness of the African peoples, and that consequently guarantees to the Native peoples that the tenure of their lands is absolutely secure. This is essential to ensure peace and goodwill among all Native communities and must be the basis of all endeavours to promote Native welfare.

It is therefore urged that all Native lands should be (a) clearly delimited and (b) protected by title deeds or vested in a trust providing a security not less valid in law than under which non-Natives hold titles.

It is further urged that it is of great importance for the well-being and development of Native life that sufficient land should be secured to the Native community to afford it adequate opportunity for economic cultivation and for stock breeding and other forms of agricultural or pastoral pursuits suitable to the locality.

II. LABOUR

It is recognized, not only by missionaries but by administrators, that the future of the continent of Africa is bound up with the moral, physical and intellectual development of the African peoples.

Having reviewed the conditions prevailing in different parts of the continent, the Conference is convinced that in many localities the rapidly increasing demands for Native labour arising out of industrial enterprises may prejudice the healthy growth of Native communities cultivating their own lands under tribal conditions. Such Native communities provide the necessary basis for the evolution of a healthy African society, and are the only reservoir from which a supply of labour for economic development can be assured. When the demands for labourers for work outside Native areas, and especially for work at a distance, are excessive, tribal life is subjected to a severe strain. The absence of adult males may reduce the amount of land under cultivation, with consequent shortage of food and under-nourishment of the population, place undue burdens on the women and children, lead to the weakening of moral restraints and the spread of immorality, thereby affecting the birth-rate, give rise to a spirit of restlessness and diminish the influence of tribal discipline. All these factors tend towards the disintegration of Native society. Economic considerations, therefore, no less than Christian and humanitarian interest in the welfare of the Native peoples, require that the whole question of the effect upon Native life of the labour demands for work at a distance from home should be made the subject of careful enquiry by competent authorities.

The Conference heartily welcomes the action of the International Labour Office in establishing a commission of experts, whose advice may be sought in regard to questions affecting Native labour, including all forms of forced labour and the conditions regulating the recruitment and protection of workers under contract and industrial conditions generally.

The Conference is deeply convinced that compulsory or forced labour for private enterprises is inadmissible in any circumstances. It is also resolutely opposed to all forced labour for public purposes, the only exceptions being (a) when such compulsion is the only means of combating epidemics and floods and of dealing with similar national emergencies, and (b) reasonable communal labour in accordance with Native law and custom.

F. AMERICAN NEGROES AND AFRICA

There are not legislative restrictions specifically directed against the American Negro, but most African Governments are opposed to, or place difficulties in the way of, the sending of American Negroes to Africa.

2. Opposition to the sending of American Negroes to Africa is due mainly to three factors:

(a) The unrest caused by certain movements believed to be dangerous to order and government and to be encouraged from America.

(b) The antagonism to Government in past years of certain American Negroes in Africa resulting in serious disturbances in some areas.

(c) The failure of certain American Negroes in Africa in past years.

3. Owing to the effect of one or more of the reasons above-named, most African missionaries consulted do not think the present time auspicious for pressing upon Government such a general change in policy as would mean the sending of a large number of American Negroes to Africa in the immediate future, although strongly believing that efforts should be made to increase gradually the number of such missionaries.

4. There are at present working in various parts of Africa American Negroes of the highest character and great usefulness, whose fine spirit and devoted work will in the course of a few years greatly increase the respect in which American Negro missionaries are held, and make it easier the securing of permission for the entrance of additional missionaries.

5. There is a natural and laudable desire on the part of a large number of American missionary societies, both white and Negro, to send additional American Negroes as missionaries to Africa—thereby giving the educated Negro an outlet for his zeal to render unselfish service, and aiding in a natural and important way the cause of African evangelization, education and general welfare.

2. Recommendations

In view of the above findings the Conference adopts the following resolutions:

1. The Negroes of America should be permitted by Governments, and encouraged by missionary societies, to play an important part in the evangelization, medical service and education of Africa, and that the number of their missionaries should be increased as qualified candidates are available for needed work, and as their representatives already in the field still further succeed in gaining for their people and their societies that public confidence which is essential.

2. That every practicable form of assistance should be given in the spirit of Christian fellowship, as to colleagues of the same missionary status, by white missionaries to qualified American Negroes working in Africa, and that the same spirit of cooperation should be expected by white missionaries from American Negro missionaries.

3. That Governments should be supported in requiring that American Negroes wishing to enter Africa for missionary purposes should go out under the auspices of

responsible societies of recognized and well-established standing; and that owing to the difficult and delicate inter-racial situation in Africa, exceptional care should be used in the selection of men and women of strength of character and a fine spirit of co-operation able to meet the same tests as white missionaries.

4. That in the interests of comity and co-operation American missionary societies not now represented in Africa should work as far as possible through well-established societies already in Africa, and that, in accordance with the general rules of missionary procedure, they should give special attention to unevangelized districts.

5. That when missionary societies of established reputation are unable to secure the admission to Africa of American Negroes needed for important work and qualified to perform it, the matter may properly be taken up with the International Missionary Council for the use of its friendly offices.

6. In adopting these resolutions the Conference recognizes that the above recommendations are not an ideal or a complete solution of the problem under consideration, but believes that they represent the 'next steps' which may be wisely taken, and that they should, in the providence of God, gradually bring about a highly significant and important contribution by the Negroes of America to their distant kindred in Africa.

G. RACIAL PROBLEMS IN SOUTH AFRICA

The Conference desires to express its profound sympathy with the people of South Africa, both white and black, in the racial problem of relations between different races, which is one of the world problems of the twentieth century, presents itself in South Africa in an exceptionally difficult and acute form.

The Conference believes that only in the teaching and spirit of Jesus Christ can a true solution be found for racial adjustments, and that this teaching requires us to desire and seek for all the fullest opportunity for growth and progress.

The Conference is convinced that the welfare and prosperity of every community is inseparably bound up with the welfare and advancement of all its parts.

The Conference desires to assure the Christian Churches of South Africa of its deep interest in their endeavours to discover how the Christian spirit may express itself in relation to the racial problems of that country, and of its prayers for the success of these endeavours. It cherishes the hope and confidence that the Christian mind of South Africa will out of the reality, greatness and acuteness of the difficulties be able to make a contribution of special value towards the improvement of the relations between the black and white races throughout the world, which is the concern of the whole Church of Christ.

H. THE TRAINING OF WOMEN MISSIONARIES

The Conference endorses the following resolution submitted to it by the women members of the Conference:

The women members of the International Conference on the Christian Mission in Africa, meeting in Le Zoute, realize that work among African women has advanced to such a point that in order to conserve the remarkable results already achieved there is more than ever an urgent need for special attention to be given to the training of new women missionaries. A sympathetic approach to the life of African women depends upon understanding and insight which can only be built upon knowledge. The mystery and dread expressed in tabus and reflecting fear can best be penetrated by the well-informed missionary.

The women of the Conference ask that more emphasis be put by all missionary boards and agencies upon training for missionary service, and that time be allowed for the study of phonetics and the principles of language, manners, customs and religion before going to the field, as well as on furlough.

I. TRANSMISSION OF RESOLUTIONS

The Conference requests the officers of the International Missionary Conference to take the following actions in regard to the resolutions:

1. To transmit the resolutions to the Missionary Conferences in Africa with the request that the Conferences in each area will at its next meeting or at a special meeting review the conclusions reached at Le Zoute and report to the International Missionary Council how far local missionary opinion is in agreement with the resolutions and, in so far as it is in agreement, what steps can be taken in the areas in question to give effect to the resolutions.

2. To transmit the resolutions of the Conference to the national missionary organizations in the home countries with the following suggestions:

(a) That the resolutions, with such comments and explanations as may be thought necessary, be brought to the attention of the boards and societies for their consideration and for such action as they may deem appropriate.

(b) That consideration be given to the best means of securing the widest publicity for the Report of the Conference.

(c) That the boards be asked to consider the desirability of placing a copy of the Report in the hands of all their missionaries.

(d) That the boards be asked to consider the means of bringing the needs and opportunities in Africa, as revealed at the Conference, before the home Church in such a way as to enlist a larger response in the offering of prayer, service and gifts.

(e) That special consideration be given to the means by which the enlarged conception of the Christian Mission in Africa reached at the Conference may be used to enlist the sympathy and service of those who are not yet committed to the missionary cause, and to appeal to the adventurous spirit of the younger generation.

3. To bring to the attention of the Governments in Africa, in the ways that seem most appropriate, the resolutions of the Conference dealing with health and Native welfare, education, literature and languages, and economic questions affecting Native well-being.

APPENDIX 2

IMPRESSIONS OF LE ZOUTE 1926*

1. By Miss Jean Kenyon Mackenzie, Board member and former missionary of the Board of Foreign Missions of the Presbyterian Church in the United States in the Cameroons.

There is Monsieur Louis Franck, and as he speaks he is laughing. A feeling for . . .Africa. . . . There is Father Callaway praying. To many a one with the memory of Father Callaway praying, Africa will knock at the door of the heart. . . . There is Mr Max Yergan, with his mingled look of youth and of control, and he is holding his peace—speaking of South Africa, he is holding his finely-wrought peace. . . . There is Mr Oldham with his look of saint and man of reason; he is with simplicity and passion preaching a new mission. . . . There is the dark Welshman, Dr Jesse Jones, chanting those incantations that have awakened sleepers and the very dead. . . . There is Dr Gilks, speaking off his left shoulder, juggling assiduously with a bit of paper and dealing with diets and harvests, with rats, with goats as money and goats as meat, building up out of its component parts the programme of African health, and curiously effective, as a difficult speaker sometimes is. . . . There is the brilliant and erudite Mademoiselle Homburger, suddenly present when her voice, with its indestructible, definite quality, penetrates the male deliberations. . . . There is Monsieur Couve, looking like a Gascon, which perhaps he is, and speaking humbly of humility. . . . There is a beautiful Englishwoman who passionately laments the suffering of African women.

It was strange by the North Sea to be so much in Africa. How many promises were there made to Africa! How many projects for her health and education, the protection of her rights, both civil and human, the preservation intact and inviolate of her immortal soul! We must remember these things and the act of faith by which we received the great resolutions put before us. Happy shall we be if we carry them out! It may be then that Africa will not entreat us to leave her, not to cease from following after her; whither she goes we may go and her God shall be ours.

2. By John Dube founder and principal of the Ohlange Institution in Natal, South Africa.

The Conference has re-created me. If it had meant going ten thousand miles farther I would willingly have gone. I would have gone to Greenland. I return to

Africa with newborn hopes in my heart. I know now as I never knew before what friends Africa has. As I listened to administrators and missionaries talking as they did, I knew that the future of my people is assured. We are passing through a perplexing period in South Africa. What with colour bars and restrictions of one sort or other, the white people are sitting upon us very tightly. But Le Zoute has given me fresh courage. I never knew how many and how difficult African problems are; but I never knew, on the other hand, that so many men were seeking to understand them and to find a solution. This brings me good cheer. You have faith in us, and we shall win through. Perhaps it is that without oppression people cannot climb. It may be with us as it was with the Israelites. They were in bondage in Egypt—yet they came into the land of promise. We shall come through our struggles a stronger, purer people. That is what Le Zoute has meant to me.

---

*Source: Edwin Smith, *Christian Mission*, pp. 30-31, 33.

APPENDIX 3

INTERNATIONAL MISSIONARY COUNCIL, SPECIAL AFRICA PROGRAM, OCTOBER 1929*

The International Missionary Council at its meeting at Williamstown last July, in response to requests from groups representing the mission boards in different countries and from the Congo Missionary Conference and other groups and individuals in Africa, resolved to include in its programme of work special attention to the needs and problems of Africa. While missionary conferences already exist in many areas of the continent, and it is hoped that these may be further developed, the great distances and the difficulties of communication preclude the formation in Africa itself of a body which would link up these conferences, and it would appear that in existing conditions it is possible for the International Missionary Council to render certain services which in fields like China or India are performed by the National Christian Council. It was further agreed that in the distribution of work among the officers of the Council the responsibility for carrying out this part of the programme of the Council should be assigned to the signatories of this letter. The resolution adopted by the International Missionary Council was as follows:

The International Missionary Council approves of the furtherance of international co-operation in the advancement of the Christian cause in Africa along the following lines:

1. Exploration of the best means of furthering and realizing the evangelistic aims of the Christian missions in Africa.

2. The development of a programme of Christian education in Africa as a means of realizing this missionary purpose, with special reference to:

    (a) The improvement of religious education.
    (b) The Christianization of Africa's womanhood and home life.
    (c) The development of African leadership.
    (d) The meeting of the needs of rural communities.

---

*Source: IMC Papers, WCC Library, Geneva.

And in connection with this the study of educational policies of governments and of the relation between the educational policy of missions and that of governments.

3. The development of a health programme for African missions with special reference to:

(a) A comprehensive programme for use in schools.

(b) Co-operation with governments in attack on disease.

(c) The creation of an African health staff of doctors, medical assistants, dressers and nurses.

4. Furtherance of the work of the International Committee on Christian Literature for Africa.

5. Co-operation with other agencies in the endeavour to understand, conserve and develop what is valuable in African cultures and institutions.

6. The occupation of the field and the avoidance of overlapping.

7. The encouragement and development of Christian councils in the continent of Africa and co-operation with existing councils.

8. Approach to governments where necessary in regard to questions involving the relations of missions and governments.

9. The bringing to bear of Christian influence for the establishment of right racial relations, and co-operation for this purpose with the proposed Department for Social and Industrial Research and Counsel.

10. Prayer for the raising up of men and women of outstanding gifts for positions of leadership in Africa, and support for efforts in different countries to secure for African missionaries the best possible equipment for their task.

The Committee agreed that a statement be prepared setting forth the needs of Africa in the matter of Christian leadership and the preparation and equipment required by missionaries in Africa.

We shall try to indicate the objectives which we have immediately in view, and what we think can be undertaken in the near future. Africa is a great continent. Christian missions are working under more than twenty separate and distinct administrations, pursuing policies that differ in various degrees. It is obvious that the whole of the programme which has been outlined cannot be undertaken at once. In sketching so large a plan the Committee aimed at laying down the lines along which we should like to see some progress made in, say, the next ten years. The execution of the plan is the task of the whole Christian forces working for Africa, and the help that the staff of the International Missionary Council can give is chiefly in keeping those in different parts of the continent in touch with one another and in touch with the movements of thought elsewhere. If the time and strength available are not to be dissipated, they must in the beginning be devoted mainly to one or two items in the programme, and when something has been achieved in regard to these it will be possible to give increased attention to other parts of the programme. Similarly, if the needs of a group of missions in particular area at a given time require the co-operation of the International Missionary Council, and their co-operation makes heavy demands on the officers, they will not be able simultaneously to give the same kind of help to missions in other parts of the continent. But while these limitations of time and strength are inevitable, it must be remembered that, in spite of differing conditions in different parts, the African continent has an underlying unity, that its problems are closely related, and consequently that the successful working out of problems and the gaining of experience in one area will in the long run be of help to those working in other areas. In thinking of Africa as a whole we must take the long view.**

Signed J. H. Oldham and B. D. Gibson.

**The remaining pages sketch the IMC's view of Africa. The view expressed there is a further elaboration of all the teachings of the Conferences held from 1922 to 1928. This view of Africa later crystallized in a book authored by Oldham and Gibson; see *The Remaking of Man in Africa* (London: Oxford, 1931).

APPENDIX 4

MESSAGE TO THE CHURCHES OF AFRICA ISSUED BY IBADAN 1958*

We, the delegates of the first All-Africa Church Conference that has ever been held in Africa, rejoice that God has called us together and in His Name we send greetings from Ibadan in Nigeria to all the churches of Africa.

We come from the countries of Sierra Leone, Gambia, Nigeria, of French West Africa, Liberia and Togo, Cameroun, French Equatorial Africa, Belgian Congo, Angola, Rhodesia, Nyasaland, South Africa, Mozambique, Egypt, Ethiopia, and Madagascar, as well as other countries of Africa and other parts of the world. But although our languages are many, our reason for coming here is the same, that we love the Lord Jesus Christ and are witnesses to His Gospel, that in Him we are one people whether we speak Ibo, Yoruba, Douala, English, Afrikaans, Zulu, Sesuto, Portuguese, French, Kikuyu or any other language that is spoken by the people who live in Africa. We are one in him who was born a Jew in Bethlehem, fled from Herod into Egypt, grew up in Nazareth, died in Jerusalem, arose there and lives today in Ibadan and in every other city and village in the world that His Father created. Of this oneness in Christ we have been given such a rich experience at this Conference that not one of us is likely to forget it.

To be here is to have abundant cause to thank God for the way that the Gospel has been brought to so many countries, and to be filled with astonished joy that it has transformed the lives of so many men and women of Africa.

In a continent where such massive events lie ahead, we thank God that the Christian Church has taken such deep root. We know there are millions who have not heard the Gospel and we accept the challenge of the evangelizing of our countries, especially in the face of the dangers of materialism and secularism.

While this experience of unity has been rich and deep, we acknowledge with penitence our many divisions which have prevented us from witnessing to our unity in Him, but this we still purpose to do with His assistance. We believe that Christ challenges us to overcome these divisions in the Church and to work for the removal of all injustices based on racial discrimination which we believe to be contrary to the will of God.

We rejoice in the advance of Christian countries toward self-government and in the liberation of African energies and talents, praying that they may be used for the service of Him whom we acknowledge to be the Lord of all mankind.

The continent of Africa will see unparalleled events and changes during the rest of this century, welcomed by some, feared by others. We pray that the Christian Church of Africa will play its role as champion, teacher, counsellor and shepherd during these crucial years. We are humbly aware of our responsibilities to God and to this continent, and dedicate ourselves anew to their performance, trusting that we shall be led and supported by our fellow-Christians throughout Africa and the world.

In the name of the Father of all men, in the name of the Son who saved us all, in the name of the Holy Spirit who inspires us, we declare ourselves to be one in Christ. Amen.

---

*Source: *The Church in Changing Africa*, pp. 15-16.

ANNOTATED BIBLIOGRAPHY

GENERAL COMMENT

The sources included here have been selected from a massive collection of literature on the subject of Africa and the ecumenical movement during the colonial years. Because the sources are many and varied, no attempt is made to include all sources. In addition to the text itself, it is hoped that this listing will suggest to the reader new directions or perspectives for further study of the subject.

PRIMARY SOURCES

A. Unpublished: Archives of the IMC

These are by far the most useful sources, particularly for the period 1910–1945. The WCC Library, Geneva, houses part of the original manuscript inventory. The IIALC at the University of London possesses some materials now part of the microfiche collection made available by the Inter Documentation Company AG, Zug, Switzerland.

Most incoming and outgoing letters from 1900 to 1958 were carefully studied, as well as personal files of individual African and European figures who featured prominently in the missiological questions of the period. These individual files are found either in the microfiche edition or in the IMC Archives, WCC Library, Geneva. Together these files provide a perspective which is not easily discernible in the official Conference Reports. Moreover, they are invaluable for understanding events/issues prior to and after each Conference.

Box number refers to the microfiche edition, following the classification scheme in the *Joint IMC/CBMS Missionary Archives: Africa & India 1910–1945* (Zug, Switzerland: IDC, 1979). All unpublished sources are arranged chronologically under each subheading and without annotation. Annotation begins with published sources.

Conferences

1904:   IMC Papers, WCC Library Geneva, Report of the Proceedings of 1st General Missionary Conference, Johannesburg, July 13–20.

1906:   IMC Papers, WCC Library Geneva, Report of the Proceedings of 2nd
          General Missionary Conference, Johannesburg, July 5–11.

1909:   IMC Papers, WCC Library Geneva, Report of the Proceedings of 3rd
          General Missionary Conference, Bloemfontein, July 1–6.

1924:   IMC Papers, WCC Library Geneva, Christian Education In Africa:
          Conference At High Leigh, Hoddesdon, September 8–13.
          Conference on Christian Missions in Tropical Africa (Programme).
          IMC Papers, WCC Library Geneva, Presscuttings on High Leigh
          1924: Church Times, Methodist Times, Record.

1925:   IMC Papers, WCC Library Geneva, Conference on Education of
          African Women, London, July.
          IMC Papers, WCC Library Geneva, Africa Conference (FMCNA),
          Hartford, Conn. October 30/November 1.
          IMC Papers, WCC Library Geneva, Le Zoute Preparatory Material,
          London, New York.

1926:   IMC Papers, WCC Library Geneva, The Christian Mission in Africa,
          Le Zoute, Belgium, September 14 to 21.
          Box 217 mf. 209–211, MSS of Speeches, Reports of Sessions, etc.
          Box 217 mf. 204, "Notes of Follow-Up Meeting, Edinburgh House,
          December 20."
          Box 217 mf. 198–199, Press cuttings from Australia, S. Africa,
          Belgium, Congo, China, Britain, Sweden.

1938:   Box 203 mf. 34–35, "The Younger Church in South Africa:
          Contribution to missionary work in South Africa and to IMC at
          Madras" (findings of group of African ministers at Lovedale).
          Box 203 mf. 35, Folder: Field Study for Madras.

1939:   Box 203 mf. 37, Follow-Up of Madras in Mission Field—Africa.

Correspondence

1914:   Box 263 mf. 1, A. H. L. Fraser Memorandum on Africa Education,
          February 27. A. H. L. Fraser to L. Harcourt, April 3.

1920:   Box 263 mf. 2, Thomas Jesse Jones to Governor Guggisberg of Gold
          Coast, November 2.

1922:   Box 216 mf. 191, Emory Ross (General Conference of Protestant Missionaries in Congo), June 21.

1923:   Box 216 mf. 186, A. W. Wilkie (Scottish Mission) to Oldham, May 6.

1924:   Box 216 mf. 185, Oldham's Cable to Stokes, September 8.

1925:   Box 207 mf. 78, Oldham to Board Secretaries, July 11. Oldham to Stacy, July 24.

1927:   Box 203 mf. 34, Oldham/Mott, December 12. Further comment on possible extent of JHO's concentration on African Affairs.

1930/1:   Box 204 mf. 50, Oldham to Moss (FMCNA).

1945:   Box 203 mf. 42, Gibson/Hooper/Grace re. Need for Strong National Councils before Regional Councils can be Effectively Followed Up.

Others

1914:   Box 263 mf. 1, A. H. L. Fraser Memorandum on Africa Education, February 27.

1926:   Box 204–205 mf. 44–65, International Institute Of African Languages and Cultures.

1926:   Box 206 mf. 66–67, Population and Health in Africa.

1939:   Box 203 mf. 37, Christian Councils in Africa in Relation to IMC. Memo by B. D. Gibson.

B. Published.

Agbebi, Mojola. *Inaugural Sermon delivered at the Celebrations of the first anniversary of the "African Church."* Lagos: 1902. An invaluable document for understanding the birth of Ethiopianism.

Aggrey, James E. K. "Physical Characteristics of the native of the West Coast of Africa." IMC Papers, WCC Library, Geneva. A paper read at the meeting of the Negro Academy in 1907. Good for understanding the questions many North Americans were asking about Africa at the turn of the century.

_____ . "Aggrey to W. E. B. DuBois, July 1, 1913," in *The Correspon-
dence of W. E. B. DuBois.* Edited by Herbert Aptheker. Amherst,
MASS: University of MASS, 1973. An extant document showing
communication between two leaders of Pan-Africanism.

_____ . "The Native Students of Africa." *Student World* XVI (January
1923): 68–70. An argument for more involvement of African students
in African and world issues.

_____ . "Africa," in *Christian Students and World Problems.* New York:
Student Volunteer Mission, 1924, pp.167–177. Reflections on Africa
and its problems.

Casely Hayford, J. E. *Ethiopia Unbound: Studies in Race Emancipation.*
London: C. M. Phillips, 1911. A treatise on Ethiopianism; considered
radical by some of his contemporaries.

*Christian Action in Africa: Report of the Church Conference on African Affairs
held at Otterbein College, Westerville, Ohio, June 19–25, 1942.* New
York: Africa Committee of the Foreign Missions Conference of
North America, 1942. Indispensable report for understanding the
mood of the North American missionary community during
World War II.

*Church in Changing Africa: Report of the All Africa Church Conference held at
Ibadan, Nigeria, January 10–19, 1958.* New York: International
Missionary Council, 1958. This Report of the Ibadan Conference
should be supplemented with various articles on the Conference
published between 1958 and 1962 in the *IRM.*

Cooker, S. A. *The Rights of Africans to Organize and Establish Indigenous
Churches Unattached to, and Uncontrolled by, Foreign Church
Organizations.* Lagos: Tika Tore, 1922. An argument for
democracy in the Church and specifically self-determination for the
African Church; not particularly objective in its conclusions.

Davis, J. Merle. *Modern Industry and the African: An Enquiry into the Effect of
the Copper Mines of Central Africa upon Native Society and the
Work of Christian Missions made under the auspices of the
Department of Social and Industrial Research of the International
Missionary Council.* London: Macmillan, 1933. Excellent study of

industrialism in Africa. Its recommendations require a second look in light of their continuing relevance.

Davis, Jackson, Thomas M. Campbill, Margaret Wrong., eds. *Africa Advancing: A Study of Rural Education in West Africa and the Belgian Congo.* New York: The Friendship Press, 1945. Written by three people who were intimately related to educational missions, this work is pertinent to understanding ecumenical problems during and after World War II.

Ecumenical Missionary Conference New York, 1900: Report of the Ecumenical Conference on Foreign Missions, Held in Carnegie Hall and Neighboring Churches, April 21 to May 1. 2 vols. New York: American Tract Society, 1900. Ends the nineteenth century with a criticism of the Churches vis-a-vis missions; opens the twentieth century with exceptional confidence in the Church as agent of missions.

Ecumenical Statements On Race Relations: Development of Ecumenical Thought on Race Relations, 1937–1964. Geneva: WCC, 1965. A historical and comparative study of the subject of racism; excellent for colonial studies.

Education In Africa: A Study of West, South, and Equatorial Africa by the African Education Commission, under the Auspices of the Phelps-Stokes Fund and Foreign Mission Societies of North America and Europe. New York: Phelps-Stokes Fund, 1922. A primer in its own right. This is the first Report of the Education Commission to Africa. It inspired a new understanding of education in Africa in both the missionary and colonial circles.

Education in East Africa: A Study of East, Central and South Africa by the Second African Education Commission under the auspices of the Phelps-Stokes Fund, in co-operation with the International Education Board. New York: Phelps-Stokes Fund, [1924]. The second Report should be read or studied together with the first one. Together they helped to change the philosophy of missions in Africa for good.

Fey, Harold E., ed. *The Ecumenical Advance: A History of the Ecumenical Movement, 1948–1968.* Philadelphia: Westminster Press, 1970.

Good for understanding general ecumenical history, but useless for understanding Africa and ecumenism.

Goodall, Norman., ed. *Missions under the Cross: Addresses delivered at the Enlarged Meeting of the Committee of the International Missionary Council at Willingen, Germany, 1952, with Statements issued by the Meeting.* London: International Missionary Council, 1953. Report of Willingen 1952; the addresses indicate the continuing uncertainty regarding how best to understand post-war mission mandates.

International Missionary Council and Continental Missions and the War of 1939–1945. London: International Missionary Council, n. d. An examination of the connection between the IMC and Continental mission societies during the war years.

Jerusalem Meeting of the International Missionary Council March 24–April 8, 1928. 8 vols. New York: International Missionary Council, 1928. Reports of the Jerusalem Conference. All volumes are essential in any comparative study.

Madras Series. Presenting Papers Based upon the Meeting of the International Missionary Council at Tambaram, Madras, India, December 12th to 29th, 1938. 7 vols. New York: International Missionary Council, 1938. Part of the Madras Report. They contain reports of the various sections of the Conference.

Minutes of International Missionary Meeting, held at Crans, near Geneva, (June 22–28, 1920). Prior to Lake Mohonk 1921, several meetings were held. This was one of them. Should be read with archival materials at the WCC Library, Geneva.

Minutes of the International Missionary Council including Minutes of the Committee of the Council of the Ad Interim Committee. New York: IMC, 1921–1961. These are brief but straightforward minutes. Not the best source for understanding individual contributions.

Mott, John R. *The Evangelization of the World in this Generation.* New York: Student Volunteer Movement For Foreign Missions, 1905. Calls for immediate evangelization of the world. Excellent for understanding Christian students involvement in the birth of the ecumenical movement.

_____ . *Co-operation and the World Mission*. Concord, NH: Rumford Press, 1935. An argument for unity as a basis for world mission.

Oldham, J. H. "America's Share in the Christian Occupation of Africa." *IRM* (1918): 418–9. Developes Oldham's growing belief that America should step in and shoulder more missionary responsibility in Africa because European nations were involved in war.

_____ . "Co-operation—its necessity and cost." *IRM* (April 1919): 173–192. An argument for real unity in world mission, in view of the failure of comity.

_____ . "A new Beginning of International Missionary Co-operation." *IRM* (October 1920): 481–494. Underlines the conclusions reached at Crans, Geneva, and looks forward to the formation of the IMC in 1921.

_____ . "Christian missions and African labour." *IRM* (April 1921): 183–195. Argues for missionary involvement in African labor questions.

_____ . *The World and the Gospel*. London: United Council for Missionary Education, 1916. Makes a case for understanding Christianity in the light of post-war social realities.

_____ . *Christianity and the Race Problem*. London: SCM, 1924. A landmark study of the subject, with an examination of the social sources of the problem. It explicates the implications of racism for Christian missions. It should precede in importance all other ecumenical studies of the problem during the colonial period.

_____ . *New Hope In Africa*. New York: Longmans, 1955. Reflections of an ecumenical veteran in light of the emergence of the new Africa.

_____ . *The Missionary situation after the war: Notes prepared for the International meeting at Crans, June, 1920*. New York: n.d. An important historical document, outlining the missionary situation in Africa and other parts of the world after the war, and the options which the missionary community was to examine.

_____ . *International Missionary Co-operation: A Statement of Fundamental Questions of Policy for consideration by the Committee of*

the *International Missionary Council, January 11–15, 1925.*
Edinburgh: Morrison & Gibb, n.d. Crucial for understanding the
designation of Africa as a special province for the IMC.

_____. and B. D. Gibson. *The Remaking of Man in Africa.* London:
Oxford University Press, 1931. Grew out of group discussions.
Brings together the gospel of education and new mission ideas, and
shows why ecumenism in Africa was inevitable.

Omoniyi, Bandele. *A defence of the Ethiopian Movement.* Edinburgh: 1908.
One of the original arguments for Ethiopianism and cultural
nationalism throughout Black Africa. A statement on major themes
of Ethiopianism.

Orchard, Ronald K., ed. *The Ghana Assembly of the International Missionary
Council 28th December 1957 to 8th January 1958. Selected Papers
with an essay on the Role of the IMC.* New York: Friendship
Press, 1958. Report of Accra 1958.

*Report of the Centenary on the Protestant Missions of the World held in Exeter
Hall (June 9th–19th), London, 1888.* 2 vols. London: James Nisbet,
1888. A good point of departure for examining missionary image of
Africa and the struggle between comity and denominationalism, amid
rising racial tensions.

*Report of the 29th Conference of Foreign Mission Boards in North America,
Atlantic City, January 11–13, 1922.* New York: Foreign Missions
Conference, 1922. The FMCNA published its conference reports
annually. This issue provides intriguing angles to the problem of
nationalism and missions as well as the Report of the African
Education Commission.

*Report of the Forty-eighth Annual Meeting of the Conference of Foreign Mission
Boards In Canada and In the United States, Hotel Hildebrecht,
Trenton, New Jersey, January 12–15, 1942.* New York: FMCNA,
1942. An important report because of the role it played on behalf of
the IMC due to the war situation.

Rouse, Ruth and Stephen C. Neill., eds. *A History of The Ecumenical Movement
1517– 1948.* Philadelphia: Westminster, 1954. An essential ecumenical
study from the Reformation to the formation of the WCC. Should be
used with caution because it completely ignores the Church in Africa.

Sinclair, Margaret. "Survey Of The Year, 1956." *IRM* (January 1956): 3–85. Social, political, and economic news as they affected Christian missions in Africa and elsewhere. Similar surveys were done for the years 1913–1955, and 1957–58.

Visser 't Hooft, W. A., ed. *The First Assembly of the World Council of Churches held at Amsterdam August 22 to September 4, 1948.* New York: Harper & Brothers, 1949. A special study edited by the first secretary of the WCC.

_____ . *The Evanston Report. The Second Report of the World Council of Churches, 1954.* London: SCM, 1954. Part of the Evanston Report. Its contents cannot be compared with any other book written about Evanston 1954. This is particularly true of the statement on race relations.

_____ . *The Ecumenical Movement and the Racial Problem.* Paris: UNESCO, 1954. Traces how the Ecumenical Movement has viewed racism from its inception. A necessary background for understanding *Ecumenical Statements on Race Relations* listed above.

_____ . *The Genesis and Formation of the World Council Of Churches.* Geneva: WCC, 1982. A historical analysis of the development of the WCC from the pen of an insider.

Witness of a Revolutionary Church Statements Issued by the Committee of the International Missionary Council, Whitby, Ontario, Canada, July 5–24, 1947. New York: International Missionary Council, 1947. Part of the Whitby Report.

World Mission of the Church: Findings and Recommendations of the International Missionary Council, Tambaram, Madras, India December 12th to 29th, 1938. New York: International Missionary Council, 1939. Incorporates all the findings and recommendations at Madras 1938.

World Missionary Conference, 1910. 9 vols. New York: Revell, 1910. All the volumes in this Report are very helpful in understanding the premises of the Conference recommendations.

Wrong Margaret. *Africa and the Making of Books.* London: ICCLA, 1934. An important contribution to the understanding of Africa's impact on the development of Christian literature.

SECONDARY SOURCES

Adams, John. *Sketches Taken During Ten Voyages To Africa Between The Years 1786–1800*. New York: Johnson Reprint, 1970. Its availability helps to refute the traditional image of African societies as undynamic. Contains rare information on the Efiks of Calabar, Nigeria—their business acumen, initiative, and modernization efforts during and because of the slave trade.

Ajayi, J. F. A. *Christian Missions in Nigeria 1841–1891: The Making of a New Elite*. Evanston: Northwestern University, 1969. A pioneer work on missions in Nigeria. Argues that missionaries used the "mission house" as the center of making a new African elite.

Allen, Roland. *Le Zoute: A critical review of "The Christian Mission in Africa."* London: World Dominion Press, 1927. As indicated by the title, the book took Le Zoute 1926 to task, rejecting its emphasis on social Christianity and the equation of missions with colonialism.

Allen, Roland and Alexander McLeish. *Devolution and its Real Significance*. London: World Dominion Press, 1927. A critical review of the devolution question, seeing it as an inevitable part of church planting.

Bassham, Rodger C. *Mission Theology: 1948–1975 Years of Worldwide Creative Tension Ecumenical, Evangelical, and Roman Catholic*. Pasedena, CA: William Carey, 1979. A comprehensive examination of mission theology.

Beaver, R. Pierce. *Ecumenical Beginnings in Protestant World Mission: A History of Comity*. New York: Thomas Nelson, 1962. A systematic examination of the history of comity beginning in the nineteenth century, referring to Africa only in passing.

Beidelman, T. O. *Colonial Evangelism*. Bloomington, IN: Indiana University, 1982. An anthropological criticism of missions, with emphasis on the CMS in East Africa.

Blyden, E. B. *Africa's Service to the World*. London: Doulton, 1880. An important work emphasizing Africa's contribution to the world community.

_____ . *Christianity, Islam and the Negro Race*. 2nd ed. London: W. B. Whittingham, 1888. A necessary reading for understanding how some educated Africans viewed Christianity vis-a-vis Islam, during the beginning of the partition of Africa and widespread racism against Africans.

Campbell, Patriarch J. E. *First Conference of Africans of British West Africa.* Lagos: 1920. An analysis of the historic Conference of educated Africans.

Coombe, Trevor A. "Project for a new biography of J. E. K. Aggrey." *AME Zion Quarterly Review* 93 (January 1982): 7–22. Outlines why a new biography of this pioneer African ecumenist is necessary.

Curtin, Philip D. *The Image of Africa: British Ideas and Action, 1780–1850.* Madison: University of Wisconsin, 1964. A historical study of British misunderstanding of Africa, including the views of John Wesley and other revivalists and "scientists" in the eighteenth and nineteenth centuries.

Davidson, Basil. *Africa in History: Themes and Outlines.* London: Weidenfeld & Nicholson, 1968. Examines African history in light of modern archaelogical and other findings.

Delo-Dosumu, Amos Olusonya. "Union of Students of African Descent." *Student World* XVI (January 1923): 46–48. Underscores the importance of unity for all Africans irrespective of where economic necessities had sent them.

Dike, Kenneth O. *Trade and Politics in the Niger Delta 1830–1885.* Oxford: Clarendon, 1956. An important background study for understanding the role of various African communities in the expansion of international capitalism.

DuBois, W. E. B. *The World and Africa.* Millwood, New York: Kraus-Thomson, 1976. Calls for a positive understanding of Africa and use of its vast resources for the development of its people.

Elias, T. O. *Africa and the Development of International Law.* Leiden: A. W. Sijthoff, 1972. Essential reading for understanding Africa's impact on the development of international law and how this paralleled the growth of the ecumenical movement.

Ferkiss, Victor C. *Africa's Search For Identity.* New York: George Brailler, 1966. A political analysis of Africa's quest for identity in a new world order. It should be read with caution because of its unbalanced treatment of the nineteenth-century Africa.

Forde, D., ed. *Efik Traders of Old Calabar*. New York: Oxford Press, 1956. Provides hard-to-find information for understanding indigenous commercial initiative in a city-state in southeastern Nigeria.

Fueter, Paul D. "The All-Africa Lutheran Conference Marangu 1955." *IRM* (July 1956): 289–96. Describes the first gathering of Lutherans in Africa before Ibadan 1958.

Geertz, Clifford. *The Interpretation of Cultures*. New York: Basic, 1973. A collection of essays by a famous social scientist, dealing with a balanced understanding of cultures and social systems.

Greaves, L. B. "The All Africa Church Conference: Ibadan, Nigeria: 10th to 20th January, 1958." *IRM* (July 1958): 257–64. Provides background information on Ibadan 1958.

Hallet, Robin., ed. *Records of the African Association*, 1788–1831. London: Thomas Nelson, 1964. A collection of extant documents dealing with city-states in West Africa.

Harnack, Adolf. *The Mission and Expansion of Christianity in the First Three Centuries*. Translated and edited by James Moffatt. Gloucester, MASS: Peter Smith, 1972. Background information on Primitive Christianity and its expansion in the Roman Empire.

Hoekendijk, J. C. "Call To Evangelism." *IRM* (1950): 162–75. Argues that evangelism is a continuing task.

_____ . "The Church in Missionary Thinking." *IRM* (1952): 324–36. An argument for making the world rather than the church the focus of missionary activity.

Hoekstra, Harvey. *The World Council Of Churches and the Demise of Evangelism*. Wheaton, ILL: Tyndale, 1979. An unbalanced attack on the WCC and its emphasis on social Christianity. Ignores the impact of nontheological factors on the meaning of evangelism.

Hogg, William Richey. *Ecumenical Foundations: A History of the International Missionary Council and Its Nineteenth-Century Background*. New York: Harper & Brothers, 1952. A pioneer work on the IMC, but gives no active place for Africa as a participant in missions.

Hudson, Darril. *The Ecumenical Movement in World Affairs*. Washington, D.C.: National Press, 1969. A social analysis of the Ecumenical Movement, including the IMC and Life and Work.

Hughes, H Stuart. *Consciousness and Society: The Reorientation of European Social Thought 1890–1930*. New York: Vintage, 1961. An excellent example of how social existence conditions human ideas. Examines the thought of many leading social theorists at the turn of this century.

Jacobs, Sylvia M., ed. *Black Americans and the Missionary Movement in Africa*. Westport, CT: Greenwood, 1982. A collection of essays on black American contributions to evangelizing Africa.

Jones, Rufus N., ed. *The Church, The Gospel and War*. New York: Harper & Brothers, 1948. A collection of essays on the impact of the war on Christian missions in Africa and elsewhere.

July, Robert W. *The Origins of Modern African Thought: Its development in West Africa during the nineteenth and twentieth centuries*. New York: Praeger, 1967. Excellent background study of why contemporary African thought is traceable to the nineteenth century.

Latham, A. J. *Old Calabar 1600–1891: The Impact of The International Economy Upon A Traditional Society*. Oxford: Clarendon, 1973. An argument that capitalism preceded Christian missions in southeastern Nigeria. Indispensable for understanding indigenous efforts to better their social state, independent of missionaries.

Latourette, K. S. and William Richey Hogg. *The World Christian Community in Action: The Story of World War II and Orphaned Mission*. New York: IMC, 1949. Special study of the role of the IMC during the war.

_____. *Tomorrow Is Here: The Mission and Work of the Church as Seen from the meeting of International Missionary Council at Whitby, Ontario, July 5–24, 1947*. New York: Friendship Press, 1948. An attempt to expound the theoretical assumptions at Whitby 1947.

Levefer, Ernest. *Amsterdam to Nairobi: The World Council of Churches and the Third World*. Washington, D. C.: Georgetown University, 1979. A conservative attack on the WCC and its liberal tendencies.

Leys, Norman. *The Color Bar In East Africa*. London: Hogarth Press, 1941. An analysis of racism in East Africa, including Kenya and Uganda.

Machen, J. Gresham. *Christianity and Liberalism*. Grand Rapids, MI: Eerdmans, 1923. A conservative attack on the rapid growth of Liberalism after World War I.

Mathews, Basil. *Road to the City of God: World Outlook from Jerusalem*. London: 1928. An interesting look at Jerusalem 1928 from the pen of an insider.

Monroe, Paul, E. Michael, and J. H. Oldham. *Papers on Educational Problems in Mission Fields*. n.p.: International Missionary Council, 1921. An outline of educational problems in Africa and elsewhere presented to the IMC.

Moss, Leslie B. *Adventures in Missionary Co-operation*. New York: Foreign Missions Conference of North America, 1930. A study of FMCNA with intriguing insight into the inner-working of that body.

M'Timkulu, Donald G. S. "All-Africa Church Conference." *IRM* (January 1962): 63–6. Written by the first secretary of the AACC, this study is a brief account of events after Ibadan 1958.

Murphy, E. Jefferson. *History of African Civilization*. New York: Delta, 1982. A balanced history of civilizations in Africa, including city-states and empires.

Nair, K. K. *Politics and Society in Southeastern Nigeria 1841–1906: A Study of Power, Diplomacy, and Commerce in Old Calabar*. London: Frank Cass, 1972. An interesting study of the Efiks of Calabar, Nigeria. It rejects the notion that social change in Efik society was brought about only by the missionaries.

Neill, Stephen. *Survey of the Training of the Ministry in Africa*. London: International Missionary Council, 1950. An outline of the needs of African Churches conducted to encourage devolution from mission to church.

_____. *Brothers of the Faith*. New York: Abingdon, 1960. A survey of ecumenism in the twentieth century.

_____ . *A History of Christian Missions*. New York, Penguin, 1964. A brief history of Christian missions from the early Church to the modern world.

_____ . *Colonialism and Christian Missions*. New York: McGraw-Hill, 1966. An attempt to put colonialism and missions in a balanced perspective.

Nkomo, Simbini Mamba. "The African Student Union." *Student World* XVI (January 1923): 54–58. An endorsement of the importance of student unionism in self-development.

_____ . "Christianity and Western Civilization: from an African standpoint." *Student World* XVII (January 1924): 14–19. An opinion on why Christianity must bear social fruits.

Oduyoye, Amba. "The Development of the Ecumenical Movement in Africa with special reference to the All Africa Conference of Churches 1958–1974." *African Theological Journal* 9, 3, (1980): 30–40. Traces the development of ecumenism in Africa, beginning at Ibadan 1958.

Roberts, C. Clifton. *Tangled justice: some reasons for a change of policy in Africa*. London: Macmillan, 1937. A good testimony to the fact that there were Westerners who rejected colonialism in Africa even before the 1960s.

Smith, E. W. *The Christian Mission in Africa: A study based on the work of the International Conference at Le Zoute, Belgium, September 14th to 21st, 1926*. New York: International Missionary Council, 1926. The Report of Le Zoute 1926 with recommendations and resolutions.

_____ . *Aggrey of Africa: A study in Black and White*. New York: Doubleday, 1929. The first biography of James Aggrey.

StrassBerger, Elfriede. *Ecumenism in South Africa 1936–1960 with special reference to the mission of the Church*. Johannesburg: South African Council of Churches, 1974. Focuses on ecumenical development in South Africa.

Student World XIX (July 1926). Special Issue on Religion and Race. An important source for background information on students and racism. Served as a basis for the resolutions on racism at Le Zoute 1926.

Thwaite, Daniel. *The Seething African Pot: A Study of Black Nationalism, 1882–1925*. London: 1936. An analysis of cultural nationalism in Black Africa.

Utuk, Efiong S. "From Wheaton to Lausanne: The Road to Modification of Contemporary Evangelical Mission Theology." *Missiology* (April 1986): 205–220. Argues that, contrary to popular thought, evangelical mission theology, like its conciliar counterpart, has undergone significant modification between Wheaton (1966) and Lausanne (1974).

_____ . "An Analysis Of John Mbiti's Missiology." *Africa Theological Journal* 15, 1, (1986): 3–15. This brings together the growing corpus of missiology as espoused by John Mbiti, a leading African theologian.

Verkuyl, J. *Contemporary Missiology: An Introduction*. Trans. Dale Cooper. Grand Rapids, Michigan: Eerdmans, 1978. A collection of essays on missiology, ideology, and ecumenics.

Vischer, Lukas., ed. *Church History in an Ecumenical Perspective*. Bern: Evangelische Arbeitsstelle Oekumene Scheweiz, 1982. A collection of essays, promoting the writing of church history from an ecumenical perspective.

Warren, M. A. C. "Nationalism as an International Asset." *IRM* (July 1955): 385–93. The collapse of colonial empires after World War II meant a new and positive understanding of nationalism. Warren, the CMS secretary, discusses this theme.

_____. *Social History and Christian Mission*. London: SCM, 1967. An analysis of Christian missions as a social system, recruiting individuals primarily from the lower classes for foreign service.

Washington, Booker T. "David Livingstone And the Negro." *IRM* (April 1913): 224–235. An evaluation of the work of a famous British missionary in Africa by an African American whose educational principles were transplanted to Africa.

Weber, Hans Ruedi. *Asia and the Ecumenical Movement, 1895–1961*. London: SCM, 1966. A historical study of the Asian impact on the development of ecumenical movement.

Webster, James Bertin. *The African Churches Among the Yoruba*. Oxford: Clarendon, 1964. A description of the Independent Churches in the Yoruba country.

Williams, Walter. *Black Americans and the Evangelization of Africa, 1877–1900*. Madison, Wisconsin: University Press, 1982. A critical examination of black American missionaries and their work in Africa.

Willis J. King. "The Federation and the Negro Students of the World." *Student World* XV (July 1922): 85–92. A black American examines the relationship between the WSCF and African students throughout the world.

_____ . "The African Students' Conference." *Student World* XVI (January 1923): 48–50. An essay on a Conference of African Students. This Conference urged the IMC to help in opening more opportunities for black Americans as missionaries in Africa.

Work, Monroe N. "Contributions of Black People to the Kingdom of God." *Student World* XVI (January 1923): 43–45. An enumeration of the contributions made by black people throughout the world to the expansion of the Church.

Yergan, Max. "The Significance of the High Leigh Meeting to Negro Students." *Student World* (October 1924): 168–9. An assessment of the significance of High Leigh 1924 to black American students.

INDEX